A HANDBOOK
OF CHRISTIAN SOCIAL ETHICS

A Handbook of Christian Social Ethics

EBERHARD WELTY OP

Volume Two

THE STRUCTURE OF THE SOCIAL ORDER

HERDER AND HERDER

1963
HERDER AND HERDER NEW YORK
232 Madison Avenue, New York 16, N. Y.

This translation by Gregor Kirstein OP, revised and adapted by John Fitzsimons, is based on the first German edition of "Herders Sozialkatechismus, Band II, Der Aufbau der Gemeinschaftsordnung", published by Herder, Freiburg, 1953

Nihil Obstat: Joannes M. T. Barton, S.T.D., L.S.S.
Censor deputatus

Imprimatur: † Georgius L. Craven, Epus. Sebastopolis, Vic. Cap.
Westmonasterii, 22ª Julii 1963

Library of Congress Catalog Card Number: 59-14749

Printed in West Germany by Herder

CONTENTS

PAPAL PRONOUNCEMENTS

THE following papal pronouncements are cited in the text with the abbreviations given below. Where other papal documents are cited in the text these are given full titles.

Leo XIII (1878–1903)

D. I.	*Diuturnum illud,* 29 June 1881, on the origin of the power of the State.
I. D.	*Immortale Dei,* 1 November 1885, on Christianity and the State.
L. P.	*Libertas praestantissimum,* 20 June 1888, against Liberalism.
S. C.	*Sapientiae Christianae,* 10 January 1890, on the duties of Christians as citizens. (Image Books, New York, 1954.)
R. N.	*Rerum Novarum,* 15 May 1891, on the condition of the working classes. (C. T. S., London.)

Pius XI (1922–39)

D. I. M.	*Divini illius Magistri,* 31 December 1929, on Christian education. (C.T.S., London.)
C. C.	*Casti Connubii,* 31 December 1930, on Christian marriage. (C.T.S., London.)
Q. A.	*Quadragesimo Anno,* 15 May 1931, on social order. (C.T.S., London.)

M. S. — *Mit brennender Sorge,* 14 March 1937, against National Socialism.

D. R. — *Divini Redemptoris,* 19 March 1937, condemning the errors of Communism.

C. C. C. — *Caritate Christi Compulsi,* 3 May 1932, on the necessity of penance, and prayer to the Sacred Heart.

Pius XII (1939–58)

S. P. — *Summi Pontificatus,* 20 October 1939, on the religious decadence of mankind and the need of a religious education. (C.T.S., London.)

M. C. C. — *Mystici Corporis Christi,* 29 June 1943, on the doctrine of the Church. (C.T.S., London.)

Q. *G. V. A.* — "Address" *Questa Grande Vostra Adunata,* 21 October 1945, on women's duties in social and political life. (C.T.S., London.)

H. G. — *Humani Generis,* 12 August 1950, on preaching. (C.T.S., London.)

V. C. S. — *Vegliare con Sollecitudine,* 29 October 1951.

N. D. N. — *Nell'Ordine della Natura,* 26 November 1951, on marriage and the moral law. (C.T.S., London.)

C. B. — *Christmas Broadcast.*

P. B. — *Pentecost Broadcast.*

John XXIII (1958–63)

M. M. — *Mater et Magistra,* 15 May 1961, on social problems. (C.T.S., London.)

P. T. — *Pacem in Terris,* 11 April 1963, on peace. (C.T.S., London.)

ABBREVIATIONS

C. T. S.	Catholic Truth Society, London.
C. M.	Catholic Mind
C. D.	Catholic Documents, Pontifical Court Club, London.
C. M. W.	Image Books, New York, 1954.
N. C. W. C.	National Catholic Welfare Conference.
U. A.	The Unwearied Advocate, St. Cloud, 1956.

Part One

Marriage and the Family

CONCERNING the very extensive subject "Marriage and the Family", we can only deal here with its "socially" conditioned aspects. Two points must be mentioned at the outset:

1. The importance of marriage and the family for both the personal and social life of man cannot be overestimated (Q. 2).

2. At the present time both these societies are undergoing a crisis which can only be overcome by recourse to every (natural and supernatural) effort (Q. 8).

As we might expect, there are few other matters on which the popes have issued more frequent and emphatic pronouncements as on marriage and the family. Only a small selection of papal pronouncements can be added to the following questions.

Lesson One

MEANING AND SOCIAL SIGNIFICANCE OF MARRIAGE

1. *What is marriage?*

Marriage is the perfect life-partnership of man and woman, which is rooted in mutual love and aims at the procreation and care of human life.

PIUS XI (C. C., 78).

" . . . true and sound love which is the foundation of marital happiness and tender intimacy . . . ".

Our answer expresses a definite attitude towards the controversial question of our time, whether the meaning and purpose of marriage are to be found in the offspring which is (undoubtedly the fruit of marriage), or in the person or partnership of husband and wife, that is, in their mutual love, completion and perfection. The traditional teaching of the Catholic Church describes the offspring as the primary and most important good of the marriage partnership. For example, St. Thomas Aquinas says: "The most essential thing for marriage is the offspring."[1]

PIUS XI (C. C., 12).

"Among the blessings of marriage offspring holds the first place. The Creator of the human race Himself, who in His goodness has willed to use human beings as His ministers in the propagation of life, taught us this truth when in instituting matrimony in the Garden of Eden. He bade our first parents, and through them all married persons who should come after them: 'Increase and multiply and fill the earth' (Gen. 1, 28)."

PIUS XII (Address of 12 November 1944).

"This is the domain in which slumber mysterious forces that God has placed in the organism of man and woman for the procreation of new life. The Creator has Himself determined the structure and

[1] IV. sent. 31. 1. With the greatest possible clarity the Austrian Bishops have stated in a pastoral letter (12–1–1947) on the protection of the unborn child: "Children are, and remain to the end of time, the ultimate and most significant purpose of every marriage union."

THE STRUCTURE OF THE SOCIAL ORDER

THE FIRST volume of this work* explained the basic questions of life in society. These are now developed under a twofold aspect. First, the conclusions arrived at must be applied. How is social life to be ordered in detail in accordance with general principles? Second, individual groupings must be examined in themselves and in their relations with one another. The questions to be considered are: what communities must there be, and why precisely these? How are these communities constituted individually, and how are they mutually related? What may they demand and what may they not demand of their members?

The natural order of society is of an ascending character; there is growth from lesser to greater entities (I, Q. 50). There are, as it were, three stages of this growth in accordance with natural law: from marriage and family to "society", from society to nation and State, from nation and State to the community of nations and States.

Hence our present volume is divided into four parts:

1. **Marriage and the Family (Qs. 1-45)**
2. **The Structure of Society (Qs. 46-59)**
3. **Political Order of the State (Qs. 60-111)**
4. **The International Political Order (Qs. 112-138)**

* *A Handbook of Christian Social Ethics,* Volume I: Man in Society (New York and Edinburgh-London, 1960).

essential functions of this force of nature, its particular purpose, and He has imposed upon man duties corresponding to this purpose for any conscious use made of this faculty."

For some time past the traditional teaching has been under attack, the main argument against it being that, if the offspring is the principal purpose of marriage, then the other aspects of marriage, especially the mutual love of husband and wife, are reduced to secondary ends. Yet experience shows, it is said, that what leads to marriage is not the thought of offspring, but mutual love and the desire for complete life-partnership.

1. We answer that it would be both foolish and fraught with grave consequences to overlook or to minimize the exalted value which marriage possesses as the source and nursery of human life:

Every individual is the image of God and the brother or sister of Jesus Christ, a fellow citizen of the saints and a member of God's household (cf. Eph. 2:19; and also I, Qs. 13, 18). God allows men to share in his creative power and loving providence. This is a most exalted task, which can only be fulfilled with a sense of personal responsibility.

Being "life from the life of the parents", the offspring corresponds to the natural inclination and desire of men to live on in one of their own species. Hence the original joy of the parents in their children; hence the undeniable aspect that marriage, a partnership of mutual love, is deepened and consolidated by offspring; many marriage partners therefore regard it as a bitter fate if their union remains childless.

PIUS XI (C. C., 13).

"To appreciate the greatness of this divine gift and blessing of marriage it is enough to contemplate the dignity of man and his sublime destiny.

Even his rational nature alone sets man above all other visible creatures. Add to this that God's purpose in willing human beings to be born is not merely that they may exist and occupy the earth, but far more, that they may worship Him, and that they may know and love Him and finally enjoy Him for ever in heaven."

2. Marriage is undoubtedly the most real and intimate partnership possible between two people. This fact is not denied even by the traditional teaching on procreation as the most important among the functions of marriage. The question of how both functions are related cannot be answered according to the ideas that prevail in any one age, nor according to what certain people feel about it, but solely according to what God has willed and ordained.

Marriage is possible only between persons of different sex; it is based precisely on the difference of sex. Man and woman meet and unite because and in so far as they are sexual beings, and beings of different sex.

The most basic and radical difference between human beings is that of sex. It is not merely physiological but also psychical. But the psychical differences are conditioned by the physiological. Man and woman differ psychically because they are different physiologically and not *vice versa.* The physiological differences indicate quite clearly the functions and tasks of both sexes in their common work of procreation. God has formed man and woman in this manner because they are to be father and mother to their common children. Thus, since the marriage partnership and conjugal love derive directly from the sex difference and the sex-determination of man and woman, they are essentially ordered to the offspring and receive from the offspring the primary purpose for which nature (God, the author of nature) has intended them (cf. below, No. 4).

PIUS XII (Address of 21 October 1945).

"Now a woman's functions, a woman's way, a woman's natural bent, is motherhood. Every woman is called to be a mother, mother in the physical sense, or mother in a sense more spiritual and more exalted, yet real none the less. To this end the Creator has fashioned the whole of woman's nature: not only her organism, but also and still more her spirit, and most of all her exquisite sensibility."

The conjugal act is undoubtedly both symbol and expression, effect and confirmation of the mutual love of husband and wife and the highest expression and fulfilment of their personal union. As such, it possesses, along with the pleasure and subsequent relaxation connected with it, an intrinsic dignity and a power to sustain their union. But whether it is considered in its fulfilment, purposefulness or effects, its natural character, that is, as given by nature, leaves no room for doubt that it is intended as an act of procreation; it attains its full, intrinsic purpose where it becomes fruitful and leads to the procreation of offspring.

PIUS XI (C. C., 54).

"The conjugal act is of its very nature designed for the procreation of offspring; and, therefore, those who in performing it deliberately deprive it of its natural power and efficacy, act against nature and do something which is shameful and intrinsically immoral."

PIUS XII (Address of 29 October 1944).

"If nature had exclusively or at least primarily aimed at the mutual surrender of husband and wife in joy and pleasure, and if it had designed that act only to fill their personal experience with a maximum of happiness, and not in order to impel them to serve new life, the Creator would surely have instituted a different design for this natural

act. Yet, on the contrary, all this has been subordinated to and integrated in the supreme law of the procreation and upbringing of offspring, that is, the realization of the primary purpose of marriage as the origin and source of life."

3. The two ends of marriage are mutually related in a beneficial unity. When rightly understood and related to each other, they complement and promote each other. Marriage can only attain its primary purpose, the offspring, in a manner according with human dignity, when husband and wife are united in deep and strong mutual affection. The natural God-intended way towards the offspring is through the conjugal act, that is, through that consummation of the marriage partnership, which in its very nature represents the highest personal surrender, presupposing genuine love. The primacy of offspring includes and heightens the personal significance of marriage. The child is an integral part of this partnership. In instituting marriage, nature intended that it should be perfected in the community of the family.

PIUS XII (Address of 18 September 1951).

" . . . The true first purpose of marriage, procreation and upbringing of children."

Pius XII has spoken unmistakably of a grading of the two purposes: the offspring is the supreme purpose. But he did not intend by that to minimize the value of the personal ends nor to revoke what had been so clearly stressed by his predecessor, Pius XI. "This mutual interior formation of husband and wife, this persevering endeavour to bring each other to the state of perfection, may in a true sense be called, as the Roman Catechism calls it, the primary cause and reason of matrimony, so long as marriage is considered not in its stricter sense, as the institution destined for the procreation and education of children, but in the wider sense as a complete and intimate life-partnership and association" (C. C., 24).

PIUS XII (Address of 29 October 1951).

"The truth is, however, that marriage, as an institution of nature according to the will of the Creator, has not as its first and innermost purpose the personal perfection of man and wife, but the awakening and upbringing of new life. While the other purposes are willed by nature, they are not on the same level as the first, nor indeed are they prior to it, but essentially subordinated to this first purpose. That applies to any marriage even when it is childless."

4. What has been said here applies also to the Christian sacrament of marriage, since grace does not destroy but rather presupposes, elevates and perfects nature. Both purposes are elevated by grace and the sacraments, but they remain unaffected in their interconnection.

As an argument to the contrary, the words of St. Paul are cited: "Yes, those words are a high mystery, and I am applying them here to Christ and his Church" (Eph. 5:32). This is a citation from the list of duties of the married state which St. Paul is dealing with for pastoral reasons. The Apostle speaks of the order of the family; he opposes the pagan attitude which ascribed inferior status to the wife, and enjoins upon husbands the duty of true love and consideration: Christ loves his Church, so also should men love their wives "as they love themselves". The whole tradition of the Old Testament and St. Paul's own attitude forbid our reading into the admonitions in verses 28 et seq. ("that is how husband ought to love wife as if she were his own body"; "It is unheard of, that a man bears ill-will to his own flesh; no, he keeps it fed and warmed") pronouncements on the order of the ends of marriage. In the Old Testament a childless marriage was looked on as unnatural and as a punishment from God. St. Paul did not think otherwise, and we should not read into his views new problems that have arisen only with later developments.

2. *What follows from the nature of marriage?*

It follows from the nature of marriage that mankind is strictly obliged to protect this "sanctuary" with the utmost care.

1. THE sacredness of marriage follows both from its origin and from its ends. Both the natural and the Christian sacramental marriage derive directly from God. Marriage between non-baptized persons is itself something sacred and full of mystery; marriage between baptized persons is a sacrament, that is, the sign and the source of supernatural grace and the symbol of the union of Christ with his bride, the Church which he founded (Eph. 5:25ff.).

PIUS XI (C. C., 5).

" . . . Matrimony was not instituted or re-established by men but by God; not men, but God, the Author of nature, and Christ our Lord, the restorer of nature, provided marriage with its laws, confirmed it and elevated it."

According to Catholic teaching, every marriage is established by what is called the marriage contract, that is, by the free consent of the two parties (C. C., 6). This holds good also for Christian marriage, since Christ elevated the marriage contract to the dignity of a sacrament (ibid. 31, 39). So-called "contract marriages" have been widely criticized in recent times. It is maintained that marriage is not a contract, which is always a matter of services and demands, but rather a union of good comradeship, a partnership based on free consent and governed by the common will of the parties. But this argument misunderstands the nature of the marriage contract. The marriage contract is by no means a mere undertaking to perform certain services (acts) as an obligation, but rather the willing consent wrought by grace to the most intimate personal union appropriate to all the ends, obligations and trials of this unique sacramental partnership.

2. The marriage partnership affords the partners personally the orderly satisfaction of the sexual instinct, the strongest of all human instincts, as also mutual help in the tasks, cares and difficulties of life. Both are excelled and must be supported by mutual love, the understanding and the basic force of the marriage partnership. For this reason, St. Thomas Aquinas says that "deepest, unselfish love" must unite husband and wife.[2]

In order to understand the depth of conjugal love we must distinguish between:

Sexus: man's natural sexuality, including sexual instinct and sexual love. Sex is not something sub-human nor demoniacal. Rather it must be valued as a God-given disposition, as a vital, procreative force. But man must not allow himself to be dominated by sex. He must rather control it and use it in a manner befitting his dignity as a person, as the image and child of God. With this qualification, conjugal love fully admits of sexual love and surrender.

[2] Cf. St. Thomas Aquinas: "Amor nihil aliud est quam quaedam transformatio affectus in rem amatam", III 27. 1. 1.; III C. G., 123; in 1 Cor. II, lect. 1.

Eros: This Greek word originally signified a love which strives to rise from the human to the divine, from the earthly to the heavenly. It is self-centred and lustful; the individual strives after a good or desires a person in order to overcome his own insufficiency and to attain his own happiness. Eros is affected with all the inconstancy and all the insufficiency of earthly and transitory things. It is excited by the sensual and finds pleasure in natural excellencies. It may be "ideal and ardent", even necessary for the conjugal union, but in the long run it is too weak and unstable to support marriage, especially in times of grave crisis.

Agape: love in the supernatural Christian sense. Agape signifies God's bounteous and merciful love which descends upon the world, the redeeming love of God who sends his own Son and sacrifices him. Hence Agape signifies charity (brotherly love) in God and in Christ crucified. This love is motivated by faith and the operation of the Holy Spirit. It gives to conjugal love an unshakable stability and a mysterious radiance. At the same time, it purifies and inspires the intensity, ardour and vivacity of natural love so that marriage may withstand any menace and burden.

3. Regarding the social significance of marriage, we might note the following three points:

i. Marriage is "the source and foundation of the family and of all human society".[3] Sound marriage leads to sound familiy life, which is the primary condition not only for the continued existence and expansion of the human race and of the Church, God's people, but for every kind of community and civilized development.

[3] Leo XIII, *Arcanum*; Pius XI, C. C., 1.

PIUS XII (Address of 21 October 1946).

"The whole of civilization in all its ramifications – nations, the community of nations, the Church herself – in a word, all human values feel the good effects of married life, when it is in a flourishing and orderly condition, and when youth becomes accustomed to look up to it, to honour it, and to love it as a holy ideal."

ii. The purity and strength of marriage, the courage to enter into this state and preserve fidelity in marriage have the most decisive influence on the important sphere of sex, and indeed on the whole field of public morality. Epochs and peoples will be prone to, or proof against, sexual aberrations according to their ideal and practice of marriage.

iii. We should not overlook the importance of marriage as the testing-ground of love, that basic force which brings the greatest blessing to men. It is as earthy, strong and courageous as it is gentle, considerate and self-sacrificing.

4. Everything possible must be done today to preserve the purity and strength of marriage:

i. Those who are preparing for marriage or who are living in the married state are responsible for their marriage and are strictly obliged to make their marriage into a real life-partnership of love (cf. Pius XI, C. C., 99-120).

ii. Society and the State must provide favourable conditions and give the necessary assistance for making and preserving sound marriages.[4]

[4] Most of the ways and means mentioned here will be more fully discussed later. Here we give only a brief summary of the most important points.

For example, the removal of economic distress; decent housing conditions; direct assistance for marriages and families of healthy stock; the fight against public immorality, especially against the flouting of marriage and conjugal morality; the legal protection of marriage (good marriage laws, abolishing divorce or rendering it difficult to obtain etc.); promoting all genuine endeavours for the rehabilitation of marriage.

3. *What are the essential characteristics of marriage?*

The essential characteristics of marriage are unity and indissolubility.

UNITY: marriage between one man and one woman only. Indissolubility: "till death do us part". Unity and indissolubility are the essential characteristics, since they are inseparable from marriage.

1. It has been maintained that men originally lived in sexual promiscuity, or that the original form of marriage imvolved several wives (polygamy) or several husbands (polyandry). These assertions are demonstrably false. Modern anthropology has shown that everywhere the original form of marriage was monogamous, and that it was often indissoluble.

2. In the Christian West, too, there have repeatedly been individuals and movements desirous of replacing monogamy by polygamy. But, generally speaking, the Western world has up to the present day preserved monogamy. On the other hand, it has abandoned indissolubility in an alarming manner. It is easier to accept that marriage cannot include a third partner than that it ought to remain valid for life.

Despite all attacks and reproaches, the Catholic Church has not deviated from her standpoint that a Christian marriage, that is one between baptized persons, having been consummated in the conjugal act, cannot be dissolved by anyone in the world, not even by the pope. Certain prominent Catholic theologians maintain even to the present day it has not been definitely proved that a marriage between non-baptized persons, that is, a non-Christian (non-sacramental) marriage is an indissoluble bond. Yet the popes say on this point:

PIUS XI (C. C., 91).

" . . . These words of Christ apply to any marriage whatsoever, even to a legitimate marriage of the natural order. Indissolubility is the attribute of every true marriage, and therefore so far as the dissolution of the bond is concerned it is independent of the will of the parties themselves and of every secular power."

PIUS XII (Address of 6 October 1946).

"But marriages legitimately entered into between unbaptized persons are also sacred according to natural law, and secular courts of law are not empowered to dissolve them. Never in such cases has the Church recognized the validity of divorces."

3. Indissoluble monogamous marriage is important because "the freedom of man has no power whatever over the nature of matrimony itself, and therefore when once a person has contracted matrimony he becomes subject to its essential laws and properties" (Pius XI, C. C., 6). This means that we are not entitled to put a particular construction on the life-partnership of man and woman, and to alter it as the conditions of the times or other circumstances might suggest. The divinely intended structure of social order must thus be based on indissoluble

monogamy. To express it in a negative way: society offends against its God-given order every time it loosens the bond of indissoluble monogamous marriage, whether by facilitating divorce or by recognizing other forms of sexual cohabitation ("compassionate marriage", "trial marriage").

4. Who has the right to marry?

Every fit person has the natural right to marry.

LEO XIII (R. N., 9).

"No human law can abolish the natural and original right of marriage."

PIUS XII (Christmas Broadcast 1942).

" . . . The right, in principle, to marriage and to the attainment of the purpose of marriage, the right to wedded society and home life."

A NATURAL right is given by nature, that is, by God. It is not something granted by men; consequently it cannot be denied or altered by men (I, Q. 64).

1. Since every human being is born and lives as male or female, nature itself has fitted him for marriage. It has so formed him that he is designed in body and soul for a life-partnership of love with one of the opposite sex. Whoever is so formed and designed is also fitted by nature to enter into and live the partnership that conforms with his nature. Thus the right to marry has the character of an original basic right (I, Qs. 83/84).

2. The right to marry does not mean that nature obliges every individual to marry, that the person who renounces marriage offends against a natural moral law. St. Thomas Aquinas dis-

tinguishes between two kinds of precepts of the natural law, corresponding to a twofold necessity imposed by nature[5]:

i. There are precepts that oblige every single individual. They demand something that every individual must do if he is to live and act as a morally good person. For instance, every individual must live justly and temperately, believing in God and serving him; otherwise he offends against his ultimate goal. Everyone must eat and drink in order to sustain life.

ii. There are precepts that directly oblige mankind as such, that is human society. They refer to what is demanded for the existence and the favourable development of the human community; either they do not bind the individual at all or they bind him only in certain circumstances. For example, society cannot get on without a certain number of trades, but the individual can, since he can find a living apart from them. The obligation of marriage comes under our second heading. Without marriage and the family human society would certainly perish, not only morally (that is, as a civilized community) but physically, that is absolutely. On the other hand it is possible for the individual to live honourably and to fulfil his obligations as a man and as a Christian even if he renounces marriage and family (Q. 9).

However, in certain cases the individual also may be obliged to marry:

i. If he personally needs marriage in order to cope with the tasks and trials of life, including mastery of sex.

ii. If he can fulfil imperative obligations only by marriage, for example, caring for old or sick parents or for children (illegitimate, or by a former marriage).

[5] Suppl., 41, 2.

iii. If the continued existence of the human race (or of the nation or the ruling house) depends on *his* marriage and offspring. These are reasons of the common good which, however, are most unlikely to arise today.[6]

3. A right can only be exercised by one who is in a position, that is, fit, to do so. Hence only one who is fit to marry has the right to marry.

According to natural law the following are (absolutely, or for the time being) unfit for marriage:

i. Those who do not possess the amount of knowledge and freedom necessary to contract a marriage, irrespectively of the reasons for this. (For instance, when the use of reason has not yet been attained or has been lost; when normal reason has been completely destroyed, or is wanting through fear, coercion, intoxication, hypnosis etc.):

ii. Those who have not yet reached the age of puberty, and those functionally incapable of coition (impotence, sexual incapacity); marriage is unalterably a sex-partnership; hence where the possibility of coition is not (or not yet) present, the necessary natural basis of marriage is wanting:

iii. Those who are still validly married. Since marriage is intrinsically indissoluble, no one can contract a new marriage as long as the other marriage partner is still alive (Qs. 5, 7).[7]

As a sacrament Christian marriage, that is marriage between baptized persons, is subject to the judgment and authority

[6] The question arose in former times in connection with hereditary monarchies and dynasties. In order to preserve the throne for a ruling house an only child could have been obliged to marry.

[7] Other natural impediments to marriage do not prevent marriage absolutely but only with certain persons, for example, with near relatives.

of the Church, which is empowered and obliged to formulate possible impediments to marriage. In doing so she is guided by very serious considerations and motives, which are demanded of her by the holiness of the sacraments, her solicitude for immortal souls, the way of life and the tasks of the priestly and the religious state (Marriage and the State, cf. Qs. 5–7).

4. Man is free in his decision to marry and in his choice of a partner. "But the only function of this human freedom is to decide that each of the contracting parties in fact wishes to enter the state of matrimony, and to marry this particular person" (Pius XI, C. C., 6). This freedom is taken for granted by the people of our time and civilization. It is an important achievement of modern anthropology to have shown that the earliest forms of marriage were not abduction and marriage by purchase but marriage by choice, in which both young people had complete freedom in choosing a partner for life: And yet it is not in accordance with the facts that, for example, where the parents decide the partner for their children no harmonious marriage can result. What is called a "love-match"[8] has its own dangers, as is shown by divorce statistics.

The following may be mentioned in particular as prerequisites of a sound marriage:

i. Spiritual and moral conviction and attitude. Only those with a religious conviction, a well-formed character and a spirit of self-sacrifice are equal both to the mystery and to the trials of the marriage partnership.

[8] We are not here objecting to love-matches as such. One can only wish that marriages would be motivated by a deep and strong mutual affection. But *mere* affection which is not based on reverence and combined with a spirit of self-sacrifice offers no secure basis.

ii. True, genuine love and sincere affection (Pius XI, C. C., 121): not ignoble or purely material motives, but deep respect and strong, unselfish love for each other.

iii. Sufficient good health (Q. 41) and economic security that will enable the couple and their children at least to enjoy a modest living standard (Q. 14, III).

As human persons and as God's children man and woman are equal. Hence they have an equal share in all rights which belong to man as a person and a child of God (I, Q. 18; Qs. 70–71; Q. 87). This is the primary and decisive meaning of the equality of the sexes which is so widely talked about today (cf. Q. 15). From their equal origin man and woman are destined for one another; the partnership of marriage unites them in a most intimate and unselfish love. They are pledged to one another, each giving himself (herself) to the other, and each meant to attain the fullness of his personality in partnership with the other. The offspring is the purpose and fruit of both in so far as they have become one. Hence in respect of the marriage partnership as such, which is a life-partnership of love, there are the same rights for both: the right of free choice of a partner, the right to absolute fidelity, the right to conjugal union in the narrower sense, the right to offspring. Notwithstanding this equality, the entire communion within marriage must have a different character for each of the two partners, because the sexual differences reach down into the depth of man's being.

PIUS XI (C. C., 76).

"Such demands for equality of rights between husband and wife are pretentious and exaggerated. But there is a true equality between them, which is to be recognized in all that pertains to the person and dignity of a human being, and in all that is implied by the marriage contract

and is inherent in wedlock itself. Here, admittedly, each party enjoys exactly the same rights and is bound by the same obligations."

PIUS XII (Address of 21 October 1945).

"As children of God, man and woman have a dignity in which they are absolutely equal; and they are equal, too, in regard to the supreme end of human life, which is everlasting union with God in the happiness of Heaven . . . . But man and woman cannot maintain or perfect this equal dignity of theirs unless they respect and make use of the distinctive qualities which nature has bestowed on each sex."

5. Is marriage a concern of the State?

Admittedly, the State has certain rights in regard to marriage, but it has far more obligations.

THE modern State assumes to itself an almost unlimited authority in the question of marriage. It is most deplorable that many people nowadays actually concede to the State this usurped competence.

PIUS XI (C. C., 129).

"But it is not only in the temporal order, Venerable Brethren, but in the spiritual order as well that the interest of the State is concerned in firmly establishing the foundations of marriage and the family; it is to the advantage of the civil community that just laws regarding conjugal fidelity and reciprocal help should be made and faithfully observed."

PIUS XII (Address of September 1946).

"If a sense for the common weal is the soul of any sound and strong nation, the dignity and sanctity of marriage and family life are its back-

bone. If this is damaged severely, the strength of this nation suffers and sooner or later the ruin occurs of its people."

1. In dealing with this question the following facts and principles must be considered:

i. Even as a natural partnership, as pertaining to the order of nature and of creation, marriage is not created by men. Therefore in its essential nature, in its goals and properties it is independent of every human authority.

ii. Obviously the State cannot ignore marriage. It draws its strength from marriage; also there are certain conditions and effects of marriage in civil law (cf. 3, 4, below).

iii. According to God's will all men are obliged to the entire Christian way of life which, while being essentially supernatural, yet includes natural values and communities (I, Q. 18). The State has no right to oppose, or to exclude itself from, this order.

2. Since marriage between baptized persons is a sacrament as such, it is not subject to the authority of the State but of the Church. Hence it is not the State's business to restrict freedom in this matter by forbidding marriages or by laying down impediments. The Church will not refuse to consider the just wishes of the State, but she alone is the competent authority (Q. 6).[9] Thus in regard to Christian marriage civil law may regulate only

[9] The Church has more than once taken over civil impediments to marriage and incorporated them in her marriage legislation, that is, she has for her part declared them to be impediments. But occasionally she has refused to do so because the impediment specified by the State derived from a consciously un-Christian ideology and way of life, as for instance in the case of the marriage legislation of the German National Socialist regime, which forbade marriages between persons of different race and those suffering from hereditary diseases.

what concerns the civil consequences of marriage,[10] that is, those legal effects which are proper to the marriage contract in a purely temporal and external way, and are directly connected with the common good. Hence civil law lays down the formalities of the marriage contract; it used to safeguard the marriage bond by punishing adultery; it defines the rights and duties of the marriage so far as they affect society, especially those which affect the care of the children and the economic position of the members of the family, *e.g.*, as heirs.

3. Marriage between non-baptized persons is to a far greater extent subject to civil authority which nevertheless can never have absolute control of non-Christian marriage. It is commonly held by Catholic moralists that the State has power also to lay down nullifying impediments for non-Christian marriage,[11] but only to the very limited extent that is really demanded by the common good (for example, defining minimum age, forbidding marriage between near relatives).

4. Thus there exists civil marriage legislation that is justified and even necessary, and accordingly civil marriage law and civil jurisdiction in matters pertaining to marriage. By this positive legal regulation the State should seek methodically and comprehensively, even though only indirectly, to further marriage – a point to which too little attention is paid in modern society. Here we might note (cf. Q. 2, No. 4): i. The State furthers marriage most effectively by supporting the efforts and, in general, the spiritual and moral power of the Church (cf. Pius XI,

[10] For Christians also the State may corroborate marriage impediments in natural law by positive legislation, since it is not thereby enacting a new law, but merely making "established" law obligatory in a new form. Cf. Q. 41.

[11] Nullifying or diriment impediments are those that render a marriage not only illicit but invalid. Where they exist a marriage is simply impossible: in spite of being made freely the declaration of consent is null and void.

C. C., 130). ii. The State may allow its health services to be used for the purpose of marriage guidance, but itself to advise on marriage is not a matter for the State, since religious and moral considerations are involved which do not come under its supreme authority. At the same time the State should curb the activity of illicit marriage advisory centres. Under certain circumstances the State may require certain professions (teaching, welfare work) to be filled by unmarried persons, provided, however, that the profession thus freely chosen can be relinquished at any time.

6. *What of "civil" marriage?*

In its present-day form civil marriage is a usurpation on the part of the State and must be rejected.

1. The State can require of its citizens the announcement and official registration of their marriage, because certain consequences of marriage come within the province of civil law. But modern civil law and public opinion nearly everywhere look on civil marriage as the only proper and valid form of contracting marriage. The State (or in its name the registrar or justice of the peace) accepts the declaration of the parties, and by this fact the marriage is supposed to be contracted.

The difference between these two views must be very carefully noted. If the State merely wishes to be assured that the marriage has been contracted so that as a result the civil legal consequences may take effect, then it is not claiming to judge or to be competent concerning the marriage itself. It recognizes the marriage (contracted privately or in church) as valid also for the State, and merely establishes that the civil legal rights and consequences now take effect, or are to be granted. On the other hand, if the declaration before the registrar has the purpose and the legal force of joining man and woman in marriage so that they are only then married at all, and of conferring civil rights on this union, then church marriage is replaced by civil marriage, and marriage is secularized.

2. Regarding civil marriage the following must be noted:

i. The Church has the right to lay down the conditions (the "form") under which alone a valid sacramental marriage is contracted. This marriage must also be recognized as valid by the State and by civil law, otherwise a crying injustice is done.

ii. Christians who are not bound to the Church form[12] can express their consent in any form they like, also before the registrar if they so wish. This marriage is valid of itself, that is, by reason of the mutual consent, but not by reason of its acceptance by the registrar.

iii. Absolutely speaking non-baptized persons may declare their will to marry in any form they like, since the natural law does not stipulate a definite form of contracting marriage. However, as guardian of the natural law the State has authority to make a definite form of contracting a non-Christian marriage obligatory, for example, before the registrar and two witnesses.[13]

3. Civil marriage is obligatory in many States. The State decrees by law that all who intend to marry, even those who are getting married in church, must be married by a registrar in order

[12] Baptized persons who have never belonged to the Catholic Church.

[13] This was the general opinion held up to the nineteenth century. Again today it may be considered the "general and safe" opinion. The matter may become quite important, as the number of non-baptized persons is steadily increasing amongst us.

to be recognized as married persons in civil law and to share in the civil legal effects. Sometimes, as in some totalitarian States of the present day, the State absolutely forbids church marriages; sometimes it forbids under penalty the church marriage to take place before the civil marriage has been performed (as in some European countries). With regard to obligatory civil marriage, there is this to be said: It is a grave injustice against God and the Church, as also against the individual Catholic whose freedom of conscience is thereby infringed. Nevertheless, the Church obliges the faithful to submit to compulsory civil marriage. But the church marriage must precede (or follow) it, and the civil act may be performed by the contracting parties solely because of its civil (legal) effects.

4. Besides the obligatory, there is also the optional civil marriage. The state may allow the contracting parties the option of a church or a civil marriage. Both forms are recognized by the State and bring about the civil legal effects.

i. Basically the optional civil marriage is not as bad as the obligatory one, since it makes the church marriage, when the contracting parties decide on it, binding also for the State. Nevertheless, it must be rejected because it gives church and civil marriage equal standing.

ii. In practice the Church has to forbid the faithful to be married before the registrar wherever civil marriage is optional, provided the church marriage includes all civil legal effects and advantages.

5. Concerning the introduction of, and assistance at, civil marriage the Catholic teaching is that in view of the difficulties and the general situation obtaining today:[14]

[14] Cf. Code of Canon Law, can. 2334, 2336.

i. A Catholic may not co-operate in the first legal introduction of civil marriage, for that would be an unjust, indeed anti-God legislation. On the other hand, where it is a question of mitigating or abolishing the severities of existing laws the Catholic may vote in favour of the measures even though they do not fulfil all the demands of his Church (for example, if compulsory civil marriage were to be replaced by optional civil marriage). Every now and then the whole body of civil marriage law comes up for review, not seldom in connection with a comprehensive legal reform. If the new law is no worse than the old, and if nothing more can be attained, then the Catholic can justify his co-operation (voting for it); and provided that the law in question is not clearly anti-God, it is permissible to support or vote for it in order to prevent worse evils.

EXAMPLES of anti-God laws. Rejection of sacramental marriage; holding marriage and concubinage as on the same level; legal recognition of polygamy.

ii. The Catholic registrar may be officially present in the name of the State at a civil marriage if he is convinced (and states this publicly should the occasion arise) that he is co-operating in a legal act which can establish civil effects only. In the law of the Church the declaration before a registrar has no significance. But it is permitted as the only means of securing to sacramental marriage the legal effects due to it in civil law. For this reason a Catholic registrar may accept such a declaration where there are weighty reasons, even when he knows that a church marriage will not take place, or because of existing matrimonial impediments cannot take place.

7. *What is the Catholic view on civil divorce?*

Civil divorce conflicts with the natural law and must be condemned unreservedly as one of the worst evils.

LEO XIII (19 March 1902).

"For the State alienated from the Church oversteps the boundaries and aim of its powers, interferes with the marriage bond, deprives it of its sanctity, injures the natural right of parents to educate their children and in many places harms the indissolubility of the marriage union by the legal approval of divorce."

PIUS XI (C. C., 87).

"But the chief obstacle to the renovation and rehabilitation of marriage willed by Christ the Redeemer lies . . . in the constantly increasing facility of divorce."

PIUS XII (Address of 6 October 1946).

"None can doubt that today it must be one of the main concerns of the Church, with every means, to arrest the growing decline of marriage and the family."

THIS question concerns divorce as meaning dissolution of the marriage bond. In virtue of its own authority the State dissolves marriage so that the parties can contract a new marriage. In doing this it assumes absolute authority over Christian and non-Christian marriage alike.[15] It declares the parties to be free in virtue of its own authoritative decision. And this sovereign authority is supposed to belong to the State in virtue of its own

[15] This is the situation at least in many countries, e. g. in England and in the United States. Some countries confine themselves to marriage between non-baptized persons or between non-Catholics.

right, that is, of itself: one of the greatest presumptions of which a State can be guilty. In modern times divorces have increased greatly. From year to year divorce has been made easier and the grounds are becoming more and more trivial.

It is often said that, while in theory the Catholic Church rejects all divorce, in practice anyone who pays enough money or is well enough "connected" in Rome can obtain a divorce. This is a base falsehood. The Church knows only two cases in which a valid marriage may be dissolved.[16] Apart from these she never dissolves a valid marriage. At most she declares after a most searching examination of these cases that the marriage in question was never valid (a declaration of nullity, but not divorce).

1. Civil divorce conflicts with the natural and the divine law. That is, the State has not the power to dissolve a valid marriage; and no authority or no association of nations even with "world authority" can bestow this power upon it.

This principle depends entirely on the intrinsic indissolubility of marriage (Q. 3). No power on earth, neither ecclesiastical nor civil nor international, is competent without a divine mandate (which, in fact, does not exist) to abolish, invalidate or alter such a natural and divine law.

2. Viewing the situation as a whole, the alarming increase in divorce may be attributed to the spirit of our age. Men lack the religious faith, moral strength and determination to accept the demands and sacrifices of an indissoluble marriage (Pius XI,

[16] The cases are well known: the sacramental marriage which has been contracted but not consummated; and what is known as the Pauline privilege. For this and all further questions concerning the Church's marriage laws and Catholic moral teaching on marriage, the relevant literature must be consulted.

C. C., 87/92). Considering individual cases, we see that various reasons may lead to divorce, for example, when the parties fail to reach a deep mutual understanding of each other's temperament (often due to over-hasty marriage), infidelity, intemperance and extravagance. Today attention is drawn particularly to the tragedy of these marriages in which the parties fail in spite of their most sincere efforts to find (or recapture) real love for each other. The view is held that it is as false as it is cruel to insist that these people should continue to live together, since their marriage is already dissolved from within and does not exist any more. But even in such cases the Catholic Church cannot allow divorce in spite of all the tragic and painful circumstances involved which she regrets most deeply. She is not above the law of God and of Christ.

3. The effects of divorce are indeed tragic:

i. Reverence for the laws of nature (of God) and for all that is sacred is generally lost because the profanation of marriage (and of the family) inevitably spreads to other things; the power of the State is increased unnecessarily; respect for the dignity of the human person decreases.

ii. The parties themselves suffer. In almost every case divorce deeply affects the parties spiritually and often also in health.

iii. Society suffers. There is a decrease in population, morality is weakened (signs of moral degeneracy); the family is broken up and the values for which it stands are lost.

4. Catholics are strictly bound to oppose civil divorce by all legitimate means. For very grave reasons they may go through the formality of civil divorce, but on the clear understanding that this is done for the sole purpose of obtaining the civil legal

effects, and not with the intention of marrying again (except in the case where their marriage has been declared invalid by an ecclesiastical court). For a Catholic judge a conflict of conscience may arise when he has to grant a divorce according to the civil norms (grounds for divorce) although this conflicts with his conviction as a Catholic. The standpoint of Catholic ethics has been formulated by Pius XII as follows:

PIUS XII (Address of 6 November 1949).

"The Catholic judge may, only on grounds of special significance, pronounce the verdict of a civil divorce (in countries where this exists) for a marriage that has been concluded validly before God and the Church. He must not forget that such a verdict in practice concerns not only matters of civil law, but actually leads to the real bond being mistakenly regarded as broken and the new one as valid and in duty bound."

In connection with this statement of the Pope it is possible to specify three guiding principles:

i. The Catholic judge may give judgment in favour of divorce if the marriage was never valid. (This holds also in the case of Catholics who were not married by the Church.)

ii. If the judge knows personally, but not from the records of the case, that the parties are validly married in the eyes of the Church, he may, nevertheless, give judgment in favour of divorce.[17]

[17] This view is held by some Catholic authorities and is based principally on a statement of St. Thomas Aquinas (II, II, 67, 2) where he teaches that the judge must give judgment according to the facts as they are known to him in his official capacity, and not as they are known to him as a private person. In a prudent manner, and if necessary by making a statement, the judge should endeavour to avoid possible scandal.

iii. Even when the judge knows from the records of the case that the marriage is valid in the eyes of the Church he may for sufficiently grave reasons give judgment in favour of divorce.[18]

8. How is the modern marriage crisis to be overcome?

It can only be overcome:

1. By instructing men again in the nature and dignity of marriage;

2. By providing suitable external conditions;

3. By married life being again made subject to the law of God.

Concerning the improvement of external conditions: Pius XII (Address 6–10–1946), Text quoted in Q. 7.

PIUS XII (Address of 2 November 1950).

"Confronted as We are by the disorder which has gone far to destroy marriage and the family, We consider that this disorder poisons and corrupts modern human society like a plague."

1. THERE are two distinct elements in the modern marriage crisis. First, the disorder in marriage itself, that is, the collapse of marriage as an institution willed by God; a divine law obliging men to hold marriage sacred is not recognized. The causes of this decay are, above all, a progressive estrangement from God, bringing with it a worldly outlook and a shrinking from self-sacrifice; growing scientific "support" for contraception, abortion, sterilization etc.; two world wars with ensuing misery and loosening of morals.

[18] Such reasons would be, for example, if the judge would otherwise be dismissed from office, if – as a probable consequence – all Catholics were forced to resign from the office of judge.

Second, difficulties arising not from a want of good will, but from the development in outlook and in living conditions:

i. The preponderance of the "love-match" form of marriage; it makes such high demands on the power and sincerity of love that the modern individual is largely incapable of coping with them.

ii. The extraordinary decline in infant mortality; the family increases much more rapidly today than formerly, since it is normal nowadays for children to survive. As a consequence we get a wastage of sex instincts. (Fear of conception; cf. 2 ii, and also Q. 37.)

iii. Decrease in practical duties. Many things were formerly done in the family which are now done outside (in clubs, offices, factories etc.). The result is that married people are much less directly dependent on each other.

2. It is both foolish and irresponsible to try to rehabilitate marriage by facilitating divorce and by loosening the moral principles that must, according to the divine will, govern sex relations.

i. Marriage must be carefully considered beforehand. But only morally unprincipled men and times can approve of sexual intercourse, "trial marriages" etc. as means of establishing physical and temperamental fitness for marriage.

ii. Marriage will not recover without strength of will and a determined return to matrimonial fidelity. Making light of adultery is one of the most dangerous of modern errors. The Catholic Church alone clearly condemns any form of contraception by which the matrimonial act is performed consciously and deliberately in a manner contrary to nature (cf. 3). The Church knows that she is bitterly criticized for this, and that she is asking extraordinary sacrifices from many of the faithful (cf. 3). But it is against the basic views of Catholic ethics that men should decide whether, and when, the natural way of performing the conjugal act is to be adhered to or departed from.

3. Since married people are not actually obliged to bring children into the world (Q. 10), they may by mutual agreement practise voluntary continence. If there are grave reasons why they should not have (more) children, then according to Catholic ethics there are only two legitimate ways open to them, either voluntary continence,[19] or the use of the "safe period". Concerning the safe period Pius XII cleared up many doubts.[20]
His most important points are summarized in the following principles: First, a marriage is invalid if, when it is being contracted, the conjugal right is restricted to the safe period. The Pope says the right; not the use of the right.

[19] Undoubtedly to renounce completely the "full expression of their natural disposition" can mean a difficult and even heroic sacrifice for married people. In full appreciation of such a situation Pope Pius XII wrote: "It may, however, be objected that such continence is impossible, that a heroism of this sort is impossible to carry out. You will hear and read of this objection everywhere and it derives from those whose obligations and competence ought to cause them to judge differently. It would be doing an injustice to the men and women of our age if they were thought to be incapable of continued heroism. Today and for many reasons – perhaps under the impact of hardship or in the service of injustice – heroism is being practised to a degree and extent that was considered impossible in past times" (Address of 29–10–1951).

[20] In the address of 29–10–1951; the text is too long to quote in full. Pius XI had already (C. C., 59) given the reason for the standpoint of Catholic ethics when he pointed out that it is quite legitimate "to have the secondary ends of matrimony in view" without doing violence to nature: "Both matrimony and the use of the matrimonial right have secondary ends – such as mutual help, the fostering of reciprocal love, and the abatement of concupiscence – which husband and wife are quite entitled to have in mind, so long as the intrinsic nature of that act, and, therefore, its due subordination to its primary end, is safeguarded."

Second, for sufficient, sound reasons married people are permitted to keep to the safe period; there must be grave reasons to justify its permanent use. Third, the reasons need not derive from external circumstances. Pius XII names the following reasons[21]: medical (disease or the danger of disease); eugenic (danger of hereditary disease to the offspring); economic (lack of means: insufficient income); social (arising from social considerations).

PIUS XII (Address of 26 November 1951).

"Therefore, in Our last Allocution on conjugal morality, We affirmed the lawfulness and at the same time the limits – in truth very wide – of a regulation of offspring, which, unlike so-called 'birth-control', is compatible with the law of God. One may even hope (yet in this matter the Church naturally leaves the judgment to medical science) that science will succeed in providing this lawful method with a sufficiently secure basis. The most recent information seems to confirm such a hope."

Among the "saving forces" of the marriage crisis sound instruction deserves particular mention (cf. C. C., 110–114; as prefatory note to this cf. 100–109). The prevalent ignorance is all the more menacing and difficult to overcome because men, partly for want of good will, seek to ignore the truth. Instruction today must cover the whole problem of marriage, particularly the "guiding thoughts of God".

[21] The papal addresses cited show that the Holy Father wishes to explore all possible avenues in order to help men in a generous fashion. It must never be overlooked, however, that the use of the safe period is an exception which is largely conditioned by the unfavourable situation of the present time.

9. What is the Catholic view on celibacy?

Whether it is adopted voluntarily or not the celibate life, lived in the right spirit is of great importance for the life of society.

OUR answer expressly concerns celibacy rightly understood and rightly lived. It does not deal with those who avoid marriage from such motives as aversion, unwillingness to make sacrifices and the like – the confirmed bachelor, for instance. It is often maintained that the celibate must necessarily become frustrated. Pius XII rejected this assertion as an "aberration of reason and emotion". That the celibate can possess extraordinary spiritual riches is shown by the history of Christianity (Christ himself, his blessed Mother and many other saints), and also by common experience.

PIUS XII (Address of 29 October 1951).

"... As though a human being who did not use the generative faculty would suffer some loss of dignity. To renounce the use of that power does not mean any mutilation of personal and spiritual values, especially if a person refrains from the highest motives."

If only as a strong force in the formation of personality the celibate life is most important for the life of society. The celibacy of Catholic priests and religious will always be a stumbling-block. It deprives the nation (and mankind), so it is often stated, of a precious heritage. Innumerable children who might have justified the highest expectations thus remain unborn. On this point we offer the following considerations:

The Church has derived the ideal of virginity from divine revelation. She has good reasons for making it a law that her priests should be celibates. We must not overlook the enormous blessing which priests and religious bring to humanity precisely because of celibacy.

There will always be certain individuals whose particular task in life is to give God the honour due to him and to make atonement on behalf of the world (cf. 1 below) – but which the world cannot understand.

The "loss" of descendants, which, we might add, is grossly exaggerated, would be amply made up for if the willingness to have children were everywhere present, especially among those who make such accusations against the Catholic Church. The losses through birth-control are appalling, and they are not counterbalanced by any positive values or services.

I. Voluntary celibacy

PIUS XII (Address of 21 October 1945).

" . . . These generous souls recognize as a great good the union of the two sexes in wedlock. But if they depart from the ordinary road, if they leave the beaten track, it is not to desert the service of humanity, but rather to devote themselves to it with complete detachment and self-denial, and by an activity which is incomparably more extended, indeed all-embracing and universal."

PIUS XII (Address of 2 November 1950).

"But wherever pure marriage blossoms, disciplined in a Christian way, there also flourishes virginity which receives its strength from the love of Christ."

1. The Church accords the state of virginity dedicated to God a higher value than that of matrimony. This has its source in

Holy Writ itself (cf. Matt. 19:12; 1 Cor. 7: 1–2, 25–38). But this does not mean:

i. that the Church in any way belittles marriage; she would be contradicting the entire divinely instituted order of creation and salvation and the Word of God in the Sacred Scriptures (cf. Gen. 2:24; Eph. 5:22–23; 1 Tim. 4:3–5);

ii. that the unmarried person (celibate) is simply better, more virtuous than the married person. Holiness (perfection) consists in the love of God and one's neighbour, and not in the fact that one belongs to this or that state in life. We might point out that in marriage the love of one's neighbour is put to the test in a special manner. Marriage and celibacy form the two ways of life which together represent the fullness of the Christian life.

2. Voluntary celibacy exercises an extraordinary influence for good on social life. It is a constant support to marriage. It is an inspiring force for all that is ideal in marriage. There must be challenge in marriage, if it is to be roused to climb the heights where Christ would have it. It provides an example of great self-sacrifice, of external and internal renunciation of the world, undivided devotion to the service of God and neighbour, of love purified. By prayer and penance it offers God the supreme Lord the honour and atonement due to him, also in the name of society. It commends to God our social concerns great and small. Those leading a life of celibacy carry out innumerable social tasks throughout the world including many which require, or at least involve, the renunciation of the ties of marriage and family life: the education of youth, social welfare work, nursing (contagious diseases), help in time of war, as well as many great achievements in science and culture. The care of souls, for

instance, is of the greatest social importance both in its direct and indirect effects (preaching and instructing; confession and other forms of counsel in matters of conscience, activity in religious sodalities, in study groups, conferences etc.).

II. Non-voluntary celibacy

Because of the normal excessive proportion of women in the population, of ill-health and other disabilities, of obligations towards parents and other relatives, and because of various other causes, there always have been men and women who wanted to marry but who in fact have had to renounce marriage. Today the fate of the unmarried woman has become a great social problem, and it is extremely difficult to find a right solution for it. The twofold desire which forms the core of this whole problem, that is, the desire for a husband's love and the desire for a child, remains unfulfilled; it remains unfulfilled for these women because, through no fault of their own, they have to bear an unavoidable burden which deeply unsettles and torments them.

PIUS XII (Address of 21 October 1945).

"But there is also the Catholic girl who remains unmarried in spite of herself; . . . she abandons the fair dream of her adolescence and young womanhood, surrenders her hope of having a faithful companion to share her life, of making a home and family of her own. In the impossibility of marriage she discerns her own vocation and, sad at heart, though resigned, she too devotes herself entirely to the highest and most varied forms of beneficence."

1. On this question also Catholic ethics cannot approve any solutions proposed that are incompatible with the order and

precepts of God. They conflict with the true welfare both of the woman in question and of the community. Among such so-called solutions are sexual intercourse and motherhood outside wedlock, and coupled with the latter, parity between illegitimate and legitimate children (cf. Q. 45), promiscuity, self-abuse.

2. A real, living belief in God enables us to see meaning and purpose in a life of involuntary celibacy, and gives the strength to master it. The fact that such a fate "befalls" many in no way proves that God has not his own special purpose for each of these individuals (cf. Q. 15). Spiritual resignation and dedication can make every compulsory sacrifice fruitful both for the individual involved and for others (society). Faith and piety are no cheap consolation meant merely to make palatable what is unpleasant, but rather a motivating and necessary force capable of reconciliation with the hardest lot.

3. In general the unmarried woman will get on the more easily if the occupation she takes up is suited to her, and at the same time offers her economic security; in most cases the occupation which will more readily suit her will involve some form of motherly love and care, for every woman is meant to be a mother. Real conviction of a vocation will most readily overcome the feeling of leading an empty and useless life. It is very important that the unmarried woman should have some appropriate form of escape from a loneliness that often can be depressing, so that she may feel sheltered and secure (being treated as one of the family, a friendly home, true companionship or friendship with those of her own type, holidays spent together etc.).

4. Left to themselves most women compelled to remain unmarried cannot cope with their lot. The problem is one that

concerns the whole of society. Understanding and the determination to help are needed in order that little personal acts of help may be done; new occupations and openings suited to the temperament and the natural bent of women must be created. Much could be achieved without taking employment away from men and consequently endangering families: more women personnel for welfare work in factories and workshops; employing additional staff to relieve those with too much to do; substituting unmarried for married women in various occupations. The political activity of women can also become important in this respect. In parliaments and in very many public bodies women are far from being represented in proportion to their voting power and political maturity.

PIUS XII (Address of 21 October 1945).

"It has been seen that a woman's work is concerned primarily with those tasks and occupations of domestic life which contribute so powerfully, and more powerfully than is generally appreciated, to the true interests of the social community. But the furtherance of those interests calls for a great number of women who will have more leisure at their disposal, and so be able to devote themselves to the task more directly and more completely. And where should We find these women if not especially (We do not, of course, say exclusively) among those to whom We have been alluding: those upon whom the force of circumstances has imposed a mysterious vocation; those whom events have destined to a life of solitude which was not in their thoughts or aspirations, and which threatened to be nothing more than a selfishly useless and purposeless existence?"

Lesson Two

ESSENTIAL NATURE AND FUNDAMENTAL RIGHTS OF THE FAMILY

In concise and compelling form Pius XII underlined the importance of the family as follows:

PIUS XII (Address of 15 September 1951).

"Certainly it is vain to seek to heal our endangered society unless the domestic community, the very core and basis of human society, is led back to the laws of the Gospel."

The renewal of family life is undoubtedly the key to any apostolate for the Kingdom of God.

Totalitarian States direct their strongest blows against the family; they know that they are assured of success once they have overcome the family.

10. *What is the family?*

The family is the community of parents and their children. Arising out of indissoluble, monogamous marriage, it is the most important community and the one closest to nature.

LEO XIII (R. N., 9–11).

"Hence we have the family; the society of a man's house – a society limited indeed in numbers, but no less a true society, anterior to every kind of State or nation, invested with rights and duties of its own, totally independent of the civil community."

PIUS XI (D. I. M., 11–13).

"Now there are three necessary societies of which man becomes a member from birth, three societies distinct from one another and yet, by God's will, harmoniously connected: two of these, the family and the civil society, are of the natural order, and the third, the Church, is of the supernatural order. First comes the family. Instituted and purposely designed by God as the means for the procreation and education of children, the family takes precedence by nature, and therefore by right, of the State.

But the family is an imperfect society; that is to say, it is not provided with everything which it needs for the perfect attainment of its high purpose."

THIS section applies to the family as we normally understand it, that is to parents and children. Other persons living and working in the house and to that extent belonging to the household are unfortunately less and less accounted part of the family. Taken in a wider sense "family" embraces either the entire kinsfolk, or a very large number of persons working for the family proper and belonging to the household (*e.g.*, slaves and serfs). This type has practically disappeared from our Western society.

1. The transmission of life from parents to children, the descent of children from parents, produces the closest blood relationship. There exists between parents and children an "organic", natural unity. The family is not just an association (I, Q. 28), but a true and genuine community. It is the primary and the most natural community and promotes in an exemplary form the outlook and values proper to society, such as love and loyalty, respect and trust. Members of a family must be really devoted to each other and be always ready to help one another. Like marriage the family comes from God. It is a community willed and instituted by God.

2. Both natural and Christian ethics can acknowledge only one single basis of the family, namely, indissoluble, monogamous marriage (Q. 3). All other forms of cohabitation (polygamy, temporary marriage, intercourse outside wedlock) may result in the birth of children, but must be absolutely rejected as valid bases of the family.

PIUS XII (Address of 2 November 1950).

"But if it (the community of marriage and family) is to be called healthy and is thus in reality, then not only outward prescription determines conduct but in the first place always the order of life which springs from the inviolate nature of man and binds him to God and the divine law."

Since it is God's will that marriage should expand into the family, married people have a natural right to fecundity of their marriage. No one, not excepting the State, may forbid them to have children. Are married people obliged to have children? In accordance with the meaning of marriage (Q. 1) the following must be stated:

i. Marriage is designed for the family, it can and should develop into the family. Therefore it is undoubtedly in accordance with nature that children should be conceived and born in marriage.

ii. By mutual agreement and for a sound reason married people may forego having (more) children provided they accept the inevitable consequences for their married life (Q. 8, Nos. 2, 3).

iii. Whoever desires and performs sexual intercourse is obliged to accept from God's hand and to bring up the child that may be born of it. Thus it is clear that the obligation to have children is not absolute but conditional.

PIUS XII (Address of 29 October 1950).

"Herein we have the characteristic service which gives their state its peculiar value – the good of the offspring. But the individual and society, the people and the State, and the Church herself, depend for their existence on the order which God has established in fruitful marriage. Hence to embrace the married state, to make frequent use of the faculty proper to it and lawful only in that state, while on the other hand, always and deliberately to seek to evade its primary duty without serious reasons, would be to sin against the very meaning of married life."

3. Aristotle, St. Thomas Aquinas and others define the family as an "imperfect" society in contradistinction to the political community of the State, the "perfect" society. This definition does not mean that the family is imperfect in relation to its own proper goal and function. On the contrary, the family is perfectly appropriate to the purposes for which it exists. But the description "imperfect society" implies three things:

i. Other societies, especially the political, have goals and functions that are more comprehensive, higher and therefore more perfect than those of the family.[22]

ii. As the imperfect is related to the perfect, so the family relates to the political society of the State: it is a part, a member of the State, designed to build up the State; because it is the family that conserves and increases the nation (Q. 11); iii. Yet the family is not merely a part of the State. It is prior to the State, i.e., it is not conceived, established and endowed with

[22] The reader is referred to Q. 15. It must not be overlooked that the family as it were builds up the State: thus the State really includes the families and all other member communities living in it; a whole has a higher goal than the part, since it embraces the goal of the part and additional factors.

rights by the State. Rather it is of natural origin and hence endowed with natural rights of its own (Q. 15).

11. *What function has the family?*

The family's function is:
1. to be the cradle and school of human life;
2. to provide for wants of daily life;
3. to guard and protect what is excellent and revered among men.

ALTHOUGH the family is by nature one of the smallest communities, its functions are very varied and exceedingly important. Hence we can speak of the family as a community of life and upbringing,[23] as a domestic and economic community. All these goals and duties result from its being "the cradle and school" of human life.

1. The whole of man's life, natural and supernatural, in Church and State and in all other communities, is dependent on the family. The latter is the most important of all communities; and for this very reason it deserves to be cherished.

2. The family must embrace and provide all that man needs materially and spiritually for his daily life because, as the source and cradle of new life, it includes and continues the marriage partnership, because its duty is to protect and develop human life within itself, and because it is necessarily prior to all other societies. Hence Aristotle, St. Thomas Aquinas and many others held that the responsibility of providing for the needs of daily life lies with the family, with the

[23] On this point cf. Qs. 17ff.

"domestic community".[24] And they are not here thinking merely of material things such as living quarters, food and clothing, but also of moral and cultural goods. The family is the primary and most advantageous centre for forming man as a whole man and for the pursuit of the human ideal in its entirety. Genuine family life aims at all that is true and good and beautiful, and, in a Christian sense, all that is holy and supernatural. In respect of religion, morality and culture the family has an exalted mission, which is to oppose superficiality by depth, false liberty by divinely imposed obligation, mere material progress by the cultivation of spiritual values, the uprooted by the person rooted in the community, the cold impersonality of law by the warmth of sincere and deep charity.

PIUS XII (Address to German Catholics 4 September 1949).

"*. . . Preserve and keep with jealous care that twofold sacred heritage handed on to you by your fathers. The first is the civilized Christian family. Foster and defend it wherever it still exists especially in the country parts. Indeed, defend it, for it is in great danger of being lost. Where it has been lost already, especially in certain working class areas of the cities, build it up anew. There is nothing more precious to hand on to your children and youth than the culture of the Christian family.*"

Developments in the technical, economic and intellectual fields have tended to deprive the family of many of its former functions. But mankind must hold fast to the basic principles, that the family: i. has certain functions which cannot in any

[24] The family is called a "domestic community" because parents and children reside and live a common life in one home (Q. 14, 1). This home which to-day is very often no more than rooms in a flat, ideally should be spacious and so set out as to form a real home for the family (ibid. III, 2b).

circumstances be transferred to another community; ii. embraces the whole man, that is, the human person in the fullness of his nature and values; the whole man is child of his parents, and is first and foremost theirs, and entrusted to them (Qs. 24f.); iii. can nowhere lose the right to fulfil those functions which have been assigned to it by nature (by God).

3. Innumerable movements, influences, events and conditions, partly hidden and partly public, make it difficult today for even the most capable and most willing family to fulfil its purpose internally and externally. There is much in modern life that tends to disperse members of the family, to draw them away from the family instead of towards it. It is almost impossible to expose a family to the impact of the modern world and yet preserve in it the "eternal" values and the refined and deep character of a living community.[25]

12. *Of what kind is family unity?*

The family is a natural, moral, juridical and economic union.

THIS question and answer have been suggested by an important statement of Pius XII which must certainly play a major part in any discussion of the family.

[25] We mean all those things that add up to the modern way of living and that are not bad in themselevs, but which, because they are so manifold and practically unavoidable, present an enormous pressure upon, and danger for, family life; for example, radio, cinema, television, business worries; sport; daily commuting between home and work; in the religious domain there is the tendency to emphasize the apostolate of associations, clubs rather than of families; one important factor is the lack of sufficient preparatory instruction for those about to marry on marriage and the family.

PIUS XII (Address of 3 June 1950).

"We need to fix our attention, without narrowing the vista, on the responsible task to give a just scope in life to numerous families in their natural, moral, juridical and economic unity. Even if only in a modest, yet at least adequate fashion, such scope ought to meet the demands of human dignity."

1. Natural union does not imply that the family is a living organism like the plant, animal or man. Natural is contrasted with artificial, with what is "made" by man. Thus it implies that the nature and character of the family can only be understood from the operation of nature and its creator (Q. 10): i. The origin and goal of the family are natural. God instituted the family primarily for the procreation and education of children (Pius XI, D. I. M., C. T. S., 12). ii. The particular structure within the family is natural: the authority of the parents with the father's authority taking precedence, the children's obligation to obey (Q. 13). iii. The distinctive rights resulting from the nature and purpose of the family and binding every human authority are natural (cf. No. 3 below; also Q. 14).

2. Moral union refers to man's free will, to his being bound by the moral law, his divine vocation and responsibility to God. Accordingly moral union implies union among men whose actions can and should be morally good.

As regards the family the highest and immediate goal of the family is the eternal happiness and the morally good life of its members. The family should be man's staff and support along the way to moral perfection and to eternity. The family community is a school and testing ground of almost every virtue.

PIUS XII (Address of 2 November 1950).

"That is why there is no more important concern than to spread as widely as possible that aspect of Christian teaching which tells us that man is born to happiness in time and eternity, but will attain neither unless he does his duty and obeys the divine law."

"Moral union" points clearly to the family as a formative community. Education aims at the morally good man, demands morally irreproachable surroundings and should be only imparted by morally good people (cf. Qs. 17–33).

3. Juridical union: the family is not only a juridical institution; it also enjoys rights. There are things that are due to it in the strict sense, that must be granted to it (Q. 15).

4. Economic union: the family is united in the acquisition and use of material goods, and is thus a self-supporting community making common use of the material goods it acquires. Making provision "for the needs of daily life" (Aristotle and St. Thomas Aquinas) was always looked on as a principal function and duty of the family. Formerly both functions, production (along with distribution) and consumption, were largely exercised within the family. The family was not only a community of consumers, but also of producers. Today this very healthy situation only partly survives in agriculture and trades (handicraft). To an ever increasing extent the family has ceased to be a community of producers and has become simply a community of consumers. The reasons for this are, for example, progressive industrialization and the division of labour, increase in the number of wage and salary earners, the size of companies and businesses dictated by capital investment.

With regard to the situation existing today, we consider that the family, even as a mere community of consumers, retains its great economic importance. The use made of incomes continues to rest largely with the family, which can consequently influence decisively the commodity and money market. Even today the family can still teach thrift, simplicity and contentment through sensible "housekeeping" (especially with modest means). Unfortunately the family, by ceasing to exist as an economic unit, is endangered in its own existence. Common work, livelihood gained in common, income earned in common contribute considerably to the strengthening of family ties.

PIUS XII (Address of 15 November 1946).

"More than others you live in permanent contact with nature. It is a material contact since you live in places as yet far removed from the excesses of an artificial civilization .... But it is also an eminent social contact, since your families are not only consumer but also and especially producer communities."

13. *Of what is the family in need?*

The family is in need of the authority enjoined upon both parents, but the father's authority enjoying priority.

AUTHORITY is taken here in its proper sense, viz. as juridical and moral power to lead the community with personal responsibility, and to command accordingly (not merely to advise, recommend or request). Corresponding to the power to command is the obligation to obey, *i.e.*, to do what the other wills and decrees. Thus it is clearly a question of greater and lesser authority. Among Christians and Catholics too, family authority has suffered damage. The primacy of the authority of the father particularly is said to conflict with the equal rights of man and woman (Qs. 12 and 15). In accordance with the Scriptures, the Catholic Church teaches that parents are entitled to genuine authority, and that the father's authority has primacy in the family.

The Sacred Scriptures show us: "He went down with them on their journey to Nazareth, and lived there in subjection to them" (Luke 2:51). Christ urges the observance of the fourth commandment (Matt. 15:4). "You who are children must shew obedience in the Lord to your parents; it is your duty" (Eph. 6:1). "Children must be obedient to their parents in every way; it is a gracious sign of serving the Lord" (Col. 3:20). "Wives must obey their husbands as they would obey the Lord. The man is the head to which the woman's body is united" (Eph. 5:22–24). "Wives must be submissive to their husbands, as the service of the Lord demands" (Col. 3:18). "You, too, who are wives must be submissive to your husbands[26] (1 Pet. 3:1).

Pronouncements of the popes:

LEO XIII (D. I.).

" ... Similarly, the authority of fathers of families is, as it were, an image and copy of the authority that is in God, from Whom all fatherhood is derived in heaven and on earth."

PIUS XI (C. C., 26, 76).

" ... The bond of charity having thus set its seal upon the home, there must reign in it what St. Augustine calls 'the order of love'.

[26] It is sometimes suggested that these texts apply only to a particular age in the past, that they reflect the custom of the country and the people of that time. But there is no doubt that the popes think otherwise. They are convinced that they apply also to the present time and to the future.

This implies the primacy of the husband over his wife and children, and the ready submission and willing obedience of the wife, according to the commandment of the Apostle: 'Let women be subject to their husbands as to the Lord, because the husband is the head of the wife as Christ is the head of the Church' (Eph. 5: 22–23)."

"But there is a true equality between them, which is to be recognized in all that pertains to the person and dignity of a human being, and in all that is implied by the marriage contract and is inherent in wedlock itself. Here, admittedly, each party enjoys exactly the same rights and is bound by the same obligations. In all else, however, there must be a certain inequality and adjustment, demanded by the welfare of the family and by the unity and ordered stability which must reign in the home."

PIUS XII (Address of 21 October 1945).

"Thus the noble, sacred authority of father and mother is bereft of all its majesty."

I. Parental Authority

1. Parents have real authority over their children, since they have given them life and are thus the true and actual cause of them. The children belong to them; they are a "part" of their parents (St. Thomas Aquinas). Parental authority is what is called authority by reason of origin, authority in the highest sense, for it is based on the giving of being and dependence in being. The authority of parents begins when the children are born and continues until they are able to cope with life independently. Parental authority has the character of genuine authority to command, but being embedded in love it is not a dictatorship. Even where they have to command or forbid,

parents should allow themselves to be guided by motives of love.

2. Parental authority also arises from the nature and function of the family. Parents and children cannot possibly live together in an orderly manner without someone being responsible for this order. And without question this responsibility lies with the parents, because it is they who have established the family, and it is they who are responsible for its origin and existence. But they can only guarantee order if they have authority to command. The family is the best school of obedience, a virtue which man needs in order to lead a morally good life.

3. Since the family embraces man, not under this or that aspect (for example, as a worker or athlete), but *as man,* parental authority has, considering its scope, the widest possible field in which to operate. Parents are entitled to command their children in what is necessary: i. so that the family can live an ordered life; ii. so that the children may become accustomed to doing deliberately and at all times what is good. By this the limits of parental authority are defined; even parents are not justified in demanding of their children what is evil, or in commanding them to do everything and anything.

4. Genuine authority must be entitled to compel the refractory and punish the disobedient; otherwise it remains ineffective and unsuccessful. When parents have to punish their children they are not avenging wrong (which is the duty of the State; Q. 90), but rather helping their children to amend. It is in keeping with the character of the family to inflict only slight punishment of a transitory nature.[27]

[27] Cf. St. Thomas Aquinas, II–II, 65, 2.

EXAMPLES. Parents may not beat their children or let them go hungry to such an extent that they become ill and unable to do their work. Children can be so intimidated that they remain frightened all their lives. One of the most severe punishments that can be inflicted on a child is to be disinherited and turned out of the parents' home. Only exceptional reasons justify such punishment: incorrigibility, open and repeated rebellion, bringing serious disgrace on the family.

5. With greater maturity children outgrow the authority of their parents and have to take more numerous decisions on their own responsibility. While the parents may advise and caution, and while children are bound to listen to them, the choice of a profession, trade, or state in life (married or single), the choice of a marriage partner are matters that do not come under the authority of parents. Obviously parents have no right to obstruct the children in their religious life and in their religious and moral progress.

II. The Primacy of Paternal Authority

1. From the nature of marriage and the family the following can be directly inferred: Both father and mother have parental authority; each has it independently so that the father cannot forbid the mother the exercise of her authority. The more harmoniously father and mother weigh and decide all matters together the better.[28]

[28] In 1949 the "International Union of Catholic Women's Leagues" drew up proposals for the safeguarding of the rights of woman and of the child, among which is the following: "Instead of the idea of subordination the idea of cooperation should be introduced as the norm for legal regulations defining the rights and duties between husband and wife, yet provision should be made for investing the husband and father with the authority in case dissension between husband and wife seriously endangers the life of the family community. But it should always remain possible to include the wife." We see that in spite of

Fathers and mothers have to exercise parental authority each in his or her own way, and this is particularly so in the domain corresponding to the natural character and function of each. We must reject all proposals to guarantee equal rights by appeal, in case of differences of opinion, to an outside agency which would have to decide the matter itself or transfer the decision to one or other of the parents (for example, the Court of Chancery). Such regulations conflict with the nature and "intimacy" of the family which simply cannot tolerate outside interference in this form.

2. Collectivist ideologies which expect all salvation to come from the State strongly oppose any primacy of paternal authority. They would substitute for the Christian idea of the family a modern idea which subordinates the family to the State. In this way they would withdraw youth from the family and surrender it defenceless to the influences of politics. This struggle to bring about a change in family law is only part of the general struggle against the whole Christian social order (cf. Pius XI, C. C., 75).

As we have said, there are Christians also who have departed from the traditional teaching. They do this, as they say, in order to establish the wife and mother in those rights that have been hitherto withheld from her, and to protect the family against the arbitrariness and failure of the husband and father (cf. Q. 15). They stress quite rightly that family law as it stands must be improved in many respects. But when they support an unqualified equality of rights for husband and wife, and are prepared to submit to an outside agency all difficulties that cannot be resolved within the family, they are striking at its core.

its proposal of mediation the I. U. C. W. L. subscribes to the primacy of the father's authority.

3. Our point is this: The father's authority has primacy within the family; where it becomes necessary the father as "head" of the family has the right and the obligation to make the final decision.

Our points are supported by these considerations:

i. In every family matters will inevitably arise which are not seen and judged alike by father and mother. This is simply human. But it presupposes that either the father or the mother is competent to make the final decision.

ii. Nature confers this right on the husband (father); *i.e.*, the primacy of paternal authority is rooted in the natural temperament, aptitude and inclination of both sexes. The man is by nature more fitted to direct and to command, for external achievements, assumptions of responsibility, representation and defence; while the woman is more fitted to watch over, care for, preserve inwardly; the man woos, the woman allows herself to be wooed; the man stands in the battle of life, the woman at the cradle of life. Sacred Scripture, the great doctors of the Church and the popes clearly speak of the order of primacy and subordination (cf. the texts quoted above). This claim which, taken by itself, sounds rather severe, should not be taken out of the context of the whole Christian conception of matrimonial love. Hence paternal authority must be exercised on the basis of mutual love and in its fulfillment.[29]

It is difficult to say in detail when, and in what domains, paternal authority is primary. The natural law lays down no clearly defined limits.

On this point Pius XI: Both parties have equal rights and duties "in all that pertains to the person and dignity of a human

[29] Cf. Pius XI, C. C., 26; also St. Thomas Aquinas, I, 92, I ad 1.

being, and in all that is implied by the marriage contract and is inherent in wedlock itself" . . . "In all else, however, there must be a certain inequality and adjustment." This inequality and adjustment are more precisely defined: "as demanded by the welfare of the family and by the unity and ordered stability which must reign in the home".

In other words, there is equality in all that pertains to the contracting of marriage, to its existence and fulfillment (matrimonial love and fidelity, the right to have children), and in what pertains to human dignity and the rights of the person (the right to life and maintenance, the right to freedom of conscience and belief (cf. I, Q. 71; Q. 84). In all else Pius XI acknowledges the primacy of paternal authority, but he restricts it to what the specific situation makes necessary for order in the family. Hence the mother must not be restricted, let alone suppressed, in her functions as "heart of the family" (Pius XI) by the authority of the father (cf. Q. 15).

14. Which are the fundamental rights of the family?

The family has a natural right:
1. to existence and a life of its own;
2. to the unimpeded fulfillment of its functions, especially in the matter of education;
3. to sufficient and secure maintenance;
4. to protection and encouragement;
5. to association and self-help.

FUNDAMENTAL rights are "essential rights" (Pius XII); they are directly connected with the origin and essential nature of man and natural communities. From these further rights are inferred (I, Qs. 78, 86). Pius XII considered it his task "resolutely to defend the rights of the family", just as his predecessors after the first world war again and again proclaimed and defended "the fundamental rights of the family" (Address 21–9–1949).

I. Continuity and a Life of its Own

LEO XIII (R. N., 10).

"Provided, therefore, the limits prescribed by the very purposes for which it exists be not transgressed, the family has at least equal rights with the State in the choice and pursuit of the things needful to its preservation and its just liberty."

PIUS XII (Address of 21 September 1949).

"These tasks derive from the actual nature of the family as willed by God and therefore entitled to be for its own sake."

1. The natural communities, marriage and the family above all, form a necessary part of the order of creation; without them God's plans cannot be fulfilled. Therefore the continuity of the family must be guaranteed absolutely.

2. The right of the family to lead a life of its own is gravely threatened today, *i.e.*, its right to live in the manner appropriate to it, and as it deems good; thus i. to form a community that is really a "family", one that cultivates the outlook and values, preserves the order and behaves in the manner natural to the community of parents and children; ii. to decide itself the specific form in which all this will be realized. At the same time, the family is bound to observe the general moral norms of living together laid down by nature, *i.e.*, by God. For example, mutual love and respect and proper care of the children are part of the proper life of a family.

The obligation and blessings of a shared life must be expressly referred to. Various reasons (occupational training and work away from home, illness and convalescence) may render a shared life impossible for a shorter or longer period. The parents must take responsibility for this in each case. Seeking to deprive the family of the benefit of the shared life is to be guilty of a very grave offence. (Examples are the organization of labour in totalitarian States; economic developments that separate families because they do not provide for living accommodation at the place of employment; excessive claims of work, politics, party etc.).

Each family forms a "little world" of its own. What this world looks like and how it lives depends on place and time, tradition, cultural development, position and profession. But outside forces, "movements", authorities (officials) have no right to interfere in this intimate life of the family, or to exert an influence on its members that upsets or depresses it.

EXAMPLES. The obtrusive way in which relatives and friends meddle in family matters; in which various organizations, including religious, may exercise their claims upon family members; in which the peace of the family is disturbed by noise (radio and TV). The disparagement of the family in word, writing and illustration (press, radio, films, TV, theatre), which causes youth to lose their pleasure in family life. The practice in totalitarian States of putting children and adolescents into State employment, State schools and party formations; encouraging them to spy on their parents; compulsory attendance at lectures, courses, parades etc. with the result that no energies are left for family life.

II. Unimpeded Fulfillment of its Functions

1. Every natural community should strive after its God-given goals and carry out its functions, grow and develop in so

doing, and contribute its share to the common good. For this reason the family must not neglect those functions proper to its nature (Q. 11); parents may not pursue their professional or other external activities so intensely that family life declines. Unfortunately many professions absorb too much time and energy. Public (political) office and activities often encumber the individual to such an extent that his own family is more or less left to itself. Not least to blame for this state of affairs are those who, because of indifference or lack of courage, refuse to play their part in these common tasks.

It is well known that woman working can have bad consequences for family life, especially when the work has to be done outside the home, or when it is either too heavy or unsuitable for the woman. In general the mother's absence affects family life more unfavourably than the father's.

PIUS XII (Address of 21 October 1945).

"Equality of rights with men has led her to abandon the home, in which she used to reign as queen, and subjected her to the same burden and the same hours of work. No heed is paid any longer to her true dignity, to that which is the firm foundation of all rights: her distinctive quality of womanhood and the essential co-ordination of the sexes. The Creator's purpose for the welfare of human society, and especially of the family, has now been forgotten."

2. The family must be able to carry out its functions, by itself, and unimpeded. This is demanded by the principle of subsidiary function (I, Q. 52) and by the human order of life, if this is to accord with the nature and dignity of man and with the will of God.

Natural communities have their goals and functions prescribed by nature and these can be fulfilled only by them and by no other community. Therefore the family has no authority to surrender its functions to others, and it must defend itself if someone tries to oust it from its natural position (cf. Q. 15). Only when things are done well and according to its intentions may it entrust a part of its functions to others.[30] The family needs freedom: No one has the right to oppress it, to forbid or render impossible the unimpeded carrying out of its function (except when it should fail seriously in its duties; Q. 18).

III. Maintenance and Property

1. Improvement of conditions. Man is not the "product of his environment", of economic and social conditions. But the environment has a decisive influence on the individual and the family for good and evil, for their advancement as well as their decline. Pope Pius XII repeatedly pointed to the untenable and unjust character of modern economic and social conditions, apportioning a full measure of blame to these conditions and to those responsible for them. He declared outright that there is no hope of rehabilitating the family without an "improvement of conditions".

PIUS XII (Address of 22 January 1947).

"When one seriously considers the conditions in which you live, modern ideas and ways of life, the modern world with its misery and unhappiness, but also with its seductive and almost diabolic magic, the tyrannical pressure of organizations with immense power, one must admit that, in order always and everywhere, without reserve and compromise, to remain true to God's commandments, requires self-

[30] This is the case particularly with the education of children. The whole question of education will be discussed in detail in the next lesson (Q. 17 ff.).

control, constant effort and self-denial, which approach a heroism the characteristic sign of which is the witness of blood."

PIUS XII (Address of 2 November 1950).

" . . . however, under the pressure of misery social conditions must find improvement, impelled by justice and love everyone who calls himself a Christian must work for the improvement of these conditions. This is demanded especially where it is necessary to help innumerable men who are able to lead a proper and happy married life only after the removal of greatest hardships."

PIUS XI (C. C., 126).

"If families, especially those with many children, have no home fit to live in; if the husband cannot find work and livelihood; if commodities of daily use can only be purchased at exorbitant prices; if the mother, to the great detriment of the home, is compelled by need to earn money by her labour; and if in the ordinary or even extraordinary labours of childbirth she is deprived of suitable nourishment, medicines, the assistance of a skilled physician, and other necessities; then it is obvious that if husband and wife lose heart, married life and the observance of God's commandments become very difficult indeed."

2. Decent living conditions.

Great material worries and hardships are as a rule unfavourable soil for moral integrity and energy. Hence where material want and the uncertainty of a livelihood persists (Q. A., 61), it is only in exceptional cases that a healthy family life will thrive.

i. The family has a right to a decent maintenance of life,[31] to

[31] We do not enter upon the manner in which this claim should be satisfied. The family is first of all obliged to use its own energies and help itself by industry and thrift before it should be entitled to help from outside.

what it needs in order to nourish and clothe itself in modest but sufficient measure.

PIUS XI (D. R., 72).

"It follows that the demands of social justice will not have been met if it is not within the power of workers to earn a wage providing a secure livelihood for themselves and their families; if they cannot accumulate a modest fortune insuring them against that widespread poverty which, like a running sore, afflicts so great a part of the human race; and if measures are not devised in their interests enabling them, either through public or private insurance organizations, to make provision for old age, sickness, and unemployment."

PIUS XII (Broadcast, Christmas 1942).

"The dignity of labour demands, not only a just wage, adequate to the needs of the worker and his family, but also the maintenance and development of a social order which will render possible and secure a portion of private property, however modest, for all sections of the community; which will favour a higher education for children of the working classes who are exceptionally intelligent and well-disposed."

ii. The housing question merits particular attention today. The popes have stressed its importance.

PIUS XI (Q. A., 135).

"We are appalled about the way in which the present economic system and, above all, disgraceful housing conditions, undermine family ties and family life."

PIUS XII (Whitsun Message, 1941).

"The concept of 'Lebensraum' and the provision of living space is today at the very centre of the social and political aims. Ought we not,

in this connection, to think of the living space of the family, and to liberate and extricate it, above all, from living conditions which do not even allow the thought of a home of one's own."

From a moral point of view the following basic demands must be made: i. The dwelling must have the space, privacy and surroundings suitable as a home in which a family can live decently with sufficient freedom to move about.[32] ii. A desirable aim is a house of one's own, on its own ground, possibly with a garden. iii. The family must be allowed to choose its place of residence freely. Restrictions on changing residence are only justified for weighty reasons and as a temporary measure. iv. Public housing schemes must be really social, that is, they must first of all benefit those in need, and must be guided by the desirability of having the home as near as possible to the place of work. v. Where other means fail, help should be given for decent resettlement and emigration schemes (Qs. 35 and 120).

3. Income and property.

LEO XIII (R. N., 10).

"That right to property, therefore, which has been proved to belong naturally to individual persons, must in likewise belong to a man in his capacity of head of a family; nay, that right is all the stronger in proportion as the human person receives a wider extension in the family group."

Cf. also R. N., 34/35, and Pius XI, C. C., 123.

[32] Modern blocks of small flats conflict with this demand to provide the family with sufficient space. They are designed from the outset to provide room for only one or at most two children and are thus deliberately designed for birth-control.

PIUS XI (Q. A., 71).

"In the first place, the wage paid to the working-man must be sufficient for the support of himself and of his family (Encyclical Casti Connubii, December 31, 1930, Christian Marriage, C. T. S., Do. 1137*).... Every effort must therefore be made, that fathers of families receive a wage sufficient to meet adequately normal domestic needs."*

i. The family must be able to acquire and possess, increase and use at its own discretion, that which it needs. ii. Parents have the right (and most often the obligation) to bequeath family property to their children. iii. The family income should be sufficient to cover the needs of daily life and to build up the necessary reserve funds for the future. (Education and training of the children; the vicissitudes of life such as illness, old age, unemployment.) iv. Social justice demands that all those who have to support themselves and their families on a weekly wage alone, should receive a family wage. This family wage is not a substitute for the living wage, but rather its standard and norm. v. Where the family wage is not possible or not sufficient (economic crisis, large family) family bonuses or allowances must be introduced. It is not for the State to do this but rather for the various organized branches of the nation's economy. Only where the latter is not yet in a position to fulfil this function should it be taken over by the State.

IV. Protection and Encouragement

1. The primary duty of society towards the family consists in warding off all that threatens the existence and favourable development of the family. More than any other community the family is in need and worthy of protection (Q. 11). But all

measures are of no avail unless the public (school, press, radio, television and films) unanimously acknowledges and defends the advantages of the family and family life.

2. The interests of the family will be promoted especially by an internal reform, by greater economic, moral and spiritual stability, by sound economics which provide opportunities of livelihood; tax rebates and other forms of privilege (scholarships, loans); sound education laws and policy; support and encouragement of family enterprises (handicrafts, agriculture).

V. Self-help: Family Associations

PIUS XII (Address of 21 September 1950).

" . . . to unite families to a joint force conscious of its strength; to help the family that its voice be heard in the public affairs of every country as also in society as a whole so that it should never have to suffer from these, but on the contrary profit from them."

PIUS XII (Address of 18 September 1951).

"One of the most powerful and in the long run most effective means is the union of the fathers of families who stand together in the same convictions and the same determination."

1. The family has the natural right and the natural duty to protect itself, that is, to do everything that serves its growth and development. It can avail itself with advantage of the natural right of free association (I, Q. 27; 71). A solid front conscious of its strength has more power than any number of actions by individual families (organized family groups, family associations).

2. Pius XII advocated the union of families on both a national and international basis: "The families of the whole world should unite for the purpose of helping one another" (Address of 21 September 1950). The family must make its voice heard in public. Laws and measures, development and reform plans, schemes and projects (housing schemes, the matter of settlements, family compensation funds) that have a decisive bearing on the fortunes of many, if not all, families cannot remain a matter of indifference to these families.

15. *What are the State's obligations towards the family?*

The State is obliged:
1. to respect and defend the family and its basic rights;
2. to safeguard without discrimination those values that guarantee order, human dignity, health and happiness to the family (Pius XII);
3. to promote the family in every proper way;
4. to give rights to the family that are in keeping with the times;
5. to intervene in serious cases when family life breaks down.

OUR question concerning the obligation of the State is necessary because the State is the highest executive and legislative authority and is charged with the care of the common weal. But for a long time now the State has tended to bring the family under its control (this is particularly so in totalitarian States; Q. 104). The family is prior to, and older than, the State (Q. 10, No. 3). Its origin, nature and own proper rights do not derive from the State, rather it has all these of itself, that is, in virtue of the divinely instituted order of creation. But the social nature of man has not full scope in the family. For this reason the family is incorporated in the State and is subordinate to it. It must abide by its just laws, contribute to the common weal and instil a civic sense in youth (Qs. 30/31).

PIUS XI (C. C., 126).

"If private contributions are not enough for this purpose it is the duty of the public authority to supplement individual resources, especially in a matter of such importance to the common good as that of assuring to families and married persons conditions which befit the dignity of man."

PIUS XII (Address of 21 September 1949).

"The dignity, rights and duties of the domestic hearth which God has instituted as the life cell of society, are on that account as old as mankind; they are independent of the power of the State, but it must protect and defend them when they are threatened."

PIUS XII (Address of 18 September 1951).

" . . . The family does not exist for the sake of society, society exists for the sake of the family. The family is the basic cell, the constituent element of the community of the State . . . . For it is the State's first duty unconditionally to protect the values which assure the family of order, human dignity, health and happiness."

1. The obligation of the State to acknowledge, respect and defend the family and its basic rights is based on the closeness to nature of the family, and on the function of the State as guardian of the natural law and of human values and communities. In its constitution the State must expressly guarantee the existence and basic rights of the family.

2. For the family to develop its beneficial activities certain

conditions are necessary and it must be able to live in favourable surroundings. This is what Pius XII meant when he described it as the primary duty of the State "to safeguard without discrimination those values that guarantee order, human dignity, health and happiness to the family". On no condition may the State neglect or give up this function of being the advocate and trustee of a favourable development of the family. External circumstances may aggravate this task but never abolish it.

3. The State must give the family every possible help, and indeed positive support. There is no lack of opportunity for a positive "family policy": reduction of taxes, loans for the building of houses; proper consideration for proposals, or petitions from families and family organizations, co-operation on parliamentary committees; schools and education (cf. Lesson 3). The State may only do what is beyond the scope and powers of other communities (subsidiary function of State assistance).

4. The State should have concern for sound and modern family legislation and develop and continually supplement that section of its laws which deals with the family. This family legislation may cover only those exterior conditions and considerations for which the State has competence. To regulate the interior life of the family is not a matter for the State but for the family itself (and the Church; Q. 16). On the question of family reform we suggest that the nature and basic rights of the family must not be attacked either directly or indirectly. (Monogamy as the basis of the family; its own proper life; rights of parents: [Qs. 25/26]; parental and paternal authority; maintenance of the family, and support for the obligations of fathers.) Family legislation should be accommodated to modern conditions and changing ideas, but no human authority can do away with

natural rights or declare them to be out of date and no longer effective.

PIUS XI (C. C., 77).

"So far as the changed circumstances and customs of human intercourse may render necessary some modification in the social and economic condition of the married woman, it rests with the public authority to adapt the civil rights of the wife to the needs and requirements of modern times; but with the stipulation that regard must be had always to the needs of woman's special temperament, to moral rectitude, and to the welfare of the family, and provided also that the essential order of the home remains inviolate. This order was constituted by an authority higher than man's, that is by the authority and wisdom of God Himself, and neither the laws of the State nor the good pleasure of individuals can ever change it."

5. The State can demand that its just laws be observed, and this it may supervise. But only when it has become clear that a family has very seriously failed in its responsibilities may the State, in certain circumstances, step in, since it is its duty to protect the social order of the community as a whole. If the evil can be remedied from some other quarter the State should not interfere.

EXAMPLES. Relatives or neighbours will look after someone whose family has neglected him. Good people may take charge of a neglected child or one left to look after itself; a charitable organization protects children from cruelty.

16. What is the attitude of the Catholic Church towards the family?

The Catholic Church considers the care of the family one of her noblest and most important duties.

PIUS XI (D. I. M., 43).

"History provides examples, especially in more recent times, of governments which have infringed and are still infringing the rights which the Creator of the human race has bestowed upon the family; and history also shows incontestably how the Church has constantly risen in their protection and defence."

1. The Church works for the sanctification of the family. The Church is a redemptive society founded and commissioned for the sanctification of men and of human society. Christ sanctified the family. It is his will that his followers should live in "holy" families.

Thus for the Church it is a question of the sanctification of the family as a community. Hence the demand; i. for an apostolate devoted expressly to the family, and aimed at awakening a sense of the values of family life and developing a sense of mutual loyalty; ii. for family life inspired by religion. The family as a community ought to express its faith and piety (besides attendance at Church and reception of the sacraments, there should be family prayers in common).

The sanctification of the family implies its regeneration. The Church believes and trusts that grace gives men sufficient strength to observe the law of God (cf. Pius XI, C. C., 115ff.). The family will not be saved by having its natural bonds and obligations relaxed, but by being led back to the order willed by God. There must be a return to the divine plan which is the standard of all law and righteousness (*ibid.* 100). Hence the Church advocates and supports "family consciousness" and care of family life.

2. The Church fearlessly protects the basic rights of the family. In the past, and even more so in modern times, the basic rights of

the family have all been attacked, denied and declared invalid. In her defence against these attacks the Church has never failed, although she has been decried as unreasonable, intolerant, petty, hard-hearted and malicious. She will never give way, either to threats or enticements.

3. The Church observes the disintegration of the family with deepest regret. The weakening and decline of family life are part and parcel of the crisis which affects modern marriage. The disintegration of marriage and family life springs from the same roots (Q. 9). The American bishops have described "secularism" as the basic evil of our time and the real source of the disintegration of the family.[33] They meant the denial of all other-wordly values, the exclusion of God from man's thoughts and life, thus the complete secularization and uprooting of man and human society (I, Q. 9, No. Id; Q. 18, No. I).

Three social phenomena in particular have contributed to the dissolution of the family: a growing disorder of morals, the supremacy of science and an increasing domination of "organization-man". Science has discovered new and considerably less dangerous "methods" of birth-control. Concentration upon industrial production has devalued the place of the family in society; general trend towards socialist or welfare type of society; automation and nationalization in industry; the family reduced to an institution for procreation and the preservation of the nation.

4. The uprooted character of family life can be countered only by replanting it in the soil of the divine order of creation and salvation. The modern trend towards automation ought to be met: i. by excluding it from the sacred domain of the marriage

[33] In their statement of November 1947.

and family community where it can only cause harm; ii. by again bringing men to an appreciation of the happiness of true family life, and by showing them how in the quiet, in the interior freedom and happiness of the family, the strength to master modern life is effectively developed.

Lesson Three

EDUCATION, PARENTS' RIGHTS, SCHOOLS

As MIGHT be expected the struggle for youth today centres round the question of education. Modern totalitarian systems have shown what can be done when education is taken out of the hands of the family (and the Church) so as to improve the prospects of training youth according to some "party line". It is quite impossible for the Church to compromise with the exaggerated educational claims of any movement or community. On this point the popes leave no room for doubt.

17. *What is education?*

To educate is to try to induce man to be morally good and to act accordingly.

To educate is to foster what is good, to form a person of character and a useful individual. An educator seeks to influence those committed to his care, to convince them of the rightness of his ideal and of the uprightness of his intention.

Education can influence: i. the intellect (reason); instruction, imparting of knowledge: formation of intellect. ii. The will. The individual should learn to do good and avoid evil. Incentive, admonition and warning, entreaty, advice and command:

formation of will. iii. The feelings (the heart): awakening what is noble and beautiful in our sense capacities (the passions: love, hate, joy, sadness, desire, fear).

True education aims at the most harmonious formation possible of all three forces of the soul, appealing above all to the will. The individual can impel both himself and his fellow men to be, and to do, good: self education. The individual will become morally good only through his own willing and acting, and by co-operating with the grace of God.

18. What is the aim of Christian education?

Christian education aims at the formation of the true and perfect Christian who will fulfil his duties faithfully in respect of this world and the next.

PIUS XI (D. I. M., 7, 67, 120).

"For if the whole purpose of education is so to shape man in this mortal life that he will be able to reach the last end for which his Creator has destined him, it is plain that there can be no true education which is not totally directed to that last end."

"For it must always be borne in mind that the person who has to receive a Christian education is the whole human being: a compound of spirit and body united to form one nature; endowed with all the perfections of mind and body which belong to that nature and with others that transcend it; man, in other words, as we know him from reason and from divine revelation."

"Hence the true Christian, the product of Christian education, is simply the supernatural man: the man who feels, judges, and acts always and consistently in accordance with right reason enlightened by the example and teaching of Jesus Christ: in other words, the real and perfect man of character."

PIUS XII (Address of 1948).

" . . . to form and to educate the human person as a whole, its intellectual abilities no less than its will and instincts, the future industrious and honest citizen as much as the Christian, the children of God, who share a heavenly calling" (Hebr. 3:1).

1. THE Christian lives in and by Christ, that is in and by his grace, in his imitation, according to his intention, in the hope and expectation of his kingdom. i. The supreme aim and measure of education is the supernatural, transcendental destiny of man. All Christian education is stamped with "the sign of the eternal". Christ expressly demands the perfect man, one who takes the perfection of his Father as his model and measure (Matt. 5:48), who fulfills the will of God in all things perfectly (Matt. 7:21 ff.). ii. Christ himself is at the same time source and cause, centre and pivot, advocate and model of supernatural life and conduct (John 1:16; 13:13ff.; Matt. 11:28ff.; 19:21). Thus Christian education will lead to him and will take his example as the standard and illustration of its teaching. It will allow him to work in men by his sacrifice and sacraments; for Christian life and conduct are essentially supernatural. iii. Christian morality is receptive to our fellow-men and to society; it is altruistic in the true sense. The proof of this is Christ's principal precept of charity which, according to his own words, includes all the other precepts. Thus of itself, and not just on the grounds of "prudence" or concern for the future, Christian education is concerned with man as a social being, ready to practise active charity and to make sacrifices (I, Q. 19, No. 3; Qs. 113, 118/122).

In an address of 1 January 1948 Pius XII called for:

i. youth of strong faith with high ideals of the reality, power and value of which it is deeply convinced;

ii. youth that is "alive" and prepared courageously to translate its convictions into deeds;

iii. "holy" youth that prays daily and drinks at the fountain of supernatural life – youth filled with Christ.

2. Christian education aims at the formation of the Christian conscience, of the conscientious Christian. The Christian conscience includes: i. Right direction, that is, direction by a reason enlightened by faith that judges in accordance with the supernatural order of revelation and salvation. ii. Firm decision of the will, that is, loyalty to God's precepts through the strength of grace.

3. Christian education envisages, fosters and teaches all natural values:

i. It aims explicitly at training the individual to judge and act independently and to take full personal responsibility.

ii. In so far as what is naturally good belongs to the moral law[34] the Christian must fulfil it.

EXAMPLES. Honesty in matters of money and property (forbidding theft, embezzlement, robbery); truthfulness (forbidding calumny, detraction, false accusation, frivolous judgment); honouring agreements; obeying the just commands of legitimate authority; reverence towards God, parents, country.

iii. Specialized training in trades and professions is quite consistent with Christian ethics. The latter requires the individual to be efficient and keen in his job. It appreciates and welcomes outstanding professional achievements. But the individual must not become the slave of his profession and his work.

[34] Cf. St. Thomas Aquinas, II–II, 80.

4. Pius XI expressly demands (D. I. M., C. T. S., 116) that Christian education should take due account of modern trends, problems and dangers, instead of evading them. Hence Christian principles must be applied with understanding of changing circumstances. The teacher and educator must be conversant especially with the forces, movements and influences that seek to frustrate his work. The following in particular should be mentioned: i. Materialism: Rejection of the supernatural, one-sided and exclusive preoccupation with material values promoted as they are by fashion, advertisement, cinema, radio, TV and literature (I, Qs. 9, 62). ii. Technocracy, the mechanization of the world and of life. The interest in technical achievements and events especially among youth has increased to such an extent that the spiritual and intellectual life is almost hidden by it. iii. Collectivism, the danger of mass-democracy. From it springs the most serious threat to the independence of the individual (I, Q. 17).

19. What conditions are required for a sound education?

A sound education requires a legitimate and capable instructor and favourable surroundings.

1. EDUCATION may be imparted in two ways: i. Systematically, and in virtue of a mandate. In this sense it is understood here (and generally). Compulsory education is based on a mandate and a title in law. ii. Without a special mandate, either by simply living in society, or by a conscious, though not necessarily obliging influence that can often be very deep and lasting (parents and children, brothers and sisters, colleagues and fellow-workers).

2. A basic condition for a sound education is the competence of the instructor.

The type and extent of this competence depend on the character of the community (family, school), on age and sex, living conditions, and stages of development (child, adolescent, poor or good abilities, town or country; previous education); on the goal pursued (priest, doctor, teacher, craftsman, welfare worker). Educational competence must include knowledge and virtue, formation and character. For example, without sufficient knowledge of the truths of religion and fidelity in religious practice no sound religious education is possible; the same is true of morals.

3. Every teacher knows the good or evil effects of an individual's environment. Man is not completely at the mercy of the influences of environment (false theory of environment; I, Q. 13). But precisely because he is capable of personal decision and responsibility it is important to create a favourable environment and to protect him against an unfavourable one. By environment we mean: i. What an individual inherits at birth; whether he is born of healthy or unhealthy stock is by no means a matter of indifference to his responsiveness and later development. ii. The immediate circle in which he spends his days and especially his early years (family and school, neighbourhood, circle of friends and acquaintances etc.). The narrow or spacious character of his home; the atmosphere of the child's home; the spirit that manifests itself in the school; the outlook and habits that predominate round about. iii. Public conditions, such as the juridical and political order and its effects (for example the granting of human rights), concord or strife among social classes (for example the equal status of wage-earners), all that is said, shown, done and offered in public (what determines the state of public culture and morality: anti-religious and obscene publications, including theatre and films; forms of social life, amusements and entertainment industry).

PIUS XII (Address of 20 April 1946).

"In the natural order of things, or We might say, according to the will of the divine Providence, the child is to be born and grow up in the healthy atmosphere of a family and a Christian society, and there to develop till maturity has been reached which enables him to play his part in maintaining, spreading and perfecting a just and Christian order of society."

20. Has man a right to education?

Man (the child) has a natural right to a sound education.

PIUS XI (D. I. M., 66).

" . . . because every Christian child or youth has a sacred right to be instructed according to the teaching of the Church, the pillar and ground of truth. Any teacher disturbing his pupil's faith, and so abusing the trust which the young place in their teachers, and taking advantage of their natural inexperience and their extravagant craving for an illusory freedom and independence, is doing him a grave injustice."

1. AT THE beginning of his life and for a number of years man, helpless but in need of help as he is, faces his most important task in life, that is, his own perfection (sanctification). In order to determine the extent of his needs and of the help he requires we must take into consideration the loftiness and importance of his aim in life, the variety of individual and partial tasks, the inner conflict in man himself and the thousand and one dangers that threaten him from without (disinclination, passions, self-seeking; error, deception, temptation, corruption, cunning and trickery, brutality and force).

Education is thus an indispensable means for the attainment of the divinely appointed goal of life. Man has a natural right to such a means, and this right is not bestowed on him by men or by human communities. It is given to him by God at birth as his natural dowry.

2. Natural rights are independent of the favourable or unfavourable circumstances under which an individual is born. Every child has a right to a sound education, thus also the illegitimate child, the difficult child, the child born in poverty and want, the neglected child. It is true that nature (God) has imposed the duty of education on particular individuals and institutions, but if these should fail through inability, disinclination or indifference education must be provided by some other quarter.

3. An education is sound when it seeks to lead and induce to good; an upbringing for evil is a grave injustice to the individual, to the community, and to God.

An education is sound also when it refers to man as a whole, that is when it embraces all that belongs to the moral rectitude of human life. Faults are committed very often, and at times "systematically", through bias, through the curtailment and shifting of values and duties. The result is an unbalanced individual, one who is spoiled, eccentric, incompetent or ignorant of life, even a failure and wastrel.

EXAMPLES. Many an education blights the freshness and innocence of youth, confuses candidness with impudence, openness with an exaggerated critical sense, modesty with prudery, obedience with obsequiousness. Every form of atheistic (free-thinking) education ignores the basic values and assessment of religion. In purely political programmes of education everything is made subservient to the community and the collectivity and true independence is crushed in the individual.

It is sound when it continues until the individual is mature enough to face "the world". No one can foresee in detail the vicissitudes of the future; but we can attain the prudence and the strength of virtue to hold our own no matter what happens.

21. *Who is competent to educate?*

Church, family and State, each in a different way, are competent to educate.

PIUS XI (D. I. M., 11, 15).

"Education is necessarily a social, not an individual function. Now there are three necessary societies of which man becomes a member from birth, three societies distinct from one another and yet, by God's will, harmoniously connected: two of these, the family and the civil society, are of the natural order, and the third, the Church, is of the supernatural order."

"Since education is concerned with man as a whole, whether considered as an individual or as a member of human society, whether as constituted in the order of nature or in the order of divine grace, it follows that this function belongs in due proportion to the three societies afore-mentioned, conformably with the proper end of each and with the present order of Providence established by God."

The answer will be explained in detail in Qs. 22–31. Here we wish to say that by education we mean the complete spiritual and moral formation of the individual, and not merely training in a particular profession or subject.

The question might be formulated more precisely thus: Who, in virtue of natural or divine law, is authorized to educate men, and who is obliged in virtue of the same law to submit himself to this education?

Individuals and communities with an authorization of this kind do not need to obtain from any human authority permission or a mandate to educate.

22. On what grounds is the Church entitled to educate?

The Church is entitled to educate because she is the teacher and the supernatural mother of men.

PIUS XI (D. I. M., 17, 18).

"The first ground of the Church's right is that supreme teaching authority and office which the divine Founder of the Church delivered to her."

"The second ground of the Church's right consists in that supernatural office of motherhood whereby the Church, Christ's spotless Bride, bestows upon men the life of divine grace and nurtures and fosters it by her sacraments and teaching."

PIUS XII (Address of 8 September 1946).

"But the Church too as teacher and supernatural mother of souls has the direct and highly significantright to co-operation in education and in everything that is necessary and useful to that end."

1. THE mandate to educate is undoubtedly contained in the twofold authority and mission of the Church to teach and to sanctify men. Because in the Christian sense here intended, to educate means to co-operate in bringing man to conform with his supernatural vocation and attain his eternal salvation.

2. The right of the Church to educate is a supernatural right, since the Church is a supernatural society; it is direct and original, since it was bestowed upon the Church by Christ himself, given implicitly with her foundation and mission; it is inalienable and inviolable, for it can neither be abolished nor restricted by men. Rights conferred by God are valid because, and so long as it pleases God; it is a "perfect" right (Pius XI, D. I. M., C. T.

S., 27), *i.e.*, it is as comprehensive as required by the mission of the Church.

3. The Church cannot, either wholly or in part, renounce her right to educate. But since this right is based on her spiritual and supernatural motherhood, she exercises it with maternal solicitude. She is really concerned for those entrusted to her charge, seeking to protect them "against the danger of imbibing any poison that may corrupt pure doctrine and moral rectitude" (Pius XI, D. I. M., C. T. S., 26), and having their eternal salvation always in mind in whatever she does in the matter of education.

23. What is the extent of the Church's right to educate?

The Church's right to educate extends:
1. to all peoples, but primarily to the faithful;
2. to anything that is necessary and useful for the fulfilment of her mission.

PIUS XI (D. I. M., 25, 27).

"The Church has a further right, which she cannot surrender, a further duty, which she cannot abandon: that of exercising general vigilance over any education which is given to her children, that is, to the faithful, in public or private institutions; and this vigilance extends not only to the religious instruction given therein, but also to any other subjects taught or regulations imposed, so far as these are in any way related to religion and morals. (C. I. C. c. 1375, 1381, 1382.)"

"The Church's mission in the sphere of education extends to all peoples, to all places, and to all times, according to the command of Christ: 'Teach ye all nations' (Matt. xxviii, 19) and there is no power on earth that can legitimately oppose or hinder it."

1. ALL men are called by God to belong to the Church of Christ, there to live as Christians. Therefore the Church is authorized to address herself to every individual and to influence him positively. She is further authorized to proclaim to the world the ideals and principles of education and to make them obligatory so that the world has to listen to her and to follow her instructions. It is her own faithful that the Church seeks to educate above all.

2. In the sphere of education the Church's right extends to all that may serve to form the "true and perfect Christian" (Q. 18). God has given the Church the right to all those means that are necessary and useful for the attainment of her goal. Moreover, the Church herself decides what in particular is necessary or useful; otherwise her entire educational rights would be dependent on the arbitrary rules of secular authority. Of course, the Church will always be prepared to take account of changing conditions, and needs. But she cannot accept a proscription of the scope and limits of her educational activity.

3. The Church is competent above all for religious and moral education in so far as this is of a supernatural character and order. She is authorized to tell men with infallible certainty what is their life's goal and what ways lead to it; it is she who administers and makes available the sources of grace, the sacraments.

Natural religious and moral education is very closely connected with the supernatural. It is most essential for the spiritual and moral life both of the individual and of the community that no ideals or principles contrary to nature should be taught. It is for the Church to judge authoritatively whether the natural ideals and principles of life are true and can be justified before God.

4. Many subjects in education have only an indirect bearing on

the spiritual and moral life; they may promote or retard it considerably according to the basis, spirit and extent to which they are pursued (for example philosophy, history, geography, sociology, economics, biology and psychology).[35]

5. Pius XI did not exaggerate when he said that "education pertained to the Church by right and in fact in a very special way" (D. I. M., C. T. S., 32).

The Church[36] has the indisputable right: i. to instruct, or have instruction given, publicly in the truths of religion. She is within her rights when she insists on being allowed to give adequate religious instruction to her faithful in all state schools; ii. to teach those subjects that have a decisive bearing on the spiritual and moral education of man (for example philosophy, history, biology); iii. to found and run her own training colleges and educational establishments the aims and purposes of which are not inconsistent with her mission: primary and secondary schools; grammar schools and universities; kindergartens; hostels for apprentices and students; training colleges for teachers, welfare workers, nurses etc.; iv. to demand that the faithful should be able to attend schools that respect Catholic convictions; v. to ensure that instruction in religion as in other subjects in all public and private eductional and training establishments should not conflict with the spiritual and moral education of her faithful.

[35] We need only consider the aims, syllabus and text-books of some liberal or totalitarian types of education in order to appreciate the disastrous effects these subjects can have on religious and moral education: the view of man as the ultimate measure of all things, the view of mass man disguised as "social" man, the exaggeration of race (theory of National Socialism), military training (under the pretext of promoting a new healthy generation).

[36] I am following here the excellent summary given in the Social Catechism of Malines, No. 26.

24. *Has the family a right to educate?*

The right of the family, or of the parents, to educate cannot be disputed.

WITH this question we begin the discussion of parental rights, that is, the right of parents over their children and their children's education. Corresponding to the rights, of which so much is heard, are the duties which are too often overlooked. It is often maintained that in reality the Catholic Church cannot recognize a parental right, that her bishops and priests and politicians under her influence have invented parental rights in order to preserve the denominational school. It is said that the Catholic Church denies to parents of other ideologies (free thinkers, atheists) that right which she demands for Catholic parents. To meet these points we might note that both Leo XIII and Pius XI (D. I. M., C. T. S., 35) were able to quote St. Thomas Aquinas in support of the parental right. In fact the Catholic Church has always championed the right of parents. Naturally, a right of parents in order to be a valid right must apply to all parents irrespective of belief, race or political opinion. But the parental right by no means implies giving parents a free hand to educate their children in any ideology, political propaganda or party line they please (Qs. 26f.).

LEO XIII (Sap. Chr.).

"The parents hold from nature their right of training the children to whom they have given birth, with the obligation superadded of shaping and directing the education of their little ones to the end for which God vouchsafed the privilege of transmitting the gift of life."

PIUS XI (C. C., 16).

"And there can be no doubt that, by natural and divine law, the right and duty of educating offspring belong primarily to those who, having begun the work of nature by begetting children, are absolutely forbidden to leave unfinished the work they have begun and so expose it to inevitable ruin."

PIUS XI (D. I. M., 84).

"Evidently the first and natural environment for the child's proper education is his family, which is divinely instituted for that very purpose."

PIUS XII (Address of 8 September 1946).

"The parents have a primary right, grounded in the order of nature, to educate their offspring, a right that is inviolable and that is superior to that of civil society and the State."

PIUS XII (Address to the Mainz Katholikentag, *5 September 1948).*

"If the signs of the times are not deceptive, the future too will demand of you to fight for the freedom of the Church, for her and the parents' rights to the child, his or her education and school."

The family's (parents') right to educate the children is substantiated by two clear, natural (not artificial) facts:

1. The right of parents over their children. This right is based on the fact that the child owes its existence to the parents. Hence the child belongs to them, not as a thing (house, or a piece of land) which they can dispose of as they please, but as "life of their life", subjected to their authority, given into their charge and placed under their protection.

2. The right of the children to education and the responsibility and suitability of the family (parents) for their education. Education is the natural extension of generation. Only by education is the newly born child developed to become fitted for life (general dependence, Q. 20): Undoubtedly the parents are responsible in the first place to see that the child receives (and learns) what it needs in order to succeed in life as a human being, as man. Parents are best fitted by nature to give their child the appropriate care and education, especially in the first years of its life. Nature implants in both children and parents a fundamental and strong mutual affection and attraction: the closest blood relationship, similarity of natures (assimilation, innate dispositions). The family forms the most favourable environment possible for a good education; only foolish or malicious minds can deny this.

25. Of what kind is the family's right to educate?

The family's right to educate is:
1. natural and given directly by God;
2. inalienable and inviolable;
3. prior to the educational right of the nation and the State;
4. comprehensive;
5. subordinated to natural and divine right.

THE answer has been taken point for point from papal pronouncements (cf. the texts quoted in Q. 24).[37]

[37] Cf. Code of Canon Law, can. 1113: "Parents are bound by a very grave obligation to care for the religious, moral, physical and civic education of their children to the best of their power, and also to provide for their temporal welfare."

PIUS XI (D. I. M., 36).

"Therefore the responsibility and consequently also the right of educating children comes to the family direct from the Creator. It is a right which cannot be surrendered, because it is combined with a very serious responsibility; it is therefore prior to any right of the civil society or the State, and for that reason may not be infringed by any power on earth."

PIUS XII (Sum. Pont.).

"Almighty God has entrusted to fathers and mothers of families the duty of providing for the best interests of their several children, in this life and in the life to come; and moreover, of educating them in the true principles of religion. That is a right which no man can usurp without the gravest injury to natural justice. Such education, to be sure, aims at arousing and urging the minds of the young to a sense of the high duties which they owe to patriotism; duties, whose exact and cheerful performance is the only test by which their active patriotism can be shown. But any training of the young which neglects, of deliberate purpose, to direct their minds towards a heavenly country as well, does a grave wrong both to the souls of those who are concerned and to the rights (which are also the duties) of the Christian family."

1. *A natural right given directly by God.* The rights on which marriage and the family depend for their favourable development and fruitful activity do not derive from any human agreement (legislation, permission), but from the author of nature, God the supreme Lord. Thus these rights are part of the divine plan and therefore "incontrovertible" (Pius XI, D. I. M., C. T. S., 42). As the "community of parents with their children" (Messner) the family is an educational community in every respect.

2. *An inalienable and inviolable right.* The parents themselves cannot renounce their right, and hence their duty, to educate their children. They are, and remain, responsible for their children's education. As a rule the education of the children at least during their infancy devolves on the parents themselves.
Inviolable. The family's right to educate its children is sacred. Whoever infringes it violates a higher order. And it does not matter how the family is set aside, whether openly or disguisedly, whether by threats or cajolery, whether through the school or through service in patriotic organizations, whether by the withdrawal or "generous" grant of allowances, whether on religious or political grounds.

3. *A right prior to the educational right of the nation and the State.* The educational right of the family is prior to that of all other communities of the natural order of life:

The child belongs to its parents before it belongs to the State. Hence the right of the parents to educate their children is prior to that of the State. The State must respect the educational right of parents absolutely and without restriction (cf. Qs. 26f.). The family and the State are the two necessary communities of the natural order to which original educational rights belong. Thus all other institutions and communities (for example schools, professions) are even less entitled to exclude or ignore the parents. It must be emphasized here that the educational right of the State is subsidiary (Q. 27, No. 1, ii.).

The following principles govern the relation between the educational rights of parents and those of the Church:

i. The parents receive directly from God the right to educate their children as Christians. Christ raised marriage to the dignity of a sacrament. He sanctified the family and at the same time imposed on it the task of educating its children in his spirit and in imitation of him.

ii. Therefore the Church is not entitled to infringe the rights of the family; but she is certainly entitled and obliged to declare and to protect these rights. At all times she has been the advocate and guarantor of parental rights. Wherever doubts arise concerning the extent and the competence of parental authority she is authorized to resolve such doubts.[38]

iii. In all matters concerning religious and moral education the Church has the right to give directions to the family (parents) that are binding on it. This right is based on her mission and her spiritual motherhood (Q. 22).

iv. By divine right Church and family are bound to co-oporate in a harmonious and fruitful manner. Only in this way will God's plan for the sanctification of men be effectively realized.

v. In so far as the family belongs to the supernatural order the educational rights of the Church are higher and prior in origin to those of the family. Nevertheless the family may be described (Pius XI and Pius XII) as the primary educational community, since nature precedes the supernatural, provides its basis and is contained in it.

4. *A comprehensive right.* Family education must aim at the individual's success in life as a man whatever his calling. It must see to it: i. that the young person grows up healthy and strong

[38] In former times a subject of lively controversy was whether children may be baptized against the will of the parents. The Church has always forbidden these baptisms, except in the case where the child cannot be expected to live until it comes to the use of reason. Cf. St. Thomas Aquinas, II–II, 10, 2; also the Code of Canon Law can. 750 § 2; both are cited by Pius XI (D. I. M., C. T. S., 45).

in body; ii. that religious, mental and moral formation begins in early childhood and is resolutely continued; iii. that the individual learns to understand and fulfil his social and political obligations. The social aspect is particularly stressed by the popes, because it is so very important in itself and often very difficult to fulfil, and also because of the reproach that the Church and Christian education neglect civic education. The popes particularly stress the family's duty to develop a civic sense in their children and to foster patriotism, *i.e.*, devotion to their country.

5. *A right that is subordinated to the natural and divine right.* The educational rights of the family are subordinated to higher natural and supernatural rights.[39] Hence parents must proceed conscientiously and carefully in the education of their children so that they may not overstep the limits of their competence (which are far from narrow) and lead their children astray.

26. What if parental rights are abused?

Like any other value, the parental right may be abused by men; but this is no reason to reject or even abolish it.

IN THE struggle for parental rights (the schools question) (cf. Qs. 28/29) the "intolerable" consequences of the right are frequently referred to. It is said that if the parents are entitled to the prior right of educating their children, then the children are surrendered for good and evil to the particular religious, moral and political outlook of the parents. Thus the parents might bring

[39] The following should be mentioned in particular: Natural right (I, Qs. 73/74); the right of divine Revelation (I, Q. 76); the right of the Church (No. 3 above); civil right (Q. 27).

up their children, just as they please, to be unbelievers, anti-social, Communists etc.

1. Unfortunately the parental right may be abused. But this abuse is wildly exaggerated, as though almost all parents continually failed grievously in the sacred duty of educating their children. The great number of parents who use their educational right in every way to the advantage of their children and of human society is deliberately overlooked or minimized. The abuse of a right may justify intervention here and there, but it does not justify abolishing the right. It is not the parental right itself that is the cause of the abuse, but rather the "spirit of the age", that host of different views, situations, achievements and influences that confuse, vitiate and harass the conscience of parents.

2. God has placed on man the obligation of personal responsibility and decision. It is man's vocation and duty to solve according to his conscience the tasks imposed on him; no community, not even the Church, may violate conscience (cf. I, Qs. 17/18, 41/42). It follows from this that parents must educate their children as their conscience dictates. They will have to give an account to God that they have done all they could. But parents are also strictly bound to form a right conscience, so that they will teach their children the right, that is, the God-given, ideals and principles of life, and entrust them to suitable educational institutions only.

3. It is most distressing and alarming that many parents pay so little, if any, attention to this formation of conscience, and for this reason do not educate their children (or have them educated) properly. Unfortunately in this way the family (the home) may

become the breeding-ground for all manner of aberrations. Nevertheless, they do not justify the abolition of the parental right. The situation would not be improved by abolishing the parental right, by a State monopoly of education and schools. This can be clearly shown historically from past experience both in liberal democracy and in totalitarian States. The evil must be cured radically; the family must be reformed and made competent to fulfil its educational obligation (Qs. 15/16).

27. *What is the extent of the State's right to educate?*

The State has the right and the duty to protect education, to foster it in various forms and to supplement it in accordance with the common good; but a State monopoly of education must be definitely rejected.

PIUS XI (D. I. M., 50, 51, 52, 53).

"Accordingly in the field of education it is the right, or more properly the duty, of the State to protect the prior right which the parents possess to give their children a Christian education, and therefore also to respect the supernatural right of the Church over such Christian education."

"It is for the State, moreover, to protect this right in the child itself should the parents' action be physically or morally in default, owing to their negligence, or incapacity, or unworthiness."

"Generally speaking, it is also the right and duty of the State to protect the moral and religious education of the young in accordance with the standards of right reason and the faith, by removing any public causes that are hostile to it."

"But the chief duty of the State, in accordance with the requirements of the common good, is to foster the education and instruction of the young in many ways."

PIUS XII (Address of 8 September 1946).

"We certainly do not intend to deny or minimize the proper right of the State to its own part in education. This right has its basis in the general good which also prescribes its scope and limits. But the general good demands that the State protect and respect the right to education which belongs to the family and the Church."

1. As GUARDIAN of the common weal it is the function of the State to guarantee the general good order of human existence. Especially by means of law and authority it should foster a favourable development in human existence and culture (Qs. 61/62). From this it follows that education is not directly and properly the function of the State. It is a human, moral concern, but not really a political one. Consequently in education the activity of the State has a subsidiary, that is, a supplementary character. The State is obliged i. to respect the right and the primacy of both the family and the Church in the matter of education; ii. to provide an education that does not conflict with that of the parents (and the Church); iii. to abstain from all monopoly of education. Monopoly of education is equivalent to an exclusive right and autocracy in the field of education. There is, in a true sense, a State right in education. The popes, who are accustomed to choose their words very carefully when speaking on matters of education, expressly acknowledge "the real and just rights which the State, according to the order divinely established, possesses in regard to the education of its citizens" (Pius XI, D. I. M., C. T. S., 47), "the just right of the State to its share in education" (Pius XII, Address of 8 September 1946).[40] This right of the State in the matter of education is

[40] Text and context show that both Pius XI and Pius XII were speaking not merely of civic or special professional education, but of education in

based on, and restricted to, the temporal welfare of the community (Pius XI).

2. The primary function of the State in the field of education is to protect and foster it in various ways. The State must protect the educational work of the family and the Church (as also of other educational communities) against interference and encroachment by suitable legal means; it must make this work possible and secure by granting financial assistance; it must facilitate it by countering demoralizing influences. It affords education the best form of help in the school system (Qs. 30/31).

3. Education forms an independent province in the life of the nation; it should also foster a sense of loyalty to the State. Hence the State is entitled to give youth and the nation a civic education (patriotism, obedience, social justice etc.).

PIUS XI (D. I. M., 57).

"It is also the function of the civil society and the State to provide, not only for the young but for citizens of every age and condition, what may be called a civic education .... This civic education, which includes in its wide and manifold scope practically the whole of the State's activity for the common good, must clearly conform to the laws of equity and therefore to the doctrine of the Church, who of those laws is the divinely appointed Teacher."

4. We must expressly acknowledge the right of the State to compel or to "replace" incompetent parents or those that

general. The sad experiences of the last centuries led Catholic scholars to deny the State any just right whatever in the matter of education. But this is not being just either to the divinely established function of the State or to the pronouncements of the Holy See. The danger of monopoly in education will be banished when the State accepts the principle of subsidiary function.

neglect their duty. The State can only intervene when it is clear that the parents do not look after their children, are even a danger to them, or allow them to become morally corrupt (possibly even lead them astray and misuse them themselves). It is for the Juvenile Courts to examine and take precautions against such cases. The State is bound by the right of parents in the matter of education. It must have the children educated in accordance with the religious and moral outlook of the parents and according to their wishes (a Catholic education for children of Catholic parents, a Protestant education for the children of Protestant parents etc.). So far as the Church or other voluntary educational communities look after such children and guarantee a good education for them the State fulfils its duty by assisting these communities.

On the co-operation of the three educational communities; Church, family and State:

PIUS XII (Address of 8 September 1946).

"The aim to be attained is always that family, Church and State should work together in the teaching and educating of youth, as the natural law and the will of Christ command and as the general good requires."

28. What is the place of the school?

The school is a place of training and education; it is obliged to comply with the wishes of those competent to educate, but it carries out its function independently.

PRELIMINARY observations. The "schools question" embraces a number of very difficult and thorny individual problems. Internal and international political negotiations, agreements, elections and coalitions have been wrecked on the conflict over the Catholic schools. It is impossible to solve the schools problem without taking account of modern conditions, that is, of the modern schools system.

The modern State considers itself alone competent in the matter of school education and claims the school as its achievement. But the truth is as Pius XI showed: (D. I. M., C. T. S., 93) "... the fact that the family, alone, was unequal to the task led to the foundation of the school as a public institution; and this first came about, be it noted, through the co-operation of Church and family, and only much later with the assistance of the State. Therefore the historical origin of schools and seats of learning shows them to be by their very nature subsidiary and complementary to Church and family".

Let us consider briefly some types of school (cf. Pius XI, D. I. M., C. T. S., 95ff.): i. The denominational school (Catholic, Protestant, Jewish school) where instruction and education are given uniformly according to the ideals, principles and directions, as well as in the spirit, of a particular religious denomination. Religion is not confined to lessons of religious instruction, but permeates everything. ii. The mixed school, where children of different religious denominations are instructed and educated together, only the religious instruction is given separately. Thus what the denominations have in common forms the basic outlook. iii. The neutral, or secular school: It does not teach religion or any knowledge of God; either it is openly hostile to every form of religious belief, or it adopts an attitude of (apparent) indifference. iv. The State school: The school that is completely dependent on, and under the influence of, the State which defines its educational ideals as it thinks fit.

1. The necessity of the school as a place of training and education: The family is seldom in a position to prepare its children adequately for later life. The instruction necessary today can only be given in proper places of instruction which must at the same time be places of education. Young people who still have to learn to see and master life cannot be entrusted to an institution which appeals exclusively to the intellect, but neglects will and temperament. Like the family, Church and State are also dependent on the school. They too could not, and cannot, do without special places of training and education in view of their continually increasing tasks and problems.

Places of higher studies and research: God the supreme Lord has given men the ability and the task of penetrating ever deeper into the mysteries of nature and revelation, of getting a deeper grasp of truth and of presenting and teaching it with ever greater clarity. In order to fulfil this task systematically there was always, and is today, need of special institutions (academies, universities).

2. The function of the school. The school must always consider itself as a delegated, never as an independent, educator. It is an instrument of education. It is strictly bound to respect the goals and basic standards laid down by God, as well as the wishes of those entitled to educate. Since the educational rights of the family are prior to those of the State, the school is not entitled to set aside the family in favour of, or on instructions from, the State. It must educate in accordance with the wishes of the parents, and should continue and supplement what was begun in the home.

Although dependent and subordinate, the school carries out its function independently. It ought to be familiar with the aims and principles of education, express them in accordance with modern developments, and transmit them with pedagogical skill to its charges.

PIUS XI (D. I. M., 93).

"Therefore the historical origin of schools and seats of learning shows them to be by their very nature subsidiary and complementary to Church and family. It follows, not only that these public institutions cannot be in conflict with either family or Church, but also that they ought as far as possible to work in harmony with both. All three – school, family, and Church – must constitute one temple of Christian education, unless the school is to fail entirely in its purpose and become a pest for the ruin of the young."

3. The individual can also attain his eternal goal and do useful work for the community (Church and State) without having attended school, perhaps even while remaining illiterate. For this reason the State has strictly speaking no natural right to introduce compulsory education and to make attendance at school obligatory. On the other hand the school is a very valuable institution, and it is only fitting that education should as far as possible be made available to all, especially today when it is impossible to get on in life without attending school and to take even a modest part in any cultural activity. Today one cannot deny the State the right to introduce compulsory education. But this compulsory State education is dependent on certain conditions of which the most important is that it may not encroach on the rights of Church and parents (Q. 29).

29. What is the parents' relationship to the school?

Parents have comprehensive and inalienable rights in regard to the school.

1. PARENTS have the right to decide upon the aims of religious and moral education for all schools which their children are to attend. Otherwise they cannot fulfil their God-given educational task. Thus the school must educate youth in the principles demanded or approved by the parents. In education the right principles are most important; pedagogical skill, syllabus and teaching methods follow from these.

EXAMPLES. Children may learn to read and write from a variety of books; they may take up any kind of sport, but if God and the Church are "eliminated" from their schoolbooks or ridiculed and insulted in them, or if sports take on unbecoming forms, parents cannot remain silent.

Parents can make known their attitude in many ways: by positive demand or declaration; by approval expressed through the ballot (schools legislation); by protest and complaint; by keeping the children from school (schools strike).

2. Parents have the right to instruct their children (or have them instructed) at home, and to establish and run their own schools should they wish to do so.

This right is based on the natural primacy of the parental right over that of the State to educate. Therefore it is still valid today, although conditions do not favour it everywhere. At the same time every private school must have due regard to the State system of education. It is inevitable in view of existing conditions that the modern State should claim the right to inspect all schools. Standards of instruction, syllabi and textbooks, systems of examinations, training and appointment of teachers are all subject to civil legislation and to the regulations of the civil school authorities which are obligatory also for private schools (Qs. 30/31).

3. Parents have the right to send their children to the school

that will, in their opinion, guarantee the children a good education. This principle concerns the parents' free choice of school:

i. It concerns first of all the type of school. Whether the child should attend a denominational or a mixed school, a private or a State school is a matter for the parents to decide. The State has no right to prescribe a particular type of school; on the other hand, the Church has the right and the duty to urge parents to send their children to a school that will meet the requirements of their conscience.

ii. But it also concerns the individual school. Parents are not obliged to send their children to the local school if the latter violates their consciences as parents. The school authorities will, of course, be entitled to be informed in advance of any such objections, so as to have an opportunity of meeting them.

4. Parents can require the State's educational system to meet their wishes; thus that the principles of liberty, toleration and justice will be upheld in education laws, in the establishment and the running of schools, in educational aims and in the school syllabus. The State can only reserve to itself the organization of education if it acknowledges the rights of parents (and of the Church) both in principle and in practice.

i. Parents have a right to the denominational school. In other words, the State school ought to be denominational if the parents demand it. The wishes of the parents in this matter ought to be ascertained by means of an absolutely free vote.

ii. In cases where the State school cannot be denominational, parents are entitled to establish a private denominational school for their children. Concerning the duties of the State cf. Q. 31.

iii. Parents ought to insist that the mixed school, where this is introduced by the State, will not jeopardize their own work in educating their children. The mixed school has serious shortcomings and disadvantages, above all in the case of primary schools, since at an age when school is compulsory children have particular need of an uniform education, and they are more easily confused and more inclined to be estranged from their parents by instruction which "omits" precisely that element which is proper to parental education. Where the mixed school is unavoidable parents must ensure that there will be separate and adequate religious instructions, a reasonable objective presentation and evaluation of historical events, mutual respect and no kind of favouritism or discrimination of the children (cf. below and Q. 31, 3).

5. Parents have the right to demand or to arrange that their children will be instructed and educated by teachers who are suitably trained and of good character. Suitability primarily implies harmony with the religious conviction of the parents or children (see also Q. 34).

6. Are Catholic parents obliged to insist on Catholic schools?

PIUS XI declared (D. I. M., 103).

"Therefore let it be loudly proclaimed and generally understood that when the faithful demand Catholic schools for their children, they are not raising a question of party politics but simply performing a religious duty which their conscience rigidly imposes upon them."

Undoubtedly the pope wishes to impress also upon individual faithful that it is their duty to co-operate in achieving Catholic schools. Nowadays the mixed school is often recommended also by Catholics on the grounds that this type of school forces the different denominations more strongly to mutual toleration, serves better to bring about the much desired unity of faith, and is more likely to avoid the pedagogical pitfalls of narrowness in general outlook and character. Our view is:

i. Catholic parents must espouse the cause of the denominational school with all legitimate means. Only the Catholic school really conforms to the requirements of their Catholic belief (Pius XI, D. I. M., C. T. S., 104). Naturally the Catholic school must be up to the requirements. Objections based on a comparison between "good" mixed schools and "bad" denominational schools do not really meet the case.

ii. If the struggle for the denominational school seems of little avail, Catholic parents may opt for the school that least endangers the education of their children (provided this school does not systematically influence the children against the Catholic faith and practice (Q. 32).

EXAMPLE. A Catholic minority which, either alone or in union with other Christian bodies, could have no chance of achieving the denominational school, might, by voting for it, only bring about the defeat of the mixed school as well (which is at any rate Christian), so that it would be left with a State school that might be neutral or hostile to religion. Such a case might arise where the other denominations could at best be won over to support the mixed school but would not have the necessary majority without the Catholics.

iii. Canon Law (can. 1374) qualifies the ban on attending non-Catholic schools to the effect that, "with certain safeguards, the attendance at these schools may be tolerated in view of particular local and temporary conditions"; the decision rests with the local ordinary. This raises another question:

7. Ought Catholic parents to insist on Catholic high schools, training colleges and universities?

i. This is a much more complicated question than that of the primary schools. (The students are fewer in number but more mature; more is demanded of the teachers; higher costs of buildings and maintenance.) The course of instruction in technical schools will hardly be conditioned equally by ideologies. In the universities, centres of learning and scientific research, it is right for different schools of thought to come into contact with one another and to engage in discussion. It is there that Catholics receive their formation who will later, often in an indifferent or hostile atmosphere, have to express the intellectual, social, political and religious creative force of the Catholic faith and way of life.

ii. Catholic parents ought to be able to entrust their sons and daughters to high schools and universities in which their Catholic principles will be respected. Where this is not the case owing to the character and outlook of the existing institutions, parents are in duty bound to foster all the more at home those values which are neglected or falsified in the schools. The Catholic section of the nation has undoubtedly the right to establish its own high schools and universites to which the State may not deny recognition and support (Q. 31).

30. What rights has the State over schools?

A sole right of the State over schools must be firmly rejected. However, the State may, or must:
1. determine the standard of instruction and the range of subjects for the different types of schools;
2. establish order in the educational system by means of legislation;
3. insist on an adequate civic education.

OUR answer suggests the extent to which these rights and duties interact. For this reason we go on to the next question and shall explain both afterwards.

31. What are the State's duties in regard to the schools?

The State is obliged:
1. to protect the rights of the family and the Church;
2. to base its schools on the wishes of the parents;
3. to support private schools which guarantee satisfactory work;
4. to exercise a general control over schools in order to ensure that they fulfil their tasks in a spirit of honesty, toleration and reverence;
5. to provide (or help to provide) adequate and competent teaching personnel.

1. THE State may define more precisely the standards of instruction classifying them according to the different grades so that they may be adapted to the development and character of the school. In other words the State may determine the range and scope of school education, a task only to be entrusted to persons who know their subject and are of good character. The selection of these persons may not be made from political or other considerations alien to the domain of education, but rather according to competence and in co-operation with qualified teachers.

2. Laws may regulate an ordered system of education. They ought to be prepared with great care.

A common system of instruction and examinations (subjects, curriculum), a certain conformity in textbooks etc. is necessary in order to guarantee a unified educational system.

3. The right of the State to establish and run schools is generally acknowledged today. This right is often exaggerated to the extent of becoming an exclusive right, a State monopoly. This is a completely unjust presumption and an evil of the worst kind. In particular: i. The State's educational policy must ensure that schools are established in accordance with the wishes of the parents. ii. In a State in which the great majority of citizens are Christians State schools[41] ought to have a Christian rather than a purely secular character (cf. Q. 29, No. 4). iii. In all schools adequate religious instruction must be given in accordance with the wishes of the parents, separately for the different denominations. This religious instruction ought to be a responsibility of the Church. Instruction in general ethics can be no substitute for religious instruction.

4. The private school is a kind of scandal for some States, political parties or pressure groups, which are keen to suppress it. The State ought to recognize and support that type of school, provided the school is not inferior to its own schools as regards the standard of instruction and syllabus. Distributive justice demands that the State should contribute for each pupil attending the school at least the sum it grants in its own schools, and that the parents should receive a rebate of taxes in return for the outlay which by establishing such schools they save the State. This also applies to private schools not established by the

[41] The term "State school" may be understood in two senses: i. the (really) "public" school, established or supported by the State; without implying anything concerning the spirit of the school. ii. the kind of school which a State may consider as its own means of propagating its spirit, ideology, educational ideals contrary to those of the family and the Church. This type of school will naturally be subservient to the State. In some countries it may appear as a neutral, or secular, school in which no religion is taught, but which, if anything, is hostile to religion (Q. 32).

parents, who may, however, voluntarily entrust to them the education of their children.

5. The State's right of control is based on, and limited by, the common good. It is by no means based on any State right of ownership and control, but rather on the State's cultural function (Q. 95): i. State control extends only to matters pertaining to the educational authority of the State: for example, observing the syllabus, examinations, attaining the required standard of instruction, accord of the teaching with the educational ideal of the parents, civic education and similar matters. ii. The State may extend its control to all schools in which youth receives compulsory education, or the teaching and examinations of which it is asked to recognize. iii. Religious instruction comes under the control of the State only in respect of school regulations (regular attendance, satisfying obligations, examination results). Similarly ecclesiastical colleges, seminaries or the theological faculties in universities would be under ecclesiastical, not State supervision, because they serve ecclesiastical studies and the training of priests.

32. What is to be done if the State should impose the unchristian school?

Parents must endeavour to resist the State that imposes the unchristian school, and to repair the harm by means of a sound home education.

LEO XIII (Sap. Christ.).

"It is then incumbent on parents . . . first and foremost to keep them away from schools where there is risk of their drinking in the poison of impiety."

THIS is a reference to the very grave case in which systematically every Christian or religious element is banned from the school by the State. This is the situation in totalitarian States where the parents are kept at bay by terror and fear and by the children being induced to spy on them.

1. In theory parents have no right to send their children to such schools. They expose their children to the grave danger of apostasy and moral corruption.

PIUS XI (D. I. M., 95).

"It follows as a necessary consequence that so-called 'neutral' or 'secular' schools, from which religion is entirely banned, are subversive of the whole foundation of Christian education. For the rest such schools will be neutral only in name; they are in fact, or at any rate will become, completely hostile to religion."

2. In practice, the parents' attitude will also depend upon the circumstances (for example, the extent of the danger, prospects of reform, consequences of rebellion). At all events the parents are strictly bound to make up for what is neglected in the school by a particularly careful upbringing. The more they see that the baneful influence of the school fails against their own vigilance and counter measures, the more readily they can be permitted to bow to the unavoidable coercion and to accept the situation in silence.

3. Undoubtedly parents are in duty bound to resist such a violation of conscience by every means in their power, even when they have reason to believe that the compulsory State school does their children no harm. For the State robs them of most sacred and inalienable rights, and they must be mindful also of

other families and of the consequences to the community as a whole.

4. In totalitarian States parents are usually in the dreadful situation that every form of resistance is frustrated by the reigning terror. He who resists only makes matters worse; he can be silenced in the most wicked manner (dismissal from employment with consequent loss of livelihood; by punitive and forced labour camps; intensification of the anti-religious campaign in the schools; more police supervision and spying). In such circumstances parents will have no alternative but suffer this grave injustice in a spirit of prayer and sacrifice, provided they make use of every remaining possibility of warding off the worst from their children. At the same time they may never consent to their being trained, as it were, positively in infidelity and an unchristian way of life.

33. What is the position of teachers?

Teachers are first and foremost the representatives of the parents, no matter by whom they are trained, employed and paid.

PIUS XI (D. I. M., 109).

"But the soundness and efficiency of a school are a matter not so much of good rules as of good teachers. These should be well trained and competent in the subject they are to teach, and possess those qualities of mind and heart which their most important office requires. Moreover, for their pupils they must have a pure and divine love."

PIUS XII (Address of 1948).

"Hence the necessity of a 'fitting cultural and professional training',

in which care must also be taken that the future teacher will not lose the love for the child and the will to dedicate himself with zeal to the work in the school."

Our answer applies primarily to those teachers to whom youth is entrusted during the formative years. Teachers in the higher technical schools and universities are not to the same degree delegated by the parents, since scientific research work reaches beyond the character of a school.

1. The position, function, qualification and responsibility of teachers must be judged according to the character of the school and its relation to those entitled to educate. A school comprises teachers and pupils, but the teachers are there for the sake of the pupils. From this the following conclusions may be drawn in respect of the position of teachers. i. The teacher must realize that by his office and his profession he is the delegate of the parents. This is true even in the case where the State, the province or the municipality establishes, finances and runs the school, trains, appoints and pays the teachers (from the taxes of the citizens). Thus the teacher is bound to instruct and educate the children in accordance with the wishes of the parents, and not according to his own personal views or whims. ii. The teaching profession like any other has the right of free association. They can form organizations and unions for the purpose of raising their economic position, fostering the ideals of their profession, and perfecting themselves in pedagogical skill. But none of this should lead to the exclusion of parents and their rights, or to the usurpation of parental rights.

2. The qualification that a teacher needs, and for the attainment of which he is himself primarily responsible, is threefold:

i. professional, *i.e.,* familiarity with the subject he teaches in school; pedagogical ability and the ability to establish inner contact with his pupils;

ii. moral, *i.e.,* a moral and exemplary life in accordance with humanist and Christian ideals as well as with the particular ideals of the school in which he teaches;

iii. cultural and social, *i.e.,* the standard of general culture that one might expect from the preparatory studies, the social standing and the professional work of the teacher.

3. The training of teachers is a matter of primary importance to the whole moral, occupational and cultural life of youth and of the entire nation:

i. To the extent to which the State is obliged to establish denominational schools, it must have adequate and suitable teaching staff trained for these schools. Suitability consists first of all in this, that the teachers themselves should belong to the particular denomination;[42] the course of instruction must have a "denominational" character.

ii. Corresponding to the liberty to establish private schools is the liberty to establish private training colleges for teachers; the State has the same rights and obligations towards these as towards private schools (Qs. 30/31).

iii. In a democratic society the system of education should also be organized according to democratic principles; where it is unavoidable that children of different denominations should attend the same school, distributive justice demands that the

[42] Catholic teachers will need a deep faith and the courage to proclaim it; reverence for the Church, her hierarchy and her tradition; participation in the life of the Church (Mass and sacraments).

proportion of the teachers should correspond to the proportion of the pupils.

Lesson Four

THE RIGHT TO LIFE

Demographic Questions

1. THE right to life is intimately connected with marriage and the family, the nursery cell of human life. From it further rights are derived (cf. I, Q. 71, 1).

2. The question of man's right to life concerns both the individual and the community, because life is both a personal and a social good. The measures taken by society in the interest of human life are covered by what is known as "population policy". Thus population policy means the concern (of the State) for the existence, growth and welfare of the nation.

3. Christian moral law is bound to consider even man's natural right in the light of Revelation and faith.[43]

34. What is included in the "right to life"?

The right to life includes:
1. the right to self-preservation (the wrong of murder);
2. the right to the body's inviolate character (the wrong of bodily injury).

1. EVERY individual has an inalienable and inviolable right to

[43] Questions connected with criminal and martial law will be dealt with later (Qs. 88ff.; Qs. 128ff.).

life, that is, to preserve his existence and to do or to receive whatever is necessary for it. No individual nor any community, not even the State is entitled to kill an innocent person directly and deliberately.[44] On the duty of self-preservation:

PIUS XII (Whitsun Message 1941).

"For this is indeed man's wholly personal task, to foster and to perfect his material and spiritual life . . . . To preserve life is a heavy duty, derived from nature, and incumbent upon every man."

Life is one of the highest and most sacred values. Hence murder is considered by everyone who has not become quite brutalized, to be one of the most abhorrent of crimes. But murder means to kill an innocent person directly and deliberately. The "technique" of the murder, that is, the manner in which the person is killed, does not alter in any way the substance of the matter (shooting, hanging, strangling, poisoning, etc.).

Pius XII in his Christmas Message, 1942, began his list of the rights of the human personality with this demand:
" . . . the right to maintain and develop physical, intellectual, and moral life."

PIUS XII (Address of 12 November 1944).

"A man's life is inviolable as long as he is not guilty. Any act which directly aims to destroy it, is therefore immoral. It is immaterial whether this destruction is understood as purpose or as the means to such a purpose, whether it concerns embryonic or fully developed life or life about to end."

[44] The State may oblige its citizens to expose themselves to mortal danger only for reasons of order and security (War service, police, life-saving crews, care of victims of epidemics).

PIUS XII (Address of 29 October 1951).

"The direct destruction of the so-called 'life without value' whether born or yet to be born, such as was practised very widely a few years ago, cannot in any way be justified. . . . The life of one who is innocent is untouchable, and any direct attempt or aggression against it is a violation of one of the fundamental laws without which secure human society is impossible."

JOHN XXIII (P. i. T., 9-10).

2. Not all those who acknowledge the value of human life do so for the right reasons; but there is a compelling logic about the Christian teaching on the origin and nature of man and on the human soul.

Every human soul, because it is spiritual, is created directly by God; because the soul is intrinsically imperishable (immortal) it makes man a natural image of God: God laid his hand on man and placed him under the rule of men, yet he did not surrender him absolutely to them to be a mere article of use (cf. I, Qs. 13 and 18).

From what Revelation teaches concerning creation the Catholic Church deduces logically that men are never absolute masters over human life but always only its guardians and stewards; human life has not been entrusted to them to be destroyed, but rather to be preserved and fostered. This command is quite independent of the character of human life, the stage of its development, or by the advantages or disadvantages to be expected from it.

3. Intimately connected with the "right to life" is the "right to the body's inviolate character", that is, that the bodily organs, internal or external, must not be destroyed (either completely or partially amputated, put out of action or rendered useless).

Here also a duty corresponds to the right: the individual is entitled only for certain reasons to permit an operation on himself that is likely to damage or destroy some bodily organ. In former centuries one spoke of mutilation[45] and meant the removal or the rendering useless of parts (limbs) that belong to the whole human body, and exercise useful and necessary functions within the human organism as a whole, as for example hands and feet, eyes and ears. The development of medical science has made operations possible of which former epochs had no idea. But the question remains, whether ordinary individuals or men in power may dispose of the organs of the human body so freely as to decide themselves, when, and for what purpose, an organ may be removed or put out of action. Catholic ethics answers this question in the negative. Operations injuring the body or bodily organs are permitted only when they are necessary for health or preserving life. As we remarked already, the cases of punishment and of self-defence are not being considered here.

Everyone knows from his own personal experience, that he can, and may, train or use his bodily faculties (organs) in a variety of ways. The activity of his organs lies in his power; thus to a considerable extent it is for him to decide whether, and in what manner, he uses his faculties. But it is not in his power to decide whether he should possess these faculties or not, and what function and significance they should have. The faculty (organ) is part of his natural constitution which man cannot give himself, but which is given to him. Now man is a person (Qs. 12/13). The faculties bestowed on him by nature participate in his dignity as a person. Just as man himself is no mere article of use of which he himself or others may dispose auto-

[45] Cf. St. Thomas Aquinas II–II, 65, 1.

cratically, so also his faculties (organs) are no "ordinary" utility goods that may be preserved or destroyed just as the individual may think fit. Man can adduce no right that would entitle him to interfere in a destructive manner with his natural constitution unless to sacrifice a part in order to save the whole, that is, for reasons of self-preservation.

EXAMPLES. An individual can raise and lower, twist and turn his hand and do a hundred and one kinds of jobs with it, but he may not put it into a machine and let it be cut off. He can open and close his eye, but he may not pluck it out.

35. *What is the attitude of modern population policy to the basic rights mentioned?*

Modern population policy sanctions and promotes measures that cannot be reconciled with the right to life and to bodily integrity.

MODERN population policy is faced with difficult and serious problems, for example: In one place lack of living space due to overpopulation; in another place serious concern for the existence of the nation due to a steadily falling birth rate. The problems must be solved, but unfortunately completely reprehensible means are being used to an alarming extent (Q. 120). This applies particularly to two measures:

1. Birth-control.
2. Mercy-killing.

36. *Why must birth-control be rejected?*

Because it acknowledges no responsibility in regard to human life, and does not scruple to make use of immoral means.

1. BIRTH-CONTROL means that man takes care that fewer children are born. He thereby prevents natural fecundity being fully utilized; he "directs" nature so that less human life is conceived (contraception; Q. 37), or that the foetus is removed from the mother's womb before it has independent life (abortion, termination of pregnancy; Q. 38).

2. But there is a legitimate birth-control, which is that practised from good motives and in a morally right manner. Such motives are, for example, the illness of the mother, the fear of diseased children, economic situation (confined living quarters; small income; impoverishment), the wife practising a profession (as doctor, maternity nurse), a voluntary, mutual decision due to religious conviction.[46] The only legitimate means of birth-control recognized by Catholic ethics is voluntary continence and the use of the safe period in marriage (Q. 8, No. 2).

PIUS XII (Address of 26 November 1951).

"Therefore, in Our last Allocution on conjugal morality, We affirmed the lawfulness and at the same time the limits – in truth very wide – of a regulation of offspring, which, unlike so-called 'birth-control', is compatible with the law of God."

JOHN XXIII (M. M., 193-195).

3. There has been illegitimate birth-control in all ages. Since the end of the nineteenth century birth-control has come to threaten the existence of many nations and States. The small family has become the rule, and in many places births no longer suffice to maintain the population, let alone to increase it. There are various reasons for the general spread of birth-

[46] Insufficient motives are for example: that children are not wanted; fear of losing one's figure; social obligations.

control such as the decreasing religious and moral sense; the consequent spirit of worldliness (refusal to take life seriously, craze for pleasure), aversion to responsibility; conflicting views on the purpose and order of sex; the disintegration of marriages and family life (Qs. 8 and 11); depopulation of the land and urbanization (new housing conditions, higher material living standards); new working conditions; technological achievements; easy availability of contraceptives, greater effectiveness and less danger of surgical operations; less danger of infection and the possibility of quicker and more certain cures; influence of press, theatre and films, radio and TV., the impact of world wars.[47]
4. Modern birth-control is linked historically with the name of Malthus (1766–1834). Malthus maintained that while population increases in the ratio of 1-2-4-8-16, production of goods increased in the ratio of 1-2-3-4-5. Hence the world was threatened with over-population which would result in inestimable mass misery and the most frightful vices. In order to avoid and to forestall this fate the number of children would have to be limited, but – as Malthus himself expressly demands – in a morally lawful way. Neo-Malthusianism, which appeared round 1850 and which up to the present day wrongfully claims the support of Malthus, dropped the moral considerations and recommended contraception (Q. 37), abortion (Q. 38), and sterilization (Q. 39).

37. *How does contraception affect social life?*

Contraception:
1. desecrates and harms marriage and the family;

[47] Undoubtedly economic necessity is a strong motive today; but economics are not the cause of the development as a whole. Birh-control generally begins among the well-to-do and middle classes and gradually spreads to other sections of the population.

2. debars innumerable children from entering natural and supernatural life;
3. dissipates the moral strength of the nation.

1. Contraception is the most widely practised form of birth-control. It is the simplest way of getting rid of all worry about the child; it excludes the child from the outset. It is due to contraception and abortion (Q. 38) above all that large families are dying out and the family of three to four children is getting rare. There is nothing that can compensate for this loss; innumerable children are prevented from entering life and so from sharing in eternal happiness; our earthly home is deprived of untold values.

2. In most cases contraception is motivated by selfish pseudo-motives, such as lack of self-sacrifice, pleasure-seeking, the child being regarded as a troublesome burden. Healthy nations that are led into the evil of contraception by modern methods of canvassing, and advertising, very soon sink from their previous high moral level. Contraception is at the same time cause and effect of moral decline.

3. Public authority has the right and duty to prevent the diffusion of neo-Malthusian doctrines and the spreading of contraceptive methods. Public authority has the right and duty to repress active co-operation in the practice of birth prevention, to forbid traffic in contraceptive material and instruments.

38. Can termination of pregnancy be permitted?

Direct and deliberate termination of pregnancy is murder, which no good intention and no human authority can justify.

PIUS XI (C. C., 63).

"But can any reason ever avail to excuse the direct killing of the innocent? For this is what is at stake. The infliction of death whether upon mother or upon child is against the commandment of God and the voice of nature: 'Thou shalt not kill!' (Exod. 20:13; cf. Decr. S. Offic., 4 May, 1898; 24 July, 1895; 31 May, 1884.) *The lives of both are equally sacred and no one, even the public authority, can ever have the right to destroy them. It is absurd to invoke against innocent human beings the right of the State to inflict capital punishment, for this is valid only against the guilty. Nor is there any question here of the right of self-defence, even to the shedding of blood, against an unjust assailant, for none could describe as an unjust assailant an innocent child. Nor, finally, does there exist any so-called right of extreme necessity which could extend to the direct killing of an innocent human being."*

PIUS XII (Address of 29 October 1951).

" . . . there is no man, no human authority, no science, no medical, eugenic, social, economic or moral 'indication' that can offer or produce a valid juridical title to a direct deliberate disposal of an innocent human life; that is to say, a disposal that aims at its destruction whether as an end or as a means to another end which is, perhaps, in no way unlawful in itself."

PIUS XII (Address of 26 November 1951).

"Innocent human life, in whatsoever condition it is found, is immune from the very first moment of its existence from any direct deliberate attack. This is a fundamental right of the human person, which is of universal value in the Christian conception of life; hence as valid for the life still hidden within the womb of the mother, as for the life already born and developing independently of her; as much opposed

to direct abortion as to the direct killing of the child before, during, or after its birth."

There is the "miscarriage", that is the unintentional termination of pregnancy that can come about through various causes, for example, as a result of organic weakness or sudden excitement. Sometimes termination of pregnancy is the unavoidable and unintentional consequence of an operation or a treatment that is imperative for the recovery of the mother and which of itself serves solely this purpose; abortion is thus only "indirectly" aimed at and is permissible for correspondingly grave reasons. In the present question we are dealing with abortion that is brought about directly and intentionally; the living creature which cannot live outside the mother's womb is forcibly and deliberately destroyed.

1. Human life is present where an immortal soul has been created in a mortal body. The extent to which this body is already formed, and its parts (organs) already recognizable, is immaterial. At the moment when conception occurs in the mother's womb God infuses the soul and human life begins. Admittedly it is still "nascent life" that has yet to develop to full maturity. Nevertheless, it is a human person, an image of God. To kill this helpless creature with full knowledge and free consent is to commit murder. The argument admits of no exception, either for the mother who permits the operation, or for the surgeon and the midwife who carry it out, or for the father who has arranged or caused it to be done. No human authority either by law or by secret command can authorize a direct abortion; for none is master over life and death.

2. There has been some controversy concerning the law making termination of pregnancy a punishable offence. Some people

demand that abortion should not be a punishable offence, and even that it should be permitted by law, because they claim: i. interference with nascent life is a personal matter for the parents (the mother) in which the State must not interfere; ii. the majority of cases, including very serious ones, are not covered; frequently the law can be evaded; iii. the law is out-of-date, it is contrary to liberty.

Reply: Under no circumstances is the State justified in positively permitting direct, intentional termination of pregnancy. The law has a basic importance; it shows that the State protects the value and the right to life of the unborn child, and that it considers attacks on unborn life a punishable offence. Precisely because of the unscrupulous practice of abortion and its materialist motivation it seems both necessary and right to make it a punishable offence (also for the doctors), and at the same time to make provision for the punishment of those responsible.

3. May a woman who was raped remove the child she may have conceived or must she bear to maturity this child that she did not want and was unable to prevent? This seems to be a case of unjust aggression on self-defence. Our answer is that undoubtedly there is a case of unjust agression, but not on the part of the child but of the one who raped the woman. The child was not yet present. How then can it attack its mother who has yet to give it life? It is equally clear that the raped woman is the true and real mother of this child. The gravity of the injustice and the most bitter distress cannot gloss over this fact.

From the first moment of his life the child is a human being with the dignity and the natural rights due to a human person. This is quite independent of the manner in which it was conceived. From this follows that no one, not even the unhappy mother, has the right to procure an abortion, that is to kill the child.

The majority of Catholic moralists, therefore, hold that even in the tragic case being considered here it is the sacred duty of the mother to bear the child to maturity and that she is not permitted to interfere with the growing life within her. Such an interference would not be a real and morally good defence against the attack, but rather prevention of the consequences of the rape. The consideration of defence would validly apply only to the act of the rape; not to the exclusion of its consequences. Nowadays some moralists hold the opposite opinion. They consider the use of semen-killing agents and operations as legitimate self-defence in cases of rape, but only in such cases. They argue that while the female ovum dies and is expelled some six to eight hours after it has come to maturity and become detached, the male semen has a life of some 48 hours. Hence impregnation can take place within this period only. Only within the 48 hours in which impregnation is uncertain the raped woman may free herself from her condition (*e.g.*, by douche, injections etc.). After 48 hours she must no longer do it, because now the child, that may have been conceived, asserts its rights.

39. Is it permitted to induce sterility?

It is wrong to induce sterility in order to prevent offspring.

PIUS XI (C. C., 67).

"We refer to those who in their excessive preoccupation with salutary advice for the improvement of the health and strength of the unborn child – which is certainly quite reasonable – want to set these con-

siderations above all other ends, even those of a higher order, and would have the public authority forbid marriage to any persons who, in the light of the laws and conjectures of eugenic science, are deemed likely through heredity to beget defective offspring, even though they may be in all essential respects fit to marry. They even demand legislation to deprive such persons of that natural faculty by medical action, even against their will. They are not asking the public authority to inflict corporal punishment for some crime that has been committed, or as a preventive measure to forestall future crimes of guilty persons; they are simply arrogating to the State, against all right and justice, a power which it has never had and can never legitimately possess."

PIUS XII (Address of 29 October 1951).

"Direct sterilization – that is, sterilization which aims, either as a means or as an end in itself, to render child-bearing impossible – is a grave violation of the moral law, and therefore unlawful. Even public authority has no right, whatever justification it may use as an excuse, to permit, and much less to prescribe it or to use it to the detriment of innocent human beings."

1. BY INDUCING sterility we understand the elimination of the reproductive faculties, they are rendered impotent by human intervention; the individual is deprived of the capacity of reproduction or of conceiving children.

Man or woman can be rendered sterile. For a woman the operation is much more difficult, more dangerous and more harmful. It may be done in several ways: various kinds of operation, X-ray treatment. The principal and intended result is the same: to destroy, stop, paralyse the generative power. The individual is rendered organically incapable of reproduction although he can still have sexual intercourse in the normal way. We are here concerned with inducing sterility directly, whether temporarily or permanently. The operation must be aimed at affecting the reproductive powers. Sterility that is the necessary, but unintentional result of medical treatment may be permitted for grave reasons.

To induce sterility on eugenic grounds, for reasons of population policy, is today widely regarded as a precautionary (prophylactic) measure for the purpose of safeguarding the coming generation against hereditary disease (criminals, mentally deranged, alcoholics, neurotics), and also for increasing the number of individuals and families of healthy stock. It is argued that by inducing sterility the enormous funds that have to be provided for the care of individuals and families of hereditary disease would be available for families of healthy stock.

2. There is no doubt that families and individuals of healthy stock represent a valuable asset to any nation and State, while individuals and families with hereditary illnesses are a heavy burden. Hence the intention is certainly good to counteract hereditary disease and to grant as much help as possible to families of healthy stock. But even the best of intentions do not justify the use of means immoral in themselves (I, Q. 47, esp. No. 3). To induce sterility on preventive grounds is wrong in itself. Such interference in the human constitution is beyond man's rights.

Modern eugenic tendencies and measures are to a great extent based on the completely unchristian, and indeed inhuman, view of "worthless life". The worth of human life is evaluated solely according to material considerations, according to its usefulness (suitability for labour or military employment), or according to the cost of maintaining it. Higher points of view are deliberately suppressed. But individuals with hereditary diseases are also human beings and children of God; as such they can live and prove successful, even though perhaps more by suffering and sacrifice; and even within the earthly spheres of life many are still capable of achieving much that is useful and good. Inducing sterility may lead to the degradation of marriage. Women who are known to be sterile are in great demand by unprincipled men.

3. With regard to heredity, leading experts plainly admit that their subject is still too little explored to base universally valid laws and measures on it. From knowledge of the parents it is not possible to tell beforehand that a future child will be less suitable than the rest as a member of society. Harmful hereditary qualities can be found in many families who are proved not to be hereditarily diseased. To induce sterility compulsorily would eliminate very valuable talent. Thus Milton, Beethoven, Dostoevsky, Van Gogh might never have been born.

4. An attempt has also been made on the Catholic side to prove that the State may lawfully induce sterility in those who are hereditarily ill (especially those who are mentally diseased) since man belongs to society. Two principles are invoked: i. The individual is part (member) of society, especially of the nation and the State. ii. The whole (society) may amputate a diseased member that becomes a danger to it.[48]

There is a major error in this line of argument. Certainly a diseased member must be removed if the whole person cannot otherwise be saved (amputation of an arm or leg; removal of an appendix, a kidney or an eye). But society is not a natural organism such as is a man, but rather a moral organism in which each individual retains his own intrinsic value (Q. 31, No. 4; Q. 22). And it is only guilt that is a disease in the moral sense,

[48] Cf. I, Qs. 29-33.

and not the bodily or mental misfortune accompanying man's mortal frailty. Therefore a person fated to a hereditary disease can still be a useful member of society provided he leads an honest life, and it is plainly unjust to inflict serious harm on him by the destruction of his natural faculties (cf. Pius XI, C. C., 69).

40. Is mercy killing allowed?

To kill so-called "useless" or unwanted lives, even through pity, is to commit murder.

PIUS XII (M. C. C., 93).

"*We see to Our profound grief that death is sometimes inflicted upon the deformed, the mentally defective, and those suffering from hereditary disease, on the plea that they are an intolerable burden upon society; and, moreover, that this expedient is hailed by some as a discovery made by human progress and as greatly conducive to the common good. Is there any man of sense who fails to see that this is not only contrary to the natural and divine law written on the hearts of all* (Decree of Holy Office, 2 Dec., 1940. A. A. S., 1940, p. 553), *but also an outrage upon the noblest instincts of humanity? The blood of these unhappy creatures, especially dear to our Redeemer because especially to be pitied, 'cries to God from the earth'* (cf. Gen. 4: 10)."

THERE are many who would justify mercy killing on humanitarian grounds in order to put an end to the suffering of an incurable person. They prefer to speak of "helping one to die" (euthanasia). Not all, but most people who advocate euthanasia insist that it should be granted only to those who are incurably ill, and that these must be suffering unbearable pain, so that their life has become a torture to them.

There are two different cases of euthanasia:

i. when death is precipitated, by shortening life; the sick person dies sooner than he would otherwise have done.

ii. when only the form of death is changed. Death enters at the same moment as it would otherwise have done, but a painful death is transformed into a calm, painless, peaceful death.

1. Catholic ethics states:

i. we must wish and even pray that God may speedily release from suffering a person who is grievously ill. Pain and anguish are evils, the avoidance or termination of which we ought to desire, hope and pray for.

ii. It is right and indeed frequently obligatory to provide every alleviation that medical science can commend for the sick person (anaesthetics).

iii. The sick person or his relatives who may ask for a quicker death, as also the doctor who responds to the request, may well have the best of intentions, such as ending terrible suffering, comforting the weary relatives, but these motives justify neither the request nor the action.

2. Since in the case of euthanasia human pity is most strongly appealed to, many people allow themselves to be deceived and so reject the Catholic view. For this makes it quite clear that 'euthanasia is murder and as such can never be permitted', whether it is a case of precipitating death or of merely changing the form of death. Thus no one may ask for it, demand, order, suggest it or carry it out; it must be resolutely refused to the sick person (and his relatives), however intense his suffering, however small the hope of recovery.[49]

[49] For example, in war or in an invasion a death-bringing injection may not

God alone is lord over life and death. He has appointed the hour and the form of death for the individual. He also knows of all afflictions that befall him, and he can turn everything to good. The individual has no authority to take his own life or the life of others arbitrarily. In doing so he would usurp God's rights by setting himself up as lord over life and death.

Thus it is necessary also in these cases to distinguish between intention and action. Euthanasia must be judged according to what happens, what is actually done. Its aim is the person's dying. A drink or an injection are given to the sick person to cause his death. And in fact he dies not from his sickness but from the agents or from the act performed on him.[50] But this is deliberate and direct killing of an innocent person. The only guilt of this person consists in his being incurably ill.

3. The most recent development of the euthanasia movement actually goes so far as to demand euthanasia as a human right. As against such confusion we add the following considerations based on reason and faith:

i. It is not God's will, and is neither permitted to us mortals nor indeed possible for us, to strip death of all its terror and pain; death is meant to be the last and greatest test we have to undergo here on earth.

be given to one who is mortally wounded in order to save him from possibly being murdered by the advancing enemy.

[50] It is necessary to recognize quite clearly that this applies not only to the case where death is intentionally and demonstrably precipitated, but also where only the "form of death is changed" (so far as this is possible at all without hastening death!): the actual cause of death is the death-bringing drug administered to the sick person. Thus we have our principle: If the means, or the act performed, of its very nature is such that a person must necessarily die from it, then the action is one of murder.

ii. How weak and ill must an individual be for euthanasia to be granted to him and his right to it acknowledged? Who decides this? Conscientious doctors have always considered themselves to be guardians and healers of human life, never its grave-diggers (Hippocratic oath), and good people nurse their sick relatives, also those who are incurably ill, with complete disregard for themselves.

iii. Over every death and last struggle with death hovers the frightful, and yet the only comforting mystery of the divine ways of salvation. No man can have any idea of what God's grace works in the soul of the dying person.

41. What should a right population policy aim at?

A right population policy should seek by legitimate means favourably to influence growth and the chance in life of a healthy population.

THERE are some very effective measures for favourably influencing population movement. These measures are in part definite obligations (cf. Q. 120).

1. In the first place two conditions must be fulfilled:

i. The State must make it possible for its member societies, especially the family, to develop a successful activity of their own.

ii. The nation must recover its moral vital force; it must recover a sense of responsibility towards life and the will to live.

2. Decline in population caused principally by a falling birth-rate can only be rectified by an increase in the number of

legitimate births. Everything that is likely to counteract the disintegration of marriage and of family life serves at the same time to sustain and increase population.

3. Population increase may lead to overpopulation: too many people living in too congested conditions, the country being inadequate for their support.

Overpopulation is one of the most difficult social, political and moral problems. We may single out some of the most important ones: Too confined living accommodation and the moral dangers that accompany it; decrease in the amount of land avaible for tillage and general agricultural purposes, decline in the rural and farming class; increase of urbanization; difficulties of finding employment. Some means of checking and avoiding overpopulation are:

i. The raising of industrial capacity and production; expansion of industry, establishment of new industries and occupations, exploitation of the soil (improvement of agricultural methods, better crops etc.), exploiting the mineral wealth (mining).

ii. Increasing foreign trade: larger exports lead to a higher demand for goods and thus to more employment.

iii. Resettlement and emigration (cf. Qs. 120f.).

4. Finally every effort must be made to reduce the number of families with hereditary diseases and increase the general health.

i. The care of health is primarily the function of the family and also of particular professions and institutions. It is for the State to help create the prerequisite conditions so that these institutions and organs may be of real service to the sick; thus it is the State's duty to do whatever is too big, and too expensive to be undertaken by others.

ii. Some Catholic experts have recommended compulsory asylum at public expense for those afflicted with hereditary disease to prevent them from producing infected progeny; in return for being maintained at public expense they could do various kinds of work for the benefit of the community. Whether or not one agrees with this proposal, one can support the principle that everything should be done and all the existing resources should be made available to improve the nation's health. Artificial insemination by donor is nowadays being recommended as a measure of population policy. Artificial insemination is supposed to help the unmarried woman and also the married woman (or both husband and wife) to the child that could not be had otherwise; it is also thought to prevent progeny of tainted stock. In two addresses Pius XII has condemned artificial insemination by donor (A.I.D.) as immoral both in marriage and outside it:

PIUS XII (Address of 29 September 1949).

"Artificial insemination outside marriage is to be regarded simply as immoral. Artificial insemination within marriage, but brought about through the active intervention of a third person, is also immoral and therefore to be rejected."

PIUS XII (Address of 29 October 1951).

"To consider unworthily the cohabitaion of husband and wife, and the marital act as a simple organic function for the transmission of seed, would be the same as to convert the domestic hearth, which is the family sanctuary, into a mere biological laboratory. For this reason, in Our Address of September 29th, 1949, made to the Inter-

national Congress of Catholic Doctors, We formally rejected artificial insemination in marriage. The marital act, in its natural setting, is a personal action. It is the simultaneous and direct co-operation of husband and wife which, by the nature of the agents and the inherent quality of the act, is the expression of the mutual giving which, in the words of Scripture, results in the union 'in one flesh'."

"This is much more than the union of two life-germs, which can be brought about even artificially, that is, without the co-operation of the husband and wife. The marital act, in the order of, and by nature's design, consists of a personal co-operation which the husband and wife exchange as a right when they marry."

JOHN XXIII (M. M., 185-195).

42. What is permitted by the "right to life"?

The right to life permits man just self-defence, i.e., to defend himself against unjust attacks.

1. No one need allow another (individual, or society and its government) unjustly to deprive him of his life. Man may legitimately defend his life.[51] The right to life would fare badly if the individual were completely at the mercy of every scoundrel and every tyrant.

2. The right of self-defence is linked naturally to the following conditions:

i. The attack on life must be "objectively" unjust. The aggressor is not entitled to threaten or to kill; whether he acts out of malice, incitement or confusion of mind, whether on his own initiative or under orders, is immaterial.

Examples. Execution without previous trial by a court of justice which

[51] Cf., *e.g.*, St. Thomas Aquinas, II–II 64, 7.

has to establish guilt; crimes of violence; mass executions of innocent persons; threat of violence from persons mentally deranged.

ii. The attack must be carried out with physical means. A person may not answer calumny or perjury by killing the guilty party. He may not kill another or render him incapable of attacking "as a precautionary measure". On the other hand, he need not wait till the other has actually fired, or stabbed, or struck.

iii. The person unjustly attacked may aim at his own deliverance only (not the death of another), and may only kill the aggressor if this is necessary for his own rescue. In the terminology of Catholic ethics there is reference to *moderamen inculpatae tutelae,* that is, prudent moderation. Self-defence is not revenge, nor punishment, but self-protection, which indeed may cause the death of the aggressor if a person has no other means of saving his life. For this reason killing in self-defence is neither murder nor homicide or manslaughter.[52]

3. May the right of self-defence be extended to others, *i.e.,* may a person ward off with force and kill one who is threatening the life of another unjustly? A person may, and in certain cases even must, ward off an unjust attack on his fellowman. Con-

[52] Question and explanation deal, as one can see, with the lawfulness and not with the duty of self-defence. No one will be able to prove that there is a universal obligation to defend oneself against unjust aggression, possibly even to the extent of killing another person. This is quite clearly demonstrated by the example of our Lord who was beyond all doubt unjustly attacked, condemned and killed (cf. Matt. 26:53; John 18-23; 19:11). Renunciation of self-defence and a ready acceptance of the injustice may be an act of heroic virtue and in the highest sense pleasing to God. At the same time there is an obligation of self-defence, for example, for one who has to care for others (the father of a family), or for one who is in possession of very important secret information that must be communicated.

siderations of charity or justice may permit him or even demand of him to do so, for example, an attack on one's wife and children, on defenceless sick people.

4. A further question concerns the permissibility of self-inflicted death. Here we must distinguish between two cases: self-inflicted death as a voluntary self-sacrifice or made under obedience, for example, when a person takes his own life because the custom of his country demands it (Harakiri); the second case is one of self-inflicted death to prevent a violent, perhaps cruel, death, when the person kills himself in order to escape this frightful fate; he is merely forestalling his murder at another's hand, more than this he does not intend.

i. The Catholic Church has always considered suicide a very grave sin. By suicide we mean a person taking his own life knowingly and deliberately. His action is aimed at causing his death, for example, by firing a bullet through his temple or his heart, cutting his arteries, taking poison.

ii. Both forms of self-inflicted death, whether as self-sacrifice or as a preventive measure, are clearly suicide, since, by supposition, the self-killing is done with full knowledge and intention.[53] The distinction between the rescue that was intended and the killing that was intentional cannot be applied here, since of itself the action aims directly and formally at the person's own death.[54]

[53] It is quite another question what an individual will do in such a situation out of terror or confusion of mind. However, one must take into account how the emergency has come about. One who provides himself in good time with poison because he wants to be prepared cannot be said to act from terror or panic.

[54] There are actions, too, that *per se* (objectively) are ordained to something else, but in which the person committing them necessarily and certainly will

He does not merely accept his own death as an avoidable secondary effect, rather he causes it directly. Nor would a command issued to him essentially change his deed.

43. Has man a right to a homeland?

Man has the right:
1. not to be innocently expelled from his own country;
2. to return to it as soon as possible;
3. to find a refuge which can become his home.

PIUS XII (Christmas address, 1945, to the new German cardinals).

"Every man has a right to his own country of birth and it is wrong to expel him from there unless he has become unworthy of it by personal guilt."

PIUS XII (Letter to German bishops, 1 March 1947).

"But was it permitted in retaliation to drive twelve million men from their homes and expose them to misery? Are not the victims of that retaliation in their overwhelming majority men who had no part in the happenings and crimes which We have referred to, and had no influence on them? . . . Is it unrealistic of Us to desire and hope that

lose his life. For example, the one-man torpedo: its proper effect is the destruction of the enemy ship, and not the death of the soldier that guides it; in like manner blowing up a bridge at the sacrifice of one's own life. Again, a person who jumps from a high window to his death in order to escape being killed or raped does not commit an act of direct suicide although he (or she) may know for certain that he (or she) will be killed, because "jumping from a window" is not an action that of itself causes death; that in this instance it leads to death is due to the particular circumstance, the window being high, not to the proper object of the action. It should be clearly understood that we are here merely concerned with pointing out the difference between direct and indirect killing of self. It must not be taken to imply that actions which must be looked on as indirect self-killing should always be considered lawful. The question of moral permissibility has to be carefully examined in each case. This applies especially to the military actions referred to above which, in my opinion, are not permissible.

all those concerned might reflect calmly and undo what has been done in as far as it still can be undone."

JOHN XXIII (P. i. T., 13-14).

THAT the human right to one's own country could be questioned is due to the injustices suffered by millions of people in our own times. There is no need to insist on such a right if people are allowed to move about and setttle freely.

"Home", "native country" are closely related terms, signifying the place or country of origin of an individual and appealing to human feelings and sentiments. Home is man's narrower, native country his wider surroundings, where he belongs and feels sheltered and protected (cf. Q. 64, No. 3).

According to present-day usage, we mean by "our country"

i. that part of the world where we are born and grow up (native home), or where we reside and live (adopted home); the town or village with its surroundings; ii. the people, from among whom we originate and with whom we fit in by common outlook, sentiments, way of life; iii. that characteristic atmosphere which we call "being at home", the feeling of being protected, sheltered, not among strangers.

1. Man needs the material world about him. The many outward and inward values of his native country are part of the human life that God has given him. The individual may renounce it voluntarily. But it is unjust to expel people from their native country, not on account of some threatening catastrophe or because they are rebellious, but because they are not wanted.

2. Mass deportations are contrary to commutative justice and hence give rise to the obligation of restitution on the part of

those who order or undertake them (Qs. 96, 97). If what has happened cannot be undone, there ought to be compensation for the lost house and home, position, income, etc.

3. No one may prevent an individual from seeking a "home" elsewhere, for man has the right to provide for himself a place to live and work, where he can feel protected. Declarations of human rights are unanimous in the claim for the inviolability of man's residence. The individual must be protected against unwarrented entry of his home and similar invasions of his privacy. He needs a place which no State authority (police, political party) may enter arbitrarily.

44. What rights has youth?

Youth has:
1. those general human rights that are applicable to it;
2. special rights due to its particular character.

1. THERE are fundamental human rights that do not apply to children and juveniles, since they presuppose certain conditions and a certain age or stage of development; for example, the right to marry, to a family wage, certain civil rights. Other fundamental rights are granted to youth within, and along with, the family in which they live, for example, the right to a dwelling place, to a home. For the rest, children and juveniles, since they are human persons, possess the same rights as the grown-ups, for example, the right to life, to self-defence, to a livelihood, to honour and a good name. The exercise of some rights may be restricted for educational reasons (*e.g.*, restrictions on reading books and magazines; compulsory attendance at school etc.).

2. The years of childhood and youth are years of preparation that have their own peculiar value, however, and are subject to their own particular laws: Youth has a claim to what it needs in order to prove itself now and to prepare itself well for the future. Youth has a right[55]: i. to a good education, if possible within the family from which it comes; ii. to the opportunity of learning a suitable profession or occupation for life; iii. to protection against neglect and dangerous environments (social protection of youth; not too severe punishment, and only of a corrective nature); iv. to exemption from too heavy and inappropriate work and from military service (in peace and war) before the proper time (child labour in factories; exposing youth to moral danger in factory and workshop); v. to protection against (infectious) disease; vi. to necessary pleasures and recreation; vii. to be allowed to take that amount of responsibility in the life of the nation and the State of which it is capable.

3. Are State and society in duty bound to offer all young people the very same prospects of vocational training and of professional and social advancement? Certainly, there exists no natural right in this respect, and professional training does not come within the proper functions of the State. Moreover, the differences in talents and bent are so great that it would be absurd to attempt to give all the same opportunity. And, finally, no one can show a claim in natural right to have his talents promoted precisely in the way he wants. On the other hand, it contradicts social justice if a certain type of education and certain professional and social positions are reserved to those whose

[55] Such a list as this can scarcely be complete, since new conditions continually reveal and establish new relations in right.

parents can afford to pay sufficient money or who belong to a certain social class.

i. Provided there is compulsory education it is reasonable to ask for the abolition of school fees in state schools. But the necessary aids (school books, writing material etc.) should be provided by the parents, except in cases of real hardship.

ii. Society and the State should ensure by means of generous allowances (scholarships etc.) that genuine talent will not be frustrated for want of money. But it is not possible to say definitely when and how the right selection should be made.

45. *How does the illegitimate child stand in relation to the legitimate child?*

The illegitimate child must be given all fitting care and assistance ; but it cannot be put on a legal par with the legitimate child.

PIUS XI (C. C., 128).

"One thing in this connection We observe with regret: it often happens that the right order of things is reversed, and the unmarried mother and her child (who admittedly must be succoured, if only to avoid greater evils) receive readily and in abundance that assistance which is either refused or else granted only sparingly and grudgingly to legitimate mothers."

THE struggle for equal status for the illegitimate and the legitimate child is a true reflection of the struggle for the purity and stability of marriage. Those who deny that marriage and the family are the only proper means for begetting and bringing up children must necessarily concede equal status and equal rights to all children, whether illegitimate or legitimate.

1. Two facts deserve our serious consideration: i. It is not the child's fault that it is illegitimate. If we discriminate against it we would seem to be punishing an innocent person. ii. As it is, the position of the illegitimate child will frequently be more difficult, economically, morally and by reason of innate dispositions. Denying equal status makes its position even worse (embitterment; social inferiority; less favourable prospects and opportunities of professional career, marriage possibilities). If on the other hand the stigma of its birth were taken from it the struggle for existence imposed by "fate" is rendered easier.

2. Nevertheless, we must not isolate these facts from the general domain of marriage and the family; rather we must give a well-considered and objective answer to this question: What would happen if the distinction between the legitimate and the illegitimate child were abolished? We would be abandoning the sacredness and unique position of marriage and the family, because it would make no difference whether the children are born in marriage or outside it. The basis of human society and the bulwark of morality would thereby be destroyed. We would also be falsifying the parental relationship. The illegitimate father and the illegitimate mother are the causes, but not the parents of the child; they have begotten the child without being prepared to take on that permanent partnership which finds its purpose precisely in the child as their common task in life. Yet this necessarily belongs to parenthood.

3. From the "human" angle there is naturally no difference between legitimate and illegitimate children. Both are persons; hence both have full claim to recognition of their human dignity and human rights. Neither can the particular rights of youth (Q. 43) be withheld from the illegitimate child; however, restric-

tions will come of themselves because the child is not the natural member of a family. In particular:

i. The illegitimate child has an absolute right to a good physical mental, moral and religious training. This is primarily the duty of the mother, since it is sometimes difficult or even impossible to establish paternity. For practical reasons the mother should be assisted by a suitable guardian. Legislation will have to pay particular attention to the illegitimate child.

ii. Social esteem ought to be quite generally due to an individual's personal conduct. Nobody ought to be ostracized because of some fault for which (he or she) is not to blame. And for this reason we should certainly approve a person trying to conceal as far as possible the fact of illegitimate birth.

iii. Maintenance and occupational training of the illegitimate child ought to be ensured or secured by law. Both father and mother must share in this, since both are responsible for the child's birth. As the upbringing of the child does not devolve on the father, he must contribute an adequate sum of money.[56] If this is not possible society (municipality, State, Public Welfare) must make up the deficiency. However, the proffered assistance must be given in such a way that it will not act as a kind of silent inducement to illegitimate motherhood. The basic principle must always remain to foster and support the family.

[56] If it is not known exactly who the father is (for example, if the mother had intercourse with several men at the time of conception) it would not be unfair to impose the obligation on all those who could possibly be the child's father.

Part Two

The Structure of Society

The Vocational or Functional Order

1. WE MUST be particularly careful in this section not to confuse the "ideal" with existing reality. Here we are examining the question: what must be done for the right ordering of society? Where, and to what extent, this order has already been realized is quite another question which can only be dealt with incidentally here.

2. We begin with a few facts:

i. Men concern themselves with many things that have nothing to do with the State and politics.[1] They plough their fields, establish and run industrial enterprises, learn and practise trades; they buy this, and sell that; they build houses, roads, ships and open up mines; they write, or read, books and newspapers; they play games, go to the cinema and travel, etc.

ii. There are innumerable social structures in which these things are organized and done. These structures differ considerably in size, object and function, but common to all of them is that men cannot, or will not, do without them; that they change very much according to circumstances or to the wishes of men; and

[1] In order to avoid possible ambiguity we refer the reader to the various uses of the terms "politics" and "political" explained in Q. 65.

that, while not belonging to the domain of politics, they nevertheless exist and function within the order of the State: trades, farms, industrial enterprises and organizations, schools, educational and cultural establishments, co-operatives, professional organizations, trade-boards, welfare organizations, etc.

iii. The modern State has shown very little capability of ordering society. Instead it has brought the non-State spheres of life and activity under its direct control to an intolerable extent: for example education; various fields of economy such as trade and communications, commerce, agriculture and industry. Hence the power and influence of State bureaucracy.

iv. Human society today is divided into classes according to positions in the labour-market: the haves and the have-nots, capitalists, middle classes and proletariat, employers and employees, landlords and tenants. Meanwhile class-distinction and class-conflict have taken on new forms and embrace ever new sections of the population. It is the aim of a vocational or functional structure of society to overcome these unnatural conditions of modern society. Its object is: (a) to give back to non-State communities what rightly belongs to them; (b) to free the State for its proper functioning; (c) to bring about harmonious and fruitful collaboration among the various social groups or sectors. It will choose the only right way to this end by returning to the natural principles of social life and seeking to put into practice the "natural" order of society in a form that, taking into account the existing situation and the demands of the present time, will be in accordance with the common good. In a word a vocational order aims at increasing the right kind of structural arrangement in the social domain.[2]

[2] We are speaking here of spheres of social "achievement" within the natural

3. The term "society" may signify:

i. almost every kind of human association: *e.g.*, State and Church, unions and federations, local administrative unions, limited liability companies, even occasional social gatherings.

ii. a contrast to "community"; cf. I, Q. 28.

iii. that extensive sphere of social achievement which lies between the domain of the individual on the one hand and that of the State on the other. In other words those whole or partial non-State domains in which men cultivate in common all that corresponds with their dispositions, tendencies, obligations and desires. Hence one might speak of spheres of pre-State, or pre-political, achievement. While the family and the State are "necessary" communities (I, Q. 27), "society" embraces social structures that are predominantly voluntary (Q. 53). This third sense is intended when we say that the object of vocational organization is to create the right kind of structural arrangement in "society", or in the domain of "social" life.[3]

4. The best explanation of a vocational or functional order is given by Pius XI in the encyclical *Quadragesimo anno,* the

order. There are spheres of social "life" that are only indirectly affected by vocational organization. Cf. Nos. 3/4 of this question, and also Q. 47.

[3] The first and most important community which precedes the State is the family (marriage). Hence if the term "society" is to denote the whole range of social structures that lie between the individual and the State, it should undoubtedly include the family. But the family holds a unique position, and so it is better not to include it under "society"; it is the living cell, the root and the source of society. One might say that the Church has her place within society "as the life-principle of human society" (Pius XII). But as a supernatural and supra-temporal divine institution she is subject to her own laws and transcends both society and all natural social structures to the extent of belonging to a different order.

object of which is to restore and perfect social order. It reaches its climax in the section on vocational or functional order. For the sake of clarity we have added the pope's observations to the relevant questions.

5. To understand what a vocational or functional order means and to put it into practice is by no means easy.[4] In order to forestall certain misconceptions it may be as well at this point to emphasize that by advocating a vocational order of society we do not want to return to the medieval social order. The vocational order is, of course, derived from the perennial principles and basic ideas of the latter system, without, however, clinging to its time-bound forms.

Although one of the principal concerns of a vocational order is a properly run economy, it does not restrict itself to the economic field, but embraces all spheres of human activity.

The vocational or functional order is indeed the most natural, but not the only possible and solely justifiable order of "society" (cf. Q. 53).

JOHN XXIII (M. M., 59–67, 142–148).

46. By what is order guaranteed in society?

Not by conflict between classes but by harmony between the various groupings of society.

PIUS XI (Q. A., 81–82).

"Now this is the primary duty of the State and of all good citizens, to abolish disputes between opposing classes, and to create and foster

[4] Recognizing both the theoretical and practical difficulties, I have followed the best explanations and have left aside all questions that might distract from the main issues. It is intended to give in this section only the basic idea of the vocational or functional order. This should suffice for the purpose of a handbook of social ethics.

harmony between vocational groups. The aim of social policy must therefore be the reestablishment of vocational groups. Society today still remains in a strained and therefore unstable and uncertain state, because it is founded on classes with divergent aims and hence opposed to each other, and consequently prone to enmity and strife."

OUR terms "class" and "vocational grouping" each refer to a plurality of persons united somehow and conscious of their unity.

1. Class denotes a group with common interests whose outlook is guided by considerations of economic advantage (or disadvantage). It stresses its real or alleged rights in a one-sided manner and is consequently given to struggling in a hostile sense. Those that form a single class, or are conscious of belonging to it, may differ considerably from one another in origin, occupation, professional position and income; but basically their economic status is the same, and this determines their relations towards the others: *e.g.*, masters – slaves; haves – have-nots; capitalist employers – wage-earners or "proletarians".

i. It is a numerical quantity, an aggregate without any genuine inner structure based on differences of value and achievement.

ii. It can be recognized and distinguished by the same basic position as regards property and income, similarity of economic status and living conditions: (independent – dependent; secure existence – insecure existence).

iii. Men are evaluated according to the class to which they belong, for example, whether they are haves or have-nots. Money and wealth become the basis of social esteem. This gives rise to class-consciousness, class-distinction and class-struggle.

iv. Social classes are interested in the general welfare of the nation only inasmuch as it is useful to them.

2. It is not really surprising that there should be classes, and that they should look after their own interests or endeavour to improve their position. But the division of society into classes ought to be overcome and replaced by a genuine organic structure. Hence Pius XI asked not that classes should be abolished, but that the despicable class-struggle should be replaced by honest discussion.

PIUS XI (Q. A., 114).

"For class warfare, provided it abstains from enmities and mutual hatred, changes little by little into a justifiable dispute, based upon the desire of justice. If this is by no means the happy social peace which we all long for, it can be and ought to be a point of departure for the mutual co-operation of vocational groups."

It was Karl Marx (d. 1883) in particular who maintained that human society and its development are based on class-distinction and class-struggle, and that only the "classless society" of the socialist (communist) future would overcome this conflict. According to Marx, the class of the exploited always subjugates the opposing class of the exploiters. But this proves fatal to the former; because it will itself become an exploiting class, which in turn will again be exploited as soon as social conditions have sufficiently changed. This class-struggle will not cease unless the proletarian revolution is victorious and the classless society established. When that happens, the source of all class-warfare which is private property will have vanished. Marx's line of argument is quite logical in itself. However:

i. his approach is false. Private property is a divinely ordained institution which unhappily may be abused by men, but which cannot be abolished.

ii. Marx was mistaken about future development. Our society consists not only of capitalists (owners of the means of production) and noncapitalists (mere wage-earners, proletariat), as he envisaged it, but embraces other classes and groups that continue to be a decisive factor in the shaping of society. Contrary to what Marx believed, the working class has been able to improve its position progressively both economically and socially. The working-class of today is not a uniform mass, rather it is strongly differentiated. There exists neither a general uniform condition of the proletariat, nor a general uniform proletarian consciousness. To an increasing extent the worker is becoming the man of the lower middle class, while large groups of the "middle" classes are becoming impoverished.

PIUS XI (Q. A., 102).

"It is true that even today this economic system does not everywhere exist exclusively, for there is another system which still embraces a very large and important group of men. There is, for instance, the agricultural group in which the larger portion of the human race provides itself with an honourable livelihood."

By vocational or functional groupings on the other hand we tend to understand a more "static" social entity (one used to speak of "estates", derived from the Latin *status*) than is denoted by the term "class". While class levels down and disintegrates, a functional or vocational grouping in society (Pius XI used the words *ordo, ordines*) tends towards integration and organic unity.

A vocational or functional social order implies that the different groupings will respect and support each other like real members of a body.[5] They are in a mutual relationship not of

[5]It is obvious that the groupings we have in mind must have positive aims

enmity but of service, recognizing in one another but different parts of one whole. Each member has its place in the whole, its proper rights and activities, but each knows that it is bound up with the other and has obligations towards it. Such vocational or functional groupings will recognize their own good and the basis of their own unity in the common good of the whole nation. They are not just associations of men linked by common interests (although they will naturally have these), but rather genuine organs that have their being in the whole of society and regard themselves responsible for it. If once they fall prey to group egoism, they will be ruled by a class or caste spirit in the worst sense. Our vocational or functional group is a well-organized social body that as such acts with a sense of responsibility. It aims at harmonious and fruitful co-operation and guarantees "an orderly common life, and a common life which is tranquil" (Pius XII, C. M., 1942, C. T. S., p. 3).

47. *What kind of grouping can guarantee harmony in modern society?*

The vocational or functional grouping. It corresponds both to the natural and to the present-day requirements of society.

PIUS XI (Q. A., C. T. S., 83–84).

"But there cannot be question of any perfect cure unless this opposition be done away with, and well-organized members of the social body be constituted; vocational groups, namely, claiming the allegiance of men,

and activities. Thus thieves, prostitutes, criminal gangs, speculators, market-riggers will not be considered as vocational or functional groups in our sense, although they may very well be organized and command strong internal group loyalties.

not according to the position they occupy in the labour-market, but according to the diverse functions which they exercise in society. For it is natural that just as those who dwell in close proximity constitute townships, so those who practise the same trade or profession, in the economic field or any other, form corporate groups. These groups, with powers of self-government, are considered by many to be, if not essential to civil society, at least natural to it.

Order, as St. Thomas well defines it (St. Thomas, *Cont. Gent.*, iii, 71; cf. *Summa Theol.*, I, q. 65, art. 2 c.), *is unity arising from the proper arrangement of a number of objects; hence, true and genuine social order demands that the various members of a society be joined together by some firm bond. Such a bond of union is provided both by the production of goods or the rendering of services in which employers and employees of one and the same vocational group collaborate; and by the common good which all such groups should unite to promote, each in its own sphere, with friendly harmony. Now this union will become powerful and efficacious in proportion to the fidelity with which the individuals and the vocational groups strive to discharge their professional duties and to excel in them."*

EVEN modern society cannot exist as a "mass"or a "collectivity", but only as an ordered unity. The order, or structure, must be appropriate to the modern state of social life, but at the same time it must be natural, that is, in keeping with the principles of nature. We have, for instance, groupings by sex and age (men – women, boys – girls) groupings according to birth and social status (aristocracy, professional, working classes) groupings according to married or single status. Pius XI said that the organization of society on the basis of functional groups was the one most in keeping with our age.

1. Vocation implies first of all a serious and lasting activity, work in the sense of an honest occupation that is taken up and persisted in

for a long period, usually for a whole lifetime. Mere casual work or work done as a hobby does not establish a vocation. Vocation indicates "calling", whether interior or exterior (someone is called to the Bar). One who feels himself called to a task or an occupation has undoubtedly a great advantage over a person who has to force himself to take up the same occupation. Today many people are forced by circumstances to adopt an occupation that is contrary to their natural bent. Yet with the proper energy and perseverance they can at least give a meaning to their life or work. The Christian knows how to sanctify every kind of work and even to carry the cross of drudgery in imitation of the cross of Christ.

Vocational or functional occupation has a number of characteristics:

i. The work must demand a certain skill, it must be sufficiently interesting and exacting to engage the individual fully. A vocational occupation – in contrast to mere employment – is so rich in content that it really appeals to the individual as a person.

ii. Vocational occupation is work for the purpose of securing a living. In most cases people take up a vocational occupation in order to support themselves and their families. Quite rightly they expect their vocational occupation to provide them and their families with an existence worthy of human beings, and also to provide security in old age and in case of sickness.

iii. The work must be regarded as socially "honourable". There are types of employment that are dishonourable in themselves, and that should never be respected in society: for example, racketeering; the production and sale of pornography; (cf. Q. 48). There are other kinds of employment that quite wrongly are not considered honourable by society, as for example, innumerable functions and services that are too unpretentious to represent a vocational occupation; they are included as supplementary services in vocational organization and in this way receive due recognition: for example, untrained assistance, messengers, door-keepers, charwomen, scavengers, etc. Finally there are activities that people look on with uneasiness or distaste. They are not considered honourable, some rightly, some wrongly, acting as hangman, cleaning sewers.

iv. Vocational or functional activity is service in the social sense; it is an office or service carried out in the interest of the community, to the advantage of the common good. Formerly this social element was much more strongly emphasized; vocational occupation was first and foremost activity that had its organic place within society. It was the effect of individualism in modern history to destroy this system. Pius XI performed an important function in reminding us of the special social significance of vocational occupation and vocational groupings.

2. By their professions or trades men are distinguished, not by localities (regionally), but by the purpose and goal of their activity (functionally). The multiplicity and variety of their occupations is no mere coincidence, but is conditioned by the necessities and possibilities of social life. We might mention the immeasurable riches in values and goods entrusted to man's responsibility and care; the dependence of human society on an ever greater number of services; man's increasing ability to explore the enormous treasures of nature and to make them subservient to his needs. Trade or profession thus concerns the many partial goals (partial goods or spheres) which together comprise the total human good, the total sphere of human welfare. Thus the given basis on which to organize human society, dividing it into various service groups, is man's trade

or profession, for it is the function of society to foster the many realms that make up its totality.

3. In every trade or profession there are different positions and activities. Not all those who have the same occupation occupy the same position and do the same work. Yet all are members of the particular trade or profession, and together form one single vocational or functional group. Thus the unity of any trade or profession derives from its purpose, from the work to be achieved, the product to be won or manufactured, the needs to be met. Yet in many cases the activities as such have nothing in common;

EXAMPLE OF BRANCHES CONSTITUTING A TOTALITY OF CULTURE[6]

WRITING AND MEDIA OF INFORMATION	ECONOMY	HEALTH
Books Newspapers Periodicals Radio Television		Physicians Nurses Pharmacists Pharmaceutical industry

SKILLED TRADES	COMMUNICATION	INDUSTRY	AGRICULTURE & FORESTRY	COMMERCE
Tailors Carpenters Painters Shoemakers Plumbers	Railway Motor-car Ship Aircraft Roads Telegraph Postal services	(extraction & processing of raw materials) Coal Iron & Steel Textiles Timber Oil	Farming Horticulture Cattle raising Forestry	Imports & exports Wholesale trade Retail trade

[6] This survey is merely intended to illustrate the varied character of vocational groups: different vocational occupations form a higher unity; individual vocational groups help as members to construct the whole of human culture. There is a great deal of overlapping. This last point presents very considerable

EXAMPLES. Apprentice – master; labourer, employee, manager; university lecturer, professor. A telephone operator in a leather factory and a typist in a steel foundry may have nothing to do with the production respectively of leather or steel; since they are employed there, however, and their work directly serves leather and steel production they belong to the industries "Leather" and "Steel" respectively.

Certain industries or professions form together a single unmistakable unit; either they belong to the same stage of production, the same "type" of work, or they fulfil together a particular task, cultivate a connected "sphere" of human values, satisfy the need for a particular kind of goods. There are various larger fields of activity which in their turn comprise partial fields. We thus get a graded structure of trade or professional groupings.

4. It is quite natural that those engaged in a common task should join together and form a social unit. These we call professional or trade groupings since they are based on the concern with a trade or profession, on a functional purpose as part of the general well-being of society. The bond that unites the members of such a functional group is based on the "goods and services" which are their direct concern, and the "common good" which they unite in preserving and promoting. These two principles of unity are mutually related and are subordinated one to the other; the one or other may be more manifest and more effective according to the particular good aimed at by the trade or profession.

48. What kind of order of trades or professions are we aiming at?

We are aiming at an order of society according to vocational groupings, that is, on the basis of membership of a trade or profession and in the form of vocational or functional association.

difficulties in carrying out the plan for a society based on vocational organization (cf. Q. 56).

PIUS XII (C. B., 1942; C. T. S., p. 6).

"In a conception of society that is inspired and sanctioned by religious thought, economic and cultural activities are seen as a vast and admirable forge of energy, richly various and harmoniously coherent, in which the similarity of men as beings endowed with reason and their functional diversity receive just acknowledgement and find adequate expression. In any other conception of society labour is oppressed and the worker is degraded."

1. Neighbourliness leads quite naturally to the formation of communities, their only effective means of mutual help (Q. A., 83). Similarly, those linked in the same trade or profession can, and should, form corporate professional or trade groupings. This is natural too, for their vocational work, or service, implies that as far as their efforts, living conditions and future prospects are concerned, they are dependent upon each other.

Example. Co-operation between post and railway authorities; between railways, motor cars, ships and aircraft in transport matters.

Membership of one or another trade, industry or profession constitutes the point of departure for a vocational or functional social order. However, it is not the position someone may hold in his trade or profession, but the mere fact that he belongs to it that accounts for his membership.

Example. Gateman, gang-labourer, fireman, engine-driver, points man, station-master, ticket office clerks, employees in railway workshops, cleaners etc. all belong to the railway (vocational group: Communications).

2. The associations that naturally arise in trades and professions lead to vocational groups, "well-organized members of the

social body" (Q. A., 83). Each group is a member of this body. Its place is determined by its particular function. Undoubtedly there exist considerable differences of rank among the vocational groups, but no one group dominates over the other. Rather each has its own laws and exercises its function independently (Q. A., 52). The vocational groups almost always embrace a number of trades and professions in the modern sense of these terms. Thus they are members which in turn are themselves composed of parts, of smaller vocational units such as professional associations and groups. They are organized partial wholes that together form the social whole (Q. 49). Thus trade or profession and membership of a trade or profession constitute both the differences and the unity in the social whole. Thus they guarantee true order, the "unity in ordered multiplicity" (Q. A., 84).

3. A natural order of this kind would be deprived of its meaning and effectiveness by false egalitarianism. Membership of a whole implies graded positions. Hence the vocational or functional order of society does not seek to overcome class-distinction by getting rid of authority and its executives from its groupings; it cannot destroy the genuine equality of status which it grants (Q. 52) by an unreasonable levelling down. Status and authority depend on the service rendered. The point is not "the same to each", but "to each his due".

49. What is the vocational order based upon?

The vocational order is based upon natural fundamental rights and laws, not on the approval and order of the State.

1. VIEWED as a whole, the vocational order is derived from the organic conception of society (I, Q. 31, No. 4). Society is a

genuine vital whole that has developed by growth and has been voluntarily accepted, that has its natural arrangement and members. These members "are not absorbed by the whole", but preserve their own natural character and enjoy their own proper rights.

The vocational organization is based on the law of growth and development that governs natural social life. According to this law, there is a trend from below upwards, the greater society developing from the lesser ones (I, Q. 49). Because of their essential character the member societies are qualified and intended to become members of the higher social whole. Thus they are seen in their proper light only when this natural aptitude and this order are understood. On the other hand, it is not possible to explain or to set up the higher social whole in contrast to its individual members; to do so would do violence to the members and destroy the whole.

2. The basic law of subsidiary function is of decisive importance for a vocational or functional order. It was not without good reason that Pius XI introduced the section on vocational order with an explanation of this fundamental principle (Q. A., 79/80); cf. I, Q. 52 as well as the accompanying papal texts. In fact, we might say that vocational order is the direct application of this basic principle to the social sphere. Unless the vocational groups can exercise their own proper rights and functions, the vocational order is meaningless.[7] For it is precisely the aim of the vocational order to set free men's functional powers and to restore the so-called non-political spheres of existence to those who do not exercise functions of State government and authority. Hence the vocational groupings are not members of the

[7] Cf. in this connection the opinion of Pius XI on the corporative organization of Fascist Italy (Q. A., 91/95).

State community in a direct and proper sense, but rather of "society", *i.e.*, of the people which is united in the form of a State (Q. 55). Yet they have their place within the entire order of the State, and for this reason they must subordinate themselves to the common good (I, Q. 48; Qs. 51 and 52).

3. Finally, the vocational order is based on man's natural freedom of association. If men are entitled to form associations for purposes that are morally good, they are all the more entitled to do so in this case where their union is so natural and beneficial.

50. What functions have individual vocational groups?

Individual vocational groups are obliged
1. to look after their own interests and those of their members;
2. to contribute to the common good to the best of their ability;
3. to collaborate harmoniously with other vocational groups.

PIUS XI (Q. A., C. T. S., 85).

"From this it is easy to conclude that in these corporations the common interest of the whole vocational group must predominate; and among these interests the most important is to promote as much as possible the contribution of each trade or profession to the common good of the State. Regarding cases which may occur in which the particular interests of employers or employees call for special care and protection, the two parties will be able to deliberate separately, or to come to such decisions as the matter may require."

1. EACH community must first of all strive in loyalty to itself and with a sense of individual responsibility to fulfil its func-

tions well. Individual vocational groups should in the spheres entrusted to them serve the nation as a whole, fulfil its just expectations and meet its needs. But this is only possible according to their competence.

i. The vocational group must work for its own proper good, its own particular goal, with due zeal and earnestness of purpose; thus the vocational group "Education" will look after educational matters, the vocational group "Health" will concern itself with preventing disease and raising the standard of health of the nation, the vocational group "Agriculture" with making the land as productive as possible, the vocational group "Communications" with establishing well-ordered traffic conditions. At the same time the vocational group must look after the totality of concerns connected with it. Hence it must know how to rate the value and importance of its own function, its stage of development, prospects for the future, the threats it encounters (also from the State), ways of meeting these and sound progress etc.

ii. The vocational group must find the kind of order that best suits it and guarantees that it will work successfully (leading bodies and their powers, work rules, subscriptions, penalties for breaches of the rules etc.). Most important is the system of vocational training which should embrace both technical and character training of the members, and especially of the rising generation (fostering the particular ethos of the trade or profession; advising on trades and professions). Trade or professional groups may establish schools, and to them applies what has been said earlier (Q. 31) with regard to State subsidies. The vocational group has the right, and the duty, to have its own social policy: *e.g.*, assistance or insurance for the sick and aged; family allowance funds; employment agencies.

iii. In the assignment and fulfilment of functions the vocational group itself must not go against the principle of subsidiary function by withholding or withdrawing from its own members what is their due and what can be accomplished by them. The vocational group must concern itself with matters that affect the group as a whole, but not with what directly concerns subsidiary groups, member associations etc.

2. Pius XI (Q. A., 85) described "the contribution of each trade or profession to the common good of the State" as the "most important" interest of the vocational groups. This is quite understandable for the vocational groups are member units in the service of the nation as a whole.

i. Thus the vocational group must be conscious of its position and responsibility in respect of the common good. For this it is necessary that it should know the common good, its order of values and obligatory character, that it should awaken and deepen in its members an appreciation of the common good, *i.e.,* of the nation and State – which does not have to be done by means of "patriotic" speeches, mass demonstrations etc., the kind of thing one sees today in the countries behind the Iron Curtain.

ii. The vocational group must adapt its own activity in a reasonable manner to the requirements of the common good: the State may even enforce this (cf. Q. 55). This does not imply giving up its own rights and functions, but it does mean being prepared to make such allowances as arise from the needs of the whole (dangers of group-egotism and collective selfishness).

Examples.

Agriculture: Production must be so arranged that on the one hand holdings will give the best yields possible and, on the other hand, the greatest nutritive advantages will be achieved for the feeding of the nation (proper proportion between various branches: tillage, stock-farming, forestry; sufficient cultivation of vital products; fullest exploitation of technical progress, but without collective (kolhoz) economy or state combines, general research, inquiry and consultation for the purpose of getting the most out of the soil, providing more favourable irrigation etc.).

Health: Raising the standard of health of the nation (dealing with epidemics and contagious diseases: causes and antidotes, preventive measures); providing for sufficient good doctors and nurses (protection against exploitation and "proletarianization"; sick-funds and national health treatment).

3. Because they are members of one whole, the vocational groups are in duty bound to work together in harmony (Q. A., 81). Members are responsible for one another and are obliged to help each other (Principle of subsidiary function; I, Q. 51).

i. There must be mutual toleration among the vocational groups; one group must not destroy what the other builds up.

Examples. It would be disastrous if the groups "Art" and "Information" (literature, theatre, press, television, films) were to destroy what the group "Education" has achieved at the cost of so much effort. Or if the group "Industry" were to aim at destroying the group "Skilled Trades" (the big wholesaler destroying the small retailer).

ii. In order gradually to achieve the higher unity in the common good there is need of regular mutual contact for which in most cases special organs (committees, conferences) might be established. There is need of a chief, or central, organ of vocational organization (Q. 56).

iii. Mutual help may be of many kinds: *e.g.,* recognition of efforts made and successes achieved; advice and warning; exchange of experiences; common applications, claims, institutions, provisions, measures (protests and remonstrations; schools; conference houses and rest homes); the granting of favourable loans, perhaps "grants-in-aid".

51. What does a vocational order depend on?

An appropriate mental attitude and the fostering of such an attitude are indispensable for any vocational order.

THE vocational order as such is "institutional"; it comprises a number of institutions. By this we mean social institutions such as economic or industry councils, professional councils, courts of honour, arbitration committees etc. The vocational order is by no means solely a matter of mental attitude; nevertheless, without the proper attitude it can neither be established nor maintained or developed. Pius XI referred to two fundamental attitudes or virtues, namely, social justice and social charity (Q. A., 88). By these he meant readiness and zeal in discharging those duties that fall to the individual as member of a community and in consideration of the common good and its claims (I, Q. 110). In particular this mental attitude must include a sense of honour of the trade or profession and a rejection of false pride; courage for taking personal responsibility; rejection of dictatorships of any kind, promoting a spirit of true consideration for others; gift of adaptation and making sacrifices, genuine generosity in mutual intercourse (overcoming petty "group" bias and narrow-mindedness).

52. What is the legal position of vocational groups?

Vocational groups should be independent bodies with public-legal status; they have a natural right to independence and self-government.

THE question concerns the measure of freedom due to vocational groups (Q. 53) and the relation of the vocational groups to the State (Q. 55), and to international order (Q. 57).

1. Vocational groups may originate through voluntary association, but they are not just any kind of voluntary associations.[8] Rather they are the "natural equipment" of civil society (Q. A., 83), and are determined by three factors:

i. The various special fields are independent partial spheres of the total human good, each subject to its own laws and each developing its own activity.[9]

ii. These multifarious and exacting spheres can prosper only in common and well-ordered activity.

iii. Therefore it is "natural" (Q. A., 83) that "well-organized members of the social body" (*ibid.*) should promote these values. The autonomy and proper rights intrinsic to the particular spheres are necessarily transferred to these organs.

2. It follows from this that the vocational groups – precisely these organs – should carry out their activities independently and in virtue of their own proper rights:

i. If a right is based on a natural title and not on human endowment, it is a natural right (I, Qs. 53/54 and 64). It is the right of vocational groups to establish themselves and develop, to

[8] The vocational group "Education" is not a private circle concerned with educational questions; the vocational group "Education" is not a private school.

[9] Economy, law, education and science are obviously separate fields. Each field must be cultivated and organized in its own proper manner: *e.g.*, to satisfy economic needs is something quite different from scientific research, hence it must be handled quite differently.

carry out the functions for which they exist; to organize themselves in the way that will serve their purpose and allow them to develop.

ii. Thus the vocational groups do not receive their basic authority from the State; rather their basic authority results from the particular goods they aim at and from their own proper function, *i.e.,* from the necessity, the nature and importance of the various spheres. But the State cannot take away or refuse what is not in its power to give in the first place; hence the vocational groups can, and must, claim the right to do what they believe to be the right thing, and to do it in the way they believe to be right (Qs. 50 and 55).

iii. Nevertheless, the vocational groups are members (member communities) within the nation and State as a whole. It is quite possible for members of a society to act independently and yet be genuine members (I, Qs. 22/23).

3. This brings us to the essential definition of vocational groups as "independent corporations with public-legal status".

i. "Independent" does not mean absolute (unrestricted), but relative (restricted) independence. For each cultural sphere embraces only a limited part or section of the total human good; hence it is – together with the vocational group itself – subordinated to the common good; as guardian of the common good the State is entitled to supervision and co-operation (Q. 55).

ii. "Corporation"[10] comes from the Latin: *corpus* – body. Here

[10] The Latin text of Q. A. speaks of *collegia,* associations, and of *corpora,* bodies, corporations. It defines *corpora* or *collegia* as *consortia jure proprio utentia, i.e.,* associations enjoying their own proper rights.

it can only be understood in the sense of a living body because the vocational groups are living units capable of acting. A living body is an independent whole that possesses members (organs) and acts through them. To this extent the term "corporate" aptly expresses the proper nature of the vocational group as an "association possessing its own proper rights".

iii. "Public law" is in contrast to "private law". Those communities (institutions, corporations) enjoy public-legal status that are directly determined by the general good; their origin and standing is thus derived directly from the necessities of the common good.

EXAMPLES.

I. Individual business concerns, companies, firms (under private law).
II. The great branches of economy (under public law)
I. Hospitals, sanatoria, clinics (private law)
II. The health service (public law). Member communities of the State, *e.g.,* the individual States in the U. S. A., provinces, counties, municipalities, cantons etc. enjoy public rights, because they are proper parts of the common good of the State, of the State organization.

The two notions "public law" and "civil law" must not be confused. Civil law is that law which the State has established or which is valid within the State because the State recognizes it and wishes it to be respected. Civil law embraces both domains of public and private law; both these in turn contain many divisions.

4. Because the vocational groups enjoy their own, not any derived, right, they possess authority to issue regulations of a legal and binding character. They are entitled to make their regulations binding in civil law.

i. Their statutes, regulations apply to the entire vocational group, that is, to all its branches and its members.[11]

ii. Naturally this competence is restricted to the field of activity proper to the group in question. For example, the "Agriculture" group cannot make regulations for the mining industry.

iii. What is decreed by the trade or professional groups must be in harmony with the general good. To find the proper harmony in this is a matter for joint deliberation by the groups and the State (Q. 55).

5. To sum up: The vocational groups have the right of self-

[11] It is a very difficult question whether the regulations of the vocational groups are directly binding, *i.e.,* without the sanction of the State, on the general public and also on the other groups. Some scholars maintain that they are. Others object that such plenary powers in the hands of the vocational groups would wipe out their limitations in relation to the sovereign authority of the State; hence, if the regulations of the vocational groups are to have this force, it must be in virtue of a right delegated to the groups by the State, or else the State must make the regulations binding in each case expressly. The view has been expressed that the vocational groups must be "declared" statutory corporations; the regulations would then have the force of law for everyone. The question is crucial because the State may possibly refuse or neglect to confer these rights on the vocational groups, or to impose on the general public what they consider to be indispensable. In this way the State could seriously handicap or even frustrate the functioning of vocational groups. For example, if the "Health" group orders comprehensive and urgently necessary measures for combating epidemics, but a part of those threatened are not bound to obey them, then the whole effort may be in vain. Nevertheless, I personally am inclined to the view that vocational groups of themselves cannot bind the general public: because this is the sole right of the State (or international) authority. But the State is undoubtedly obliged to see to it that those regulations of vocational groups that are necessary for the common good are carried out. Since in any case it has the right to supervise the activity of vocational groups (Q. 54), it would incur no risk if it conferred on them the power to bind the general public; it could always intervene where necessary by virtue of its right of supervision.

determination and self-government. They are entitled to lead their own associate lives and to promote their spheres on their own responsibility.

53. How does the vocational order relate to human liberty?

Men are at liberty at any time to give the vocational order the form they consider to be right and useful.

PIUS XI (Q. A., C. T. S., 86).

"It is hardly necessary to note that what Leo XIII taught concerning the form of political government can in due measure be applied also to professional corporations. Here, too, men may choose whatever form they please, provided that both justice and the common good be taken into account" (Encyclical Immortale Dei, November 1, 1885).

1. IN THE vocational order the following are given by nature (Qs. 46/47): i. The multiplicity and order of values, ii. The mandate to men to promote these values, iii. Man's duty to establish a social order that will correspond to the abundance, multiplicity and order of these values. Therefore, as often and as soon as social development has reached the point where only a vocational order will guarantee concord and progress to society (and the State), it cannot be left to an arbitrary decision to decide whether society will be organized on a vocational basis or not.

It must be clear from what has been said that a vocational order can only be realized at a certain stage of human development and culture. A jungle tribe will not be able to have a vocational order. The transition to a vocational order will have to be gradual. Especially when, as at the present time our society has very serious defects and has to be radically reconstructed (Q. A., 128), vocational organization cannot be enforced (Q. 58).

2. Just as nature leaves it to men to choose a form of State (Q. 74), so it leaves it to men to find the particular form in which a vocational order can be realized. Vocational organization may here and there take on a different external form depending on different circumstances. This depends, for example, on the nature of the country (whether it is agricultural or industrial), on the density of population, the state of technical and civilized development, the form of State and the political maturity of the people, on the extent of international involvement, and on the "beginnings" already made. For the establishment of a vocational order Pius XI only demanded that "both justice and the common good should be taken into account" (Q. A., 86). Thus two questions arise: Is the proposed arrangement just, that is, does it respect the rights of individuals and communities? Is the common good promoted or harmed?

EXAMPLES. It would be not merely unreasonable but unjust if the equality of status due to the organs of vocational groups were denied them (Q. 54); if the personal responsibility of the individual or of the member communities were abolished or arbitrarily restricted; if regulations were made that favoured some members of a trade or profession at the expense of the others (unfortunately often the case today). It would be contrary to the common good, for example, if economic productive capacity were to diminish to the extent that the provision of goods of genuine value were no longer secure; if the dangers threatening public health or morality were dealt with in a negligent fashion; if too much "organization" and bureaucracy made the practical work impossible. Stakhanovite methods have nothing to do with vocational order; they sacrifice the dignity, liberty and talents of men to raising the production of material social products, or rather to the collectivist State.

3. Pius XI compared the origin and internal development of vocational groups with the origin and internal development of the parish community (municipality, urban or rural district):

i. Everyone who lives, or wishes to live in it belongs to the parish; and the parish has the right to demand that everyone who belongs to it or resides in it will comply with its order or otherwise depart. Through his choice of occupation a man becomes a member of the vocational group. The choice of occupation is voluntary, but membership of the vocational group is an obligatory consequence; whoever does not like the regulations is at liberty to choose some other occupation. Consideration for the common good demands that for every partial function (task) there will be only one vocational group (Q. 55), and that this will embrace all members of the particular trade or profession (Q. 54).[12]

ii. Almost everywhere the constitution (for local government) is prescribed for the parish by civil law. This is necessary for reasons of the common good. But the parish retains the right to choose its own organs (parish council, representation) and the State is obliged by virtue of the principle of subsidiary function to leave to the parish (*e.g.*, to the municipal council) all functions that it can fulfil without prejudice to the common good (communal government). Vocational groups are not formal divisions of the State; they are only indirectly subject to the State (Q. 55). So far as they are true to their own character and the basic principle of a true community of interests (Q. 54)

[12] Father Nell-Breuning remarks quite rightly that it is not a question here of "compulsory membership" in the bad sense. For right to change one's trade or profession is not affected any more than the free choice of a trade or profession. Concerning the present difficulties in this respect cf. Q. 58. For this reason compulsory guilds, compulsory unions and similar compulsory organizations (*e.g.*, the labour front) are not being advocated here. Genuine vocational groups, which unfortunately do not yet exist, would be quite differently constituted. It is true that the individual automatically becomes a member of them by reason of his choice of occupation, but nowhere is he ignored, rather he has a personal voice (Pius XII) in deciding the affairs of the vocational group (Q. 56).

they may themselves decide: what organs they wish to create and how responsibilities might best be allocated; when and where further divisions are expedient (Q. 56). Industry and skilled trades – agriculture and mining industry, health and education, commerce and communications each require a different structure, a different distribution of functions, different subsections.

iii. All members of the vocational group have the same "fundamental rights" as all members of the parish. At the same time the extent of the service rendered will also determine the extent to which a part of these rights may be exercised. Participation in election, councils and decisions is necessarily graded, it has its different levels. An apprentice will belong to the crafts group, but not with the same rights as a master craftsman.

54. What must predominate in the vocational groups?

Common interests must predominate, hence they must be discussed and decided by the entire vocational group.

PIUS XI (Q. A., C. T. S., 85).

"The most important among these interests is to promote the co-operation in the highest degree of each industry and profession for the sake of the common good of the country. Concerning matters, however, in which particular points, involving advantage or detriment to employers or workers, may require special care and protection, the two parties, when these cases arise, can deliberate separately or as the situation requires reach a decision separately."

PIUS XII (Address of 11 March, 1945; U. A. vol. 2, p. 198).

"The time has come to repudiate empty phrases and to attempt to

organize the forces of the people on a new basis; to raise them above the distinction between employers and would-be workers, and to realize that higher unity which is a bond between all those who co-operate in production, formed by their solidarity in the duty of working together for the common good and filling together the needs of the community."

1. THE vocational group embraces two kinds of concern; i. those applying to the vocational group as such, that directly interest all the members of the group precisely because, and in so far as, they constitute this particular vocational group; ii. those that directly interest certain sections within the vocational group. Of course, indirectly they have an importance both for the entire group and for the other sections within the group.

EXAMPLES. To illustrate i.: Agriculture and Industry: improved methods of production, consequently higher production, greater earnings.
To illustrate ii.: particular interests of apprentices in relation to masters and vice versa, of employees and employers, of labourers and office workers; wage and insurance questions.
It is not always possible to say whether the matter in question is of common or particular concern. Wage questions that the employee rightly considers his particular concern are of great importance both for the employer and for the whole firm, as also for the entire society: they may involve a rise in the price of products, difficulties in finding markets, recession in orders and prospects of work, diminishing profits or even losses.

2. In contrast to a society based on classes the peculiarity of a vocational order lies in this that the vocational groups:

i. recognize and acknowledge common interests, because the individual sections are conscious of being members of one vocational group and act as such;

ii. adjust these common interests in common deliberations and decisions. The higher unity of the vocational group becomes the basis of genuine agreement. Thus particular interests are not played off one against the other. Rather the primary question is always: What can, and must, be done in the interest of the vocational group as a whole and of the general public? To find the answer to this question, and to the many individual questions it involves, is the business of the vocational group organizations which are constituted on a basis of parity, *i.e.*, in accordance with the principle of equality of status (thus employers and employees, masters and apprentices, managers and staffs); they deliberate, decide and act in common; and for this reason a vocational organization cannot exist without genuine unselfishness, hence the chief danger to a society based on vocational organization is group egotism.

3. In the vocational order of society the individual groups retain their particular interests, as Pius XI pointed out; there will always be certain interests that are, for example, peculiar to employees and not to employers and vice versa. These differences in interests and aims are in the nature of things and consequently unavoidable. Morevoer, a vocational order cannot do away with all differences of opinion, wrong judgments, severities and even injustices. Any of its groups may well have to defend its just claims and ward off unjust decisions. For this reason it is necessary for each group to confer and decide for itself concerning its own particular interests. It is quite natural that voluntary associations such as trade-unions and employers federations should be formed to look after these particular interests.

The essential idea is the transfer of social disputes from the "political" plane of the national economy or even of the State to the sphere of vocational organization councils (Q. 56). Pius XII spoke of common deliberation and decision within the vocational groups, thus "at the industrial or professional level". On the other hand, he did not say that wherever men have such problems to solve there ought to be an egalitarian form of collaboration. In dealing with vocational organization Pius XI did not touch on what is called co-management in individual firms. Individual works and firms are not organs of vocational organization, but basic units of the national economy. Naturally vocational organization indirectly affects works-regulations.

55. *What is the relation of vocational groupings to the State?*

Although they are social and not political, corporations of the vocational groups are incorporated in the State and have obligations towards it.

1. THE most important interest of the vocational groups is to collaborate "in promoting the common good" (Q. A., 85). This does not turn vocational groups into political communities. But the words of the pope show clearly that as vocational groups exist within the State they are obliged to fit into, and serve the community of, the State. They will perform this service in the first place by properly carrying out their own function, and the specific nature and area of this proper function will be determined by what will promote the common good.

2. It is wrong to conceive of the State itself as a mere vocational group, and a State organized on the basis of vocational organization as a "Corporate State".[13]

[13] I agree with the view held, for example, by Father Nell-Breuning that it is

i. The State is the total community within the natural order (Qs. 60/61). It is something other and something more than a vocational group. Even though a certain class or group may in consequence of birth, talents or election be considered the support of the State in the narrower sense, it is not the State itself. (At most it is a pillar, or the strongest pillar of the State). The State is the people organized as a political unit. It is not the prerogative of particular individuals to be identified with the State, for example, those who possess political talent or interest. To identify the State with the vocational group deprives it of its proper function and plenitude of power.

ii. The vocational order of society does not produce what is called the Corporate State. In the "Corporate State" the groups are organs (parts) of the State; but that is precisely what the vocational groups are *not,* they are not organs of the State but rather of society, of the people who unite to form the State.

3. The vocational order of society is not tied to any particular form of State. Whether the State is monarchy constituted as aristocracy or democracy the people of the State and the "society" that supports the State can be organized on the basis of vocational organization:

i. The vocational order of society is in particular not opposed

much better not to speak of a "Corporate State" at all. Messner (*Die berufsständische Ordnung,* Innsbruck 1936) explains a threefold meaning of the term "Corporate State": i. where the State completely dominates the vocational groups; ii. where the State is absorbed in the autonomous vocational groups; iii. where vocational groups and State complement each other and work together in harmony. As "organized society" the vocational groups form the basis for the State. If the vocational groups were the *only* basis of the State, one might agree with Messner; but this is not the case, for it also includes families, local communities like municipalities, urban and rural districts, political parties etc.

to genuine democracy.[14] Vocational groups are not organs for the formation of the political will. They are not intended to replace or to eliminate political parties, neither are they capable of doing so.

ii. Nevertheless, legislation and government can scarcely be carried out properly if the vocational groups remain excluded from them. The vocational groups are eminently qualified to collaborate in ascertaining the requirements of the common good and in issuing the appropriate orders. Because the various spheres of the common good are in fact their proper function. The form in which they should participate in the leading functions of State must be determined by the actual situation. Whether the vocational groups should create their own senate or chamber, or whether they should merely send representatives to another body; how large the number of representatives for the individual groups should be; whether the vocational groups should only take part in the deliberations, or should have a voice in the decisions: *e.g.*, collaborate in promulgating laws, or only in preparing legislation; whether, and to what extent, Parliament (and the Cabinet) would have to meet the proposals, objections and opinions of the vocational groups. – all these questions must be determined according to circumstances (cf. also Q. 56).

An "aristocratic element" is infused into democracy by the participation of the vocational groups in the formation of State policy and in the running of the State; a select group of

[14] In his broadcast message of 1944 Pius XII indicated democracy as the form of State best suited to modern society (cf. Q. 98). He repeatedly mentioned vocational organization and expressly confirmed the teaching of his predecessor, which shows that the pope considers vocational organization to be compatible with democracy, and that in fact he considers the two to be particularly suited to eachother.

experts complements the popular representation elected according to political party views (House of Lords). Hence vocational organization does not weaken the (democratic) State; on the contrary it strengthens it.

4. What rights, and consequently also obligations, has the State in respect of the vocational groups? Three are generally mentioned:

i. The State may, and must, determine exactly the limits of self-government of the vocational groups. There is much overlapping of State and society spheres of activity; besides, "owing to changed circumstances much that was formerly done by small groups can nowadays only be done by large associations" (Q. A., 79). Thus the functional orbit of the vocational groups is not always and everywhere of like extent. Where the vocational groups do not themselves find the "golden mean" it must be indicated to them by the State:

EXAMPLES. In matters of culture and education the State nowadays has to do a great deal that in former times could be left to the member communities. The same is true in economics; without a general legislation governing economic policy neither the national economy nor its individual elements will prosper today.

ii. By appropriate measures the State must ensure that there are good relations between the different vocational groups, that the just claims of the whole community are furthered: coordinating function. The common deliberation of the vocational groups, which should exercise this significant function, will often not be sufficient, and in fact will not suffice at all, since the task is uncommonly difficult and delicate. Hence the State will first of all have to make a basic regulation from the standpoint of the common good regarding those matters which lie outside the scope of vocational groups and are easily overlooked by them.[15]

iii. The State has the right to exercise vigilance over the activity of the vocational groups, and to use compulsion where there is blatant neglect of duty. As guardian of the common good it is entitled to intervene when the member communities fail. To exercise vigilance does not mean to dominate, but rather to ensure that things develop as well as possible under the circumstances. All State measures of assistance must aim at leading (or leading back) the vocational groups to orderly activity. In times of emergency State interference will, of course, increase considerably, since then the common good is particularly endangered and consequently must be guarded with the utmost care.

56. *What kind of structure is fitting for a vocational order of society?*

The vocational order of society ought in its structure to take account of the different spheres of service and of particular conditions.

1. No definite rule can be given even about what are the principal vocational groups, and how many there are, or should be. Even this first question concerning the number of principal groups can only be answered by taking into account the circumstances of place and time. In a country that possesses little industry it may well be possible to include (for the time being) the whole of industry in a single vocational group; in a country where industry is highly developed at least the main branches of industry will each have to be given the rank of a vocational group. The division into vocational groups must be made in

[15] For example, concerning the family, State member communities, foreign policy, national defence; considerations of private property and criminal law.

accordance with the vital and cultural needs of society; the subdivisions follow the independent partial services within one complete total service.

Examples. Press and information media which at first must be considered one vocational group because of their homogeneous function, may expand and spread to such an extent that it may seem expedient to develop the individual groups, or forms, each into a proper vocational group (*e.g.*, press, radio and television; educational and light literature; printing, publishing and book-selling). Or the vocational group "Science": The individual fields, or branches, of science offer sufficient grounds for creating not merely subdivisions, but main divisions of equal rank.

2. The difference between the vocational groups in the economic field and those outside this field is hardly likely to be disputed. The former are concerned with the production and distribution (as also with the consumption) of material, or consumption, goods; the latter with goods other than these: goods that do not directly serve man's material needs.

i. It is true that the national economy represents a single field of human activity, but this field is so extensive and heterogeneous that several economic vocational groups are called for:

	Agriculture (& Forestry)
	Mining industry
Production of goods:	Trades
↗	Industry
Credit & Insurance	
↘	Trade
Distribution of goods:	(Home & foreign trade)
	(Wholesale & retail trade)
	Transport
	(Passenger & goods services)

ii. Of non-economic spheres of activity with social rather than State, characteristics there are at least the following:

Sciences
Education and general formation
Press and Information
Health services
Arts
Technology

It is obvious from this classification that a clear-cut division is very difficult. Many doubts remain that can only be resolved in practice. In certain circumstances the State may have to decide the matter. A few further points should be noted:

a. The same individual may belong to two vocational groups simultaneously. For example, a professor of medicine who runs a private practice may belong to the vocational groups of "Formation" and "Health"; a carpenter or a locksmith in a factory to the vocational groups "Trades" and "Industry".

b. The military profession and the Civil Service, both of which usually have a marked professional *esprit de corps,* are State professions but not genuine vocational groups. Undoubtedly many who are paid by the State, or out of public funds, belong to a definite vocational group by reason of their function: *e.g.,* teachers and school inspectors belong to "Education" and "Formation"; social workers to "Health". Besides, State professions and vocational groups form one single total community.

c. What are called "professional men", *e.g.,* writers, lawyers and doctors, do not constitute a vocational group of their own. It is true that they have much in common, but they differ widely in their professional concerns.

d. What is the position with regard to the administration of justice? As we know the courts act in the name, and with the authority of the State, and judges are independent officers of State. On the other hand the courts enjoy a large measure of independence, thus genuine professional independence; the judge makes his decisions independently, although these must be in accordance with law. There is no doubt that law is especially apt to engender a genuine and high professional consciousness in those that serve it; likewise, that the administration of justice does not lie in the hands of State officials alone. Scholars of law, lawyers and barristers, justices of the peace and jurymen, even clerks of the court and messengers are among those whose function, or occupation, is, or determines, the administration of justice. The question whether "law" or "administration of justice" should be recognized as a proper vocational group becomes important when, for example, it has to be decided whether, and in what manner, the administration of justice should be represented in a chamber of vocational groups.

3. It is still more difficult to say how the various vocational groups are to be further subdivided. Most of the economic and cultural spheres have grown so much in extent and depth that they need to be subdivided in order to develop an orderly and successful activity. Often there is need of subordinate associations restricted both in function and area. For this reason men must make up their minds on two points:

i. What, and how many, divisions must be made so that a satisfactory total service will be guaranteed?

ii. Which divisions are to be recognized now or later as having the character of a proper vocational group?

Examples. Press and Information media: books, daily, weekly and periodical press, broadcasting and T. V. (together with the radio industry, and broadcasting staff); Industry: iron and steel, timber, leather, textiles, iron-producing and processing industry; Chemical Industry, together with its major branches; Mining Industry: coal, ore, oil; Power Production: waterpower, electricity, atomic power; Communications: postal system, railways, motors, aircraft; Trades: the various individual trades, or groups of these; Education: primary and secondary schools, universities, technical schools (which belong more to trades, industry or mining industry according to the type of instruction given in them); Health: Doctors' groups, the pharmaceutical industry (which also belongs to the chemical industry). Some vocational groups, or sections of them, can be extended over an entire country, while others need to be territorially restricted because otherwise their functions cannot be controlled.

4. It is inevitable that the vocational groups will themselves create a supreme council or councils (cf. below ii), to which the individual vocational groups will send their own representatives, and which will regulate those matters that are the common concern of all. The name of this Chamber or Council is unimportant. But other matters are important:

i. Is this supreme organ to have only an advisory function, or should it also have power to issue obligatory directives? The individual vocational group is empowered to make regulations that have legal force for its own special field and its own members. But this competence cannot be transferred unaltered to the supreme body of vocational organization. Because its decisions would directly and formally affect the common weal in its entirety, and would clearly be expressions of the sovereign authority of the State. Here also one must consider carefully what would be the right thing: either a chamber that would have equal authority so that it would govern conjointly with the people's elected representatives: laws and other decisions would only become valid when both sides (Parliament and the vocational organization chamber) passed them or raised no objection (right of veto); or a body that would be entitled only to collaborate (to give advice, to state its views, to make suggestions, have the right to be heard, the right to postpone): this type of collaboration is by no means unimportant; expert preliminary work is absolutely necessary in order that the decisions, laws etc. will be right. If the organs of government (Parliament and Cabinet) are obliged by the constitution to consult the vocational groups and give their opinion due consideration, there is a very strong guarantee of good government and against the abuse of power.

ii. The question is disputed whether all the vocational groups should be united in one single council, or whether there should be two chambers: one for the economic vocational groups (a national economic council), and one for those outside the economic field (cultural council, or some such name). Some favour or demand a single chamber. They point out that the vocational groups belong together as members of a whole, and that one cannot separate economic affairs from those outside this field, since no vocational group can thrive without an economic basis. Others recommend, and just as vigorously defend, two chambers.[16] They maintain that economic questions have increased and would still further increase in independence and urgency as a consequence of technical progress to such an extent that they would have to be dealt with separately. It would be relatively easy to ascertain the material needs of the other cultural spheres; the other vocational groups could be represented in the "economic council". Which of these two views should be adopted? The vocational groups complement one another intrinsically, and this unity is really more effectively guaranteed when the entire "policy" of vocational organization is the responsibility

[16] Only a few recommend more than two chambers, but even this is worth considering; of course, unity would then have to be attained at a higher level.

of one single chamber. On the other hand the arguments in favour of two chambers cannot be rejected out of hand. Here again the best solution will depend on the circumstances.

5. Opinions differ also on the question as to whether representatives of the State, *e.g.*, of the municipality, the federal government, the whole country, should participate in the deliberations and resolutions of the organs of vocational organization:

i. One opinion is based on the principle that vocational groups must consider it their primary duty to collaborate in promoting the common good (cf. Q. A., 84/85). But the responsible guardian of the common good is the State, and it alone can judge and determine to what extent the decisions of the vocational groups are in line with the common good. Hence the vocational groups cannot get on without the direct participation and collaboration of the State.

ii. The other opinion fully acknowledges the obligation of vocational groups to the common good. But it considers neither necessary nor desirable that the State should have a voice in the internal deliberations and decisions of the councils of vocational organization, and this for the following reasons:

a. Expert knowledge to an ever increasing extent is becoming indispensable. But the experts are found precisely among the members of the vocational groups.

b. The State's right of supervision is sufficient to prevent the vocational groups going in the wrong direction.

c. In any case the proposed legislation and objections, possibly the resolutions and decisions of the higher councils of vocational organization only become valid in law by the consent of the government. For example, legislation proposed by the vocation-nal organization council would only become binding when it had been accepted by Parliament. Here again much can be said for and against both opinions.

57. *What is the significance of a society based on vocational organization for the community of nations?*

A vocational order prepares and ensures the way to harmonious collaboration between nations and States.

PIUS XII (Address of 6 April, 1951; U. A. vol. 1, p. 250).

"You are of the opinion that this world political organization, in order to be effective, must be federal in form. If by this you understand that it should not be enmeshed in an artificial uniformity, again you are in harmony with the principles of social and political life so firmly founded and sustained by the Church. Indeed, no organization of the world could live if it were not harmonized with the whole complex of natural relations, with that normal organic order which rules the particular relations between men and men and between different peoples. If it does not do that, then, no matter what its structure may be, it will not be able to stand up and endure."

1. If the State restores to the vocational groups what these are capable of achieving, it will free itself from the excess of power it has wrongly assumed, and will be more inclined to accept those restrictions that its incorporation in the community of nations demands of it. It can also devote itself much more thoroughly to its own internal and external affairs.

2. Vocational groups may (and should; Q. 116) form associations among themselves on an international basis. Cultural goods are made and destined to become the common property of all men, and the cultural development of individual nations is

becoming increasingly dependent on international collaboration. Men find contact more easily at the economic and cultural than at the political level where power and self-interest, fear and jealousy usually are asserted more strongly. There should be nothing to prevent the formation of international associations on a vocational group basis. Certain beginnings have been made. It would be an easy matter to increase and develop these if international politics were more liberal and did not erect so many barriers between the nations: *e.g.,* currency and passport difficulties.

EXAMPLES. Genuine vocational communities could result without much difficulty from a livelier international exchange in the sciences and arts. The United Nations have established branch organizations which in their function and field of activity have the character of vocational groups: for example, UNESCO – United Nations Educational, Scientific and Cultural Organization; WHO – World Health Organization; FAO – Food and Agricultural Organization. The European Economic Community, the aims of which are in fact political, deals with what would primarily be a matter for the "Economy" vocational groups.

58. *Could a vocational order be established easily?*

The establishment of a vocational order would undoubtedly have to contend with many and substantial difficulties.

It would be foolish to close one's eyes to the difficulties that actually exist. Even Pius XI neither expected nor prophesied that the vocational order as proposed by him would be easily and quickly achieved (cf. Q. A., 87, 138). We must distinguish between two types of difficulty: i. practical difficulties, *i.e.,* those that are in the nature of the vocational order itself (cf. in this connection especially Qs. 55–56); ii. difficulties conditioned by the times, *i.e.*, those that arise from historical development and from the existing conditions of social life.

1. The division of labour in the large-scale economy of today has created conditions that are to a large extent very unfavourable to genuine partnership and collaboration on a basis of equality; in addition a great number of reasons for distrust and suspicion, tensions and hardships have been inherited from the past. Among others we might mention present-day working methods, progressive mechanization and division of labour; the great number and differentiation of partial functions; dependence in methods, kind and time of work; the practical lack of liberty in choice of occupation; urbanization which is conditioned in large measure by modern industrial economy; the breath-taking pace at which everything happens today; economic, social and political insecurity.

i. Patriarchal conditions cannot, and should not, be re-established today in their earlier form. But where men have been alienated from one another, the spirit is lacking which must support and vitalize a vocational organization.

ii. Not only economy but also other spheres of life cannot be mastered today without what is called the manager, *i.e.*, without the determining influence of men to whom the relationship of man to man or man to things is entrusted as their proper function. Where this manager becomes a mere functionary he ignores or breaks the individual and the communities. For this reason it is very necessary that an interest should be taken in the training of these men; they must be made really fit for their work at the "cardinal points" of social life (cf. below, 4 iv).

2. Vocational organization presupposes persons who are independent yet conscious of their social obligations. Egotism and unbridled liberty are as much opposed to it as the herd instinct, the escape into the anonymity of groups and movements such as the party or the union, and in general every type of collectivity. But the capacity for personal responsibility and the courage to assume it are not exactly strong points of modern man. Egotism or a false spirit of subservience dominate large numbers in our time. They have become uprooted, the sense for a natural order of things has largely disappeared; genuine authority has largely been reduced or is, at least, disputed. Considering the continual incitements and distortions to which men are subject, we find it difficult to say how this sense of order and authority is to be awakened.

3. It is well known that some of those bodies and institutions on the collaboration of which a vocational order would depend, will have nothing to do with it:

i. The modern State, even though it may not be totalitarian, is scarcely inclined to restore the independence of the member communities that it has itself destroyed.[17] To the extent to which political parties put their own particular interests before the common good they will oppose vocational orders, because the latter is not compatible with party egotism.[18]

[17] Hence from the point of view of vocational organization those tendencies are of the greatest importance that would restore to the member communities of the State their individual responsibility and self-government.

[18] Cf. once again the opinion of Pius XI on the corporate State of Fascist Italy. Pius XI (Q. A., 95): ". . . There are some who fear that the State is substituting itself in the place of private initiative, instead of limiting itself to necessary and sufficient assistance. It is feared that the new syndical and corporative organization tends to have an excessively bureaucratic and politicate character, and that, notwithstanding the general advantages referred to above, it

ii. In many places both the trade unions and the federations of employers oppose a vocational order. Substantially their reasons are that class-distinctions have not yet been overcome; the introduction of a vocational organization would mean the end of the class-struggle: "labour-market parties" live by the slogans of class-conflict; they are afraid of the "power-politics" of the vocational groups and of a consequent diminution of free competition. Some fear a planned economy, confusing the ordered economy of a vocational order with a State-directed economy. There is the fear of losing existing powers, *i.e.*, of having to hand them over to the vocational groups.

iii. The implacable opponents of a vocational social order are to be found among all forms of collectivism, even of a moderate type, as well as among political parties sympathetic to collectivist ideas and aims. Collectivism repudiates all genuine independence both of the individual and of member communities; it detests all natural grading of position and authority, since this conflicts with its preconceived notion of absolute equality. It does not wish to see force and conflict vanquished by concord and collaboration.

Individualistic tendencies and parties also clearly oppose vocational organization. Their reasons are largely akin to those of the collectivists, *e.g.*, rejection of a natural order of values and communities; an exaggerated view of the exigencies of State policy (Q. 62, 11); group-egotism; no genuine readiness to collaborate; a false notion of "equality of rights".

4. Yet despite the great difficulties, the prospects of approaching our goal are not too bad, given but good will and sufficient per-

ends in serving particular political aims rather than in contributing to the initiation and promotion of a better social order."

severance. For this it is necessary to acknowledge and develop the beginnings already made; to instruct the people on a broad basis and educate them to the idea of vocational organization; and to induce the State to create the necessary legal conditions, to promote vigorously the formation of vocational groups and gradually to hand over to them those functions which the State is usurping.

i. Even today there are whole economic and cultural fields that are, at least in part, organized on a vocational basis or offer the best approach: *e.g.,* Trades (guilds, boards); Agriculture and Farm Workers (co-operative associations, unions, boards); commerce (chambers); among the professional classes associations of doctors and lawyers, film boards, broadcasting corporations. In education also institutions on a vocational basis may be found or could be created without difficulty, that is, on condition that the State renounces its monopoly.

ii. In the branches of economy, which are not easy of access because of their size and mechanization, there exist, nevertheless, institutions that could either be taken over or developed: *e.g.,* chambers of industry and commerce.

iii. Pius XI pointed out (Q. A., 87) that precisely these "voluntary associations" could prepare the way for vocational organization, thus forming the preliminary stage for eventual vocational groups. Among Catholic associations that consciously foster the idea of vocational organization the following deserve to be mentioned: both in England and the U. S. A.: the Young Christian Workers, the Association of Catholic Trade Unionists; in England: the Catholic Social Guild, the Association of Catholic Managers and Employers; in the U. S. A.: the National Catholic Social Action Conference, Labour Schools, etc.

iv. Once again the fostering of human relations must be mentioned, and in this connection also joint consultation and a share in management in so far as these are not meant to imply power-politics, but would guarantee employees legitimate collaboration within the economic sphere. What characterizes a vocational social order is the harmonious collaboration of all members of the vocational group. Efforts to bring about what is implied in the expression "human relations" could at least create the "atmosphere" in which men with different interests and functions would be able to live *together* (and not merely side by side): trust must form the basis of true collaboration.

59. What are the advantages of a vocational social order?

A vocational social order would abolish class-distinctions and lead to order and unity among the classes; it would overcome the exaggerated claims of the State to power and authority; it would ensure the natural rights and liberties of individuals and member communities; and it would offer to the ambitious and efficient opportunities of advancement on the basis of achievement. It would make the common good the "object of achievement" of the whole nation, and guarantee genuine cultural and economic progress to the individual nation and the community of nations.

Part Three

Political Order of the State

Nation and State

In spite of all the crimes and breaches of law which are recorded in the history of States, Catholic ethics does not look on the State as a phantom of human power, but as an essential part of the divine order of creation and providence. Nevertheless, the discussion of what concerns the State and State politics encounters considerable difficulties at the present time.

1. Many people have completely lost interest in the State; they do not realize how wrong and how dangerous such an attitude is.

2. The trend is away from the "State" and towards an international order transcending individual States. The world, alerted by events, is coming to realize gradually that the State can no longer remain "sovereign" to the same extent as it has been up to now.

3. A number of intricate questions have to be dealt with, as for example, taxation laws, political parties, man in the totalitarian State, resistance to the supreme authority of the State.

Lesson One

POLITICAL COMMUNITY AND STATE

CATHOLIC political thought links up with definitions that go back to pre-Christian times: the State is the political society, that is, the society concerned with "politics" (home and foreign policy).[1]

The word "political" derives from the Greek "polis". Originally "polis" denoted the city in the sense of a sovereign dominion like the city-States of Athens, Sparta and Corinth in contrast to the country which owed allegiance and was obliged to pay taxes to it. The urban population was composed of freemen and slaves; only the freemen had the right to engage in the political affairs of the city, such as legislation, administration and jurisdiction. The city was self-sufficient, *i.e.*, it produced all that was necessary for a full and good human existence; it was self-sufficient in the spheres of law, economics and culture. The large number of its families, allied groupings such as artisans and traders and institutions as also its security against enemies, since it was protected by fortifications and armed forces, enabled the citizens to enjoy a peaceful and happy existence in the fullness of human values. For this reason the polis was called "perfect", or the "perfect society".[2]

[1] On the meaning of the terms "politics" and "political" cf. Q. 64.

[2] For the Greeks the community of the *polis* had an all-inclusive character, *i.e.*, for the individual it was not only the supreme authority but also the highest goal that determined all values and which all were obliged to serve. At the same time arbitrariness was largely excluded in so far as the higher values like religion, custom, way of life, could not be determined authoritatively by any particular ruler, but were based on the customs and tradition of the people and on the political wisdom of the higher academies. Corresponding to the Greek *polis* was the Latin *civitas* which meant the city (Rome) or the citizens

Catholic social thought maintains that much can be learned from the nature of man and from the natural order of things that will always remain valid and basic for the political community. It has adopted from pre-Christian ethics certain terms and principles; but it has supplemented, corrected or newly defined the meaning of these terms and principles, as in the case of the terms "political" and "autarchic" or "sovereign"; or the principle that the common good comes before private interest. Catholic social thought makes a careful distinction between the validity and binding force of the *idea* and that of the specific place in which the idea is realized; today, for example, whether, and how far, the idea of the political community is put into practice in the modern State.

Antiquity and Middle Ages were unaware of the term "State" in the modern sense. The modern meaning of the term appears for the first time in Italy at the beginning of the fifteenth century when "stato" meant "order" or "constitution". It was the Italian historian and statesman Macchiavelli (1469 to 1527) who really introduced the term. But the modern form of the national State did not evolve until much later (cf. Q. 65). Before we connect "State" with political society we shall have to examine more carefully the meaning of both concepts.

(of Rome). Later on Rome came to signify the *imperium,* the whole Roman Empire. With the Greeks the educational, social and cultural aspects predominated, with the Romans it was the legal aspect. The Roman Empire acknowledged basic private rights, although not to the same extent as today. From the Romans the Empire and the idea of the Empire passed on to the Germans in the form of the "Holy Roman Empire". Later this became the much smaller "German Empire". Today "empire" denotes an extensive sovereign dominion usually embracing several peoples and territories.

60. *What is the political society?*

The political society is human society in its totality, that is, the all-inclusive order of natural social life.

1. For all its rich variety of forms, human social life basically constitutes a unity. Because human nature from which it springs is designed for the totality of the human good and therefore requires a social order in which the total good can be attained or realized (I, Qs. 44/45, 59). Thus above and beyond the many individual societies there must be, according to the design of nature, a society that can be correctly described as the whole of society. In it social life finds its natural perfection precisely because this society embraces everything that belongs to the total human good. The goal of this society will thus consist in the common good as such.[3] That this society is called "political" is due to the fact that Greek philosophers of the pre-Christian era gave it the name "polis".

2. Every society needs an order of its own. Corresponding to society as a whole would be an order that unites all other societies in a general order.

61. *What is the character of political society?*

Political society is of natural origin and therefore necessary; it is legally above member communities; it is a "perfect" society *(societas perfecta)*.

It should be noted that the answer is not applicable without qualification to existing States. It is given here as a principle.

[3] In contrast to the common good of those societies that only have a limited partial sphere as their goal. Every society has its own common good which is related and subordinated to the total human good. We are concerned here with the natural order.

I. Origin of Political Society

1. The social nature of man implies not only that men must live as social beings but also that men should by mutual and complementary assistance find and achieve, for themselves and for others, the fullness of human good. Hence the society that has this fullness of human good as its goal and function is something intended by nature. The political society is of natural origin.
2. God has given human nature its own proper goals, tendencies and powers (I, Qs. 68, 71). Hence political society is part of the divine plan. This applies not only to the fact of its existence but also to its extensive rights (cf. Lessons 2–4).

II. Legal Character of Political Society

1. In order to be or to constitute a proper all-inclusive order, political society has to be given suitable and effective means by nature, that is, by God. To these belong in the first place the right to issue and promulgate necessary laws and to order and enforce their observance. This right is not subject to any higher human right, and extends to everything that can possibly fall within the scope of man.[4]

Nature (God) has determined in a general manner only what is the human good as a whole and the corresponding political order. Men must find out for themselves what in practice will meet the goals and directives of nature; then they must ensure that the order found to be the right one is established and maintained. Medieval political society could not have the same sort of structure as modern States; the type of government of a

[4] We are not here dealing with the rights of individual States. The competence of the Church is of a higher kind than the merely human, natural competence with which we are speaking here.

monarchy will necessarily differ from that of a democracy with universal suffrage and Parliament.

To prevent a political order from being upset or destroyed either from within or without, adequate security measures are necessary and these have to have a legal basis. In virtue of natural right the political society is entitled to defend itself against its enemies. It is at the same time guarantor and trustee of the right both of individuals and of subsidiary societies; it should guarantee life in freedom.

2. In short, political society is legally placed above the individual and over other societies. It possesses sovereign powers; the members are bound to obey it (they are "subjects" cf. Qs. 79–81).

III. "Perfect" Society

We ought to be clear about the precise meaning of the term "perfect" society. A thing (an action, an institution, a structure) may be perfect:

i. in itself, if it lacks nothing of what it must possess or fulfil in order to satisfy completely the requirements of its nature; a tool is perfect when it is well made for its purpose;

ii. in comparison with another. In this case perfect means "more than", "greater", "richer", "higher"; imperfect means "less than", "less important", "smaller", "poorer", "lower" etc. But what is imperfect may well be perfect in itself, *i.e.,* of its kind. For example, a simple box camera may be perfect of its kind, but imperfect compared with a cinecamera. If political society is called "perfect" this does not mean that political societies in the past or present were, or are, in fact perfect and did, or do, in fact fulfil their functions as they should; neither does it mean that political societies must themselves own and produce everything which they do for their citizens. A country may be wealthy and yet dependent on the import of foreign goods. But it does mean that political society by nature is conceived as perfect in itself and that it is vested accordingly with a plenitude of rights and powers. It also means that political society surpasses in perfection all other societies. In the natural order there is no society the goals of which are more important, the functions of which are more extensive and the rights and powers of which are greater.

The concept "perfect society" is easily misunderstood because we tend to forget that a whole comprises its parts. If we refer to the perfection of a whole, the parts are not excluded, but are contained in it and consequently are referred to.[5]

1. The perfection of a society is based primarily on the perfection of its goal, thus on that good which the society ought to attain. The goal of political society, the human good as a whole, comprises all natural parts and individual goals; it is the "virtual" unity of all these parts and individual goods (I, Q. 29, I, 4). It can be achieved only if the other societies play their part well and fulfil their individual functions (I, Q. 52, Nos. 4–6).

First principle: The political society is called "perfect" because it has for its goal and function the fullness of human goods.

2. Corresponding to a perfect goal there must be perfectly fitting and adequate means. First, political society must be capable of providing everything that men need in order to attain together and among themselves the fullness of human good; second it must also be entitled and obliged to do everything to enable men to live in an order of unity and peace. Aristotle and

[5] For a better understanding of this cf. I, Qs. 21, 31, 45, 52.

St. Thomas Aquinas referred to the former as the amount of goods necessary for a good, that is, virtuous, life.[6] They referred to the latter (especially St. Thomas) as concord or the "unity of peace" in the order of justice. Today we speak about the "general welfare", meaning both aspects.

Second principle: Political society is called "perfect" because it posseses all the (legal) means it needs in order to secure to its subjects peace and the fullness of human good.

3. What is really perfect is autonomous, independent, while what is imperfect on the contrary is dependent and not autonomous. The highest autonomy and independence within the natural order is due to political society; it is the highest human authority and power[7] (cf. "Sovereignty" in Q. 67).

Third principle: Political society is called "perfect" because full internal autonomy and full independence externally are due to it.

Political society thus exhausts, as it were, the social nature of man to the point of its natural fulfilment. For this reason both Aristotle and St. Thomas Aquinas described man as a social or a political being indiscriminately; that is, by virtue of his social disposition man is destined for the political, or perfect, society.

We can understand now why, following Aristotle, St. Thomas and eminent scholars after him could refer to political society as pre-eminent among all entities of the natural order, as the most excellent of all human institutions. We can also

[6] *Politics* I, 1 and explanation; *De reg. princ.* I, 2, 15.

[7] That every human society, even the highest, is subject to God, to the natural moral law and to the genuine claims of the common good has already been explained (I, Qs. 27, 99, 76); we shall come back to it in Q. 66. To this extent the sovereignty, and consequently the perfection, of political society can only be relative, that is, conditional and limited, but never absolute, that is unconditional and unlimited.

understand why "politics", that is, political science, or philosophy was regarded as the supreme and most important part of the moral law. This may sound strange to us, since we can only see the modern State and are accustomed to judge things in the light of our less happy experiences of it.

It is nowadays very dangerous to speak of the "all-embracing character of politics". The "perfect" society of Christian political teaching has nothing in common with the modern totalitarian State. This will be shown in more detail in the questions that follow. St. Thomas emphasized that it is the immediate function of the secular authority to manage temporal affairs *(terrena, temporalia bona)*. These temporal affairs must be related and subordinated to the spiritual *(spiritualia)*; he argued thus that the good life *(vita virtuosa)* in which the goal of political society consists has to be understood in the sense not merely of natural but of supernatural Christian virtue.[8]

62. *What is the State?*

The State is the individual political society which comprises a group of human persons limited in numbers and area.

IT HAS been suggested that the whole of mankind ought to form a single political community (World State; Q. 113). This is evidently contradicted by history which testifies to a multiplicity of States or similar political structures in all ages and in all parts of the world. The facts of history have their deeper cause in human nature itself as well as in the necessities of life

[8] *De reg. princ.* I, 14. This work (Book One and Book Two, chaps. 1–4; the rest is by another hand) contains St. Thomas' most important and significant political teaching.

derived from it and in the developments rooted in it (*ibid.*). Hence we conclude that the multiplicity of political societies is according to nature.

I. Essential Features of the State

1. History shows us that States may in fact originate in a variety of ways, for example, by conquest, subjugation, free association, organic development from earlier social forms, divisions, declaration of independence, annexation etc. But ultimately States are of natural origin. Catholic social ethics has always agreed with Aristotle, St. Thomas and many others who hold that the State is the result of an organic development; starting from marriage, family and tribal societies to the village society or city with its neighbouring areas and estates, province or county, etc. According to the modern theory of contract, the State originates wholly through voluntary agreement, from the "general will". Men are said to have renounced part of their liberty in order to exchange for it the necessary security against dangers, attacks etc. We do not agree with this opinion. Individual States too possess the natural rights of political society for their own territory and subjects. By law they are placed over individuals and subordinate societies, having sovereign rights and authority over them.

Because there are several or many States, it is necessary, i. that their body of laws must be adapted to specific prevailing conditions; ii. that consideration is due to other States.

2. Is the individual State also to be regarded as a "perfect" society? – This is nowadays a controversial question since the modern State is far removed from the genuine political society (Q. 65). Even St. Thomas stressed the fact that political

societies are not all perfect societies in the same degree; the kingdom *(regnum)*, for instance, is more perfect than the city *(civitas)*.[9] The popes of modern times have continued to describe the State as the "perfect" and supreme society of the natural order. Undoubtedly, they refer to the modern State inasmuch as it is a constitutional State.

LEO XIII (I. D., 13).

"The Almighty, therefore, has given the charge of the human race to two powers, the ecclesiastical and the civil, the one being set over divine, and the other over human, things. Each in its kind is supreme . . . ."

PIUS XII (Address to the Rota, 1944).

"A deep difference exists between the Church and the State, although both are perfect societies in the fullest sense of the word."

Catholic political thinkers are divided on the question; some state quite frankly that the idea of the perfect society has become obsolete and impracticable, others hold fast to this idea. Our view is that, within its own frontiers, and for its own subjects, the individual State has the complete human good for its goal, and in this sense it is a perfect or complete society. Much more difficult today is the question of providing suitable and adequate means in accordance with this goal. In this respect, States now more than ever depend on one another. Hardly any State is still in a position today to supply from its own resources all that human life needs in the present state of science and civilization. But the essential point is that the State continues to be entitled and obliged to make these means

[9] Commentary on the Gospel of St. Matthew chap. 12 (ed. Marietti p. 170).

accessible to itself and its members by the use of all necessary and practicable ways. The greatest difficulties today are presented by the independence or sovereignty of individual States. In view of modern developments towards larger political units embracing several States, individual States have to surrender parts of their sovereignty. Yet in a restricted but genuine sense they remain supreme authority, and hence "perfect" society (cf. Qs. 67 and 114). Thus even for the modern State the idea of the perfect society remains the guiding principle.

II. The State as a Society of Persons

The State is without doubt an ordered unity of persons. As free persons men are members (citizens) and subjects of the State. What constitutes a State does not depend on class and occupation, on wealth and efficiency, on race or religion. Only the exercise of political rights depends on certain conditions such as age and political maturity. To form a State is grounded in the social nature of man which finds complete fulfilment in the political society (Q. 60). The concept of the State as a unity of persons gives rise to some important qualifications:

1. For the purpose of the State, which cannot be impersonal but must relate to the human person: Undoubtedly the State's aim is above persons in the sense that it is the common aim of the whole nation. Yet it is neither the laws and institutions nor the achievements of science and civilization which form the starting-point and goal of the State community but men in their dignity and aims, tasks and necessities.

2. For the scope of State's activity: The State has an obligation towards all those who belong to it as members or who reside or move within its territory in peaceful intent. Of course, this

is not an indiscriminate obligation towards all. But the State must devote its activities and care to all levels of the people and especially to those who on account of their general or particular (needs) situation are most endangered and most in need of help, for example, unemployed, refugees, pensioners (cf. Q. 96).

3. For the people of the State: The question, What is the State? is often answered simply thus: the State is the nation politically united. This is all very well, but what is meant by "the nation"? We can at once exclude two meanings of the word. i. nation or people as a mere plurality of individuals, ii. the people in contrast to the educated or the ruling classes, and sometimes used in a derogatory, *e.g.*, the common people, the plebs.

"People" may denote a biological, spiritual and cultural unity, a group of men belonging together by reason of descent, kinship, language, tradition, common origin and native land, common experience and religious beliefs, being conscious of this solidarity. Taken in this sense the people is always the upholder of its own cultural and spiritual values. It has a strong sense of community and is attached to the natural soil; (folk customs, folklore). But the people by itself does not form a political unit, because as "a people" it does not as yet possess the legal and constitutional order necessary for this. Nevertheless, it is of great importance "politically", because it is entitled to lead its own life within the State to which it belongs, for example, as a national minority (cf. Q. 114, No. 2); and also by constituting a natural basis for State entity inasmuch as it is conscious of itself (right of self-determination).

Finally, people denotes the people forming a State, *i.e.*, the totality of men living in a State and there enjoying the rights of citizens without distinction of birth, class, religion or position. (The people as representative of the political will; sovereignty of the people, Q. 70). Nationality is acquired either by birth or by naturalization. In saying that the State is the people united politically, we intend the term "people" to be understood primarily in the sense of the people forming the State, but also as a biologico-cultural unity (cf. Qs. 63 and 115).

III. Territorial Unity and Sovereignty

A State requires a definite territory, a circumscribed part of the earth's surface which the people of the State inhabit and within which the State exercises its authority.[10] The territory of the State is not the property of the State or of the people, for the right to property is primarily a natural right of the human person. Only the human person is the image of God and endowed with mind. The State possesses only a kind of supreme right of property; it can make laws and take measures to regulate in various respects the acquisition, possession and use of property for reasons of the common good. But territorial sovereignty endows the State with the following rights.

1. The State has the sole right to rule within and over its territory, that is, to exercise its sovereign authority. Limitations of this right are dealt with in Q. 115.

2. Accordingly, the State is entitled to repulse unjust attacks on its territory (just self-defence, cf. Qs. 120/121).

3. The State may, and must, make adequate provision for the development in its territory of improved ways of living (Q. A., 75), *e.g.*, by exploiting mineral wealth, providing sufficient

[10] According to modern law the interior of the earth, air space and the coastal waters are part of State territory. Further particulars pertain to the province of international law.

roads and means of transport, promoting agriculture and forestry, fighting diseases, draining and reclaiming swamps etc.

4. The general weal of mankind and its own particular weal require the State to keep its frontiers open for the most extensive possible peaceful communications (cf. Qs. 116/117).

The political community of ancient times till the late Middle Ages and sometimes till modern times recognized a form of religious consecration. The Holy Roman Empire, for example, was not just a secular power. In the seventeenth century the divine right of kings was proclaimed, concealing frequently extreme forms of the autocracy of State or princes (Louis XIV of France; [1638–1715]; the Age of Absolutism).

63. What is the modern State?

The modern State is the national State, and is mostly unduly dominated by "reason of State".

I. Nation and State

The national State is one which developed from the modern nation and national consciousness. It is an entity of historical growth. Yet there are a number of things that can be said about it from the point of view of the natural law, since in the last analysis historical developments are based on the social nature of man and must in any case be examined in accordance with the norms of the natural law (Qs. 60–62).

1. It is difficult to define "nation" precisely.[11] This is shown by the many attempts to do so and by conflicting opinions, all of

[11] The word comes from the Latin *nasci,* to be born.

which agree that a number of factors are involved in the nature and development of the nation, as, for example, descent (kinship), climate and soil, common destiny, language (very important) and religion, ties of a common culture, national consciousness and the will to self-determination. Some Catholic scholars consider the cultural factors to be primary, defining nation as a particular community of culture and destiny, with its own consciousness and with the will to cultivate its special character and to express it within communities of a similar type.

2. Nation and people, in the biologico-cultural sense, are so closely related that there is no clear distinction implied when speaking of national or of racial minorities, of the right of self-determination of nations or of peoples. While in the term "people" common descent and kinship predominate, "nation" refers rather to a common destiny or cultural unity.

3. The actual rise of the modern national State is due to the French Revolution of 1789 and to the Napoleonic wars. The struggle against Napoleonic domination awakened the self-consciousness and the will to self-preservation of the European States. The new ideals and basic rights of "liberty, equality and fraternity" replaced the sovereignty of princes by the sovereignty of peoples. An additional factor was the industrial and economic revolution, the progressive achievement of which contributed much to strengthening economic and cultural unity within the nation.

4. Nation and State are not identical, as history can show us. On the one hand, there are States including members of several nations; for example, Switzerland, the former Austro-Hungarian Monarchy and Belgium; on the other hand, members of the

same nation may be citizens of several states; for example, the Italians who were formerly citizens of Italy as well as of Austria-Hungary; there are also national groups living in foreign countries. But even within the national State there is an essential difference between the two. The State is the political order and unity of the nation. The nation is, as it were, the ground structure for the State; it is the people become politically conscious and striving to form a State. Hence nation appertains not to the political, but to the social or pre-political orbit, and as such has social, that is, cultural, rather than political functions. The national State is one, but not the only form of State community (cf. Q. 115). National unity of a people cannot necessarily guarantee the State's capacity of fulfilling its function. We have the historical example of the disintegration of the Austro-Hungarian Monarchy.

5. One of the worst errors and mischief-makers of modern times has been a false nationalism which rgossly exaggerates an otherwise quite legitimate national consciousness. The nation, its honour and power, are idolized; it becomes an end in itself. The result is national egotism, envy and hate.

PIUS XI (C. C. C.; C. T. S., pp. 5, 6).

"If, however, egoism, abusing this love of country and exaggerating this sentiment of nationalism, insinuates itself into the relations between people and people, there is no excess that will not seem justified; . . . the solid foundations of right and honesty, on which the State should rest, are undermined."

PIUS XII (C. B., 1942; C. T. S., p. 7).

"Likewise to be banned is the theory which claims for a particular

nation, or race, or class, a juridical instinct against whose law and command there is no appeal."

II. Reason of State (Raison d'état)

The term "reasonable" has the double sense of being guided by right reason, when reason judges according to the principles and directives derived by nature and God, and of being autonomous, completely independent, when man considers himself as the supreme arbiter and his will as the only valid norm. Modern reason of State implies this second sense. It decides autonomously according to what it considers will best serve its purpose.[12]

1. Reason of State is rooted in the error of absolute State autonomy, that is, in the untrammeled self-glory of the State. This error is bound up with man's progressive detachment from God. The State no longer considers itself bound to obey God and his law, rather it considers itself to be the ultimate source of law and morality. It is sole and adequate law unto itself; an end in itself. The rest follows naturally.

i. The goal of the State and of the reason of State is its own or the nation's self-preservation and self-assertion. Nation and State are the supreme human values.

ii. The State becomes power, its constitutional and legal order becomes an order based solely on power. The reason of State which is ruled by utilitarian considerations decides the extent and employment of the means of power. State law becomes divorced from natural law.

[12] The term "reason of State" will be used in this sense from now on.

iii. "Politics" become exclusively *Realpolitik;* politically right is whatever serves a particular purpose; success decides what is politically justified. The firm foundations of the moral law crumble; honesty and fidelity to contract may disappear; trickery and deception, murder and terror may become acceptable means in politics.

Fortunately, God has imprinted the basic principles of morality deep in the heart of man; otherwise the consequences of these pernicious errors would have been more frightful still. But we must admit that modern reason of State has supplied the totalitarian State with one of its most deadly weapons.

2. The rule of reason of State has unfavourably altered the internal order of the State, partly deliberately and partly because it could not fail to do so:

i. The State has usurped many functions of its subsidiary groupings by intervention and disregard for the principle of subsidiary function; the social sphere has been given a political character. This has its counterpart in the refusal of the citizens to acknowledge the State as anything more than the guarantor of private interests (The "Night-watchman-State" of Lassalle [1825–64]);

ii. Related to this is the progressive growth of centralization and bureaucracy. The "apparatus" grows, the number of official authorities increases continually, the carrying out of tasks (partly alien to the State) becomes ever more complicated and enmeshed in form-filling. The State turns into a "civil service" State, unfortunately not in the good sense of an efficient and reliable civil service supporting the State, but in the bad sense of the State becoming submerged in officialdom.

iii. Finally, conscription must be mentioned to which the

standing army and, in some countries, militarism are due (cf. Qs. 125/127).

3. How can "reason of State" be reformed or overcome? i. The State must again recognize the goals and norms of the natural law, of "human rights"; ii. It would thereby renounce its self-aggrandizement, and might would again serve right. iii. An essential condition would be for the State to restore the rights and functional spheres of subordinate societies (Q. 55), counteracting centralization and excessive bureaucracy.

64. What is a "Christian" State?

A "Christian" State is one that responds to the demands made of it by the Christian way of life.

STRICTLY speaking the State is a "natural" community, part of the created order; it never is a supernatural community or in itself Christian. For this reason we can well understand those who reject the idea of a Christian State. They very rightly stress two further points:

i. Nowadays the term "Christian" is usually taken to mean that which all Christian denominations have in common. But it is at least questionable whether this "common element" is not too little and too vague to form the basis of a really Christian State. ii. The modern State has become secularized. Because of its "pluralist" religious and political composition, including baptized and non-baptized, many indifferent or "lapsed" Christians, there is little prospect of ever again "christianizing" the State.

1. Without wishing to overlook or to belittle these reasons and doubts we would, nevertheless, urge that: i. Only Christianity

can proclaim the principles and order of the natural law with that reliability and rightness which the State needs as a firm foundation. ii. Divine Revelation can teach man about the links between the orders of creation and redemption, nature and supernature, the ultimate goal to which God has called men, and on the duties and obligations that correspond to this ultimate goal. Hence the whole Christian order of life must be taken into account when defining the position and function of the State. iii. There is only one valid concept of man, which is the Christian, and by this the State too is bound.

These facts must be considered in relation to the nature of the State as the all-inclusive natural society. By reason of its goal, its function and its powers the State, being that kind of natural society, is much closer to the supernatural Christian order of life than the many individual or subsidiary communities such as vocational groups and voluntary associations.[13] If it is conscious of this relationship and draws from it the necessary conclusions for its conduct, we may consider it a "Christian" State. By allowing itself to be guided by Christian aims, principles and precepts, it is not its nature that is being changed (it does not become a supernatural society), but in its outward form and activity it will differ so considerably from the non-Christian State, that it will in fact be of a different "kind". (Compare the medieval Empire with the modern secularized national State.)

We may now understand Leo XIII's reference to a "Christian order of the State" and to a "Christian State" although it was

[13] Apart from the community of nations (Q. 113), of which in a higher sense the same is true as of the State, only marriage and the family are exceptions because they are also concerned with human life as such (and not with only some particular aspect of it), and in origin and purpose are still closer to nature and the supernatural – in which respect they surpass the State.

he who had emphasized the natural origin and the natural, proper rights of the State.

The State's relationship to the Church has taken on very different forms in the course of history. Original hostility (persecutions of the early Christians) was followed by gradual rapprochement, although tensions continued until there was reached in the high Middle Ages a co-ordinated unity of Church and State. Later the State came into growing opposition to the Church, a development that was to lead to the "godless" State.

Although there is no such thing as a "general" Christianity and though the differences between the Christian denominations are much more fundamental than most people believe, still one may talk about a "Christian" State even when its people belong to several Christian denominations, if these denominations have preserved the belief in Christ the God-man and Redeemer of the world; if Christian belief and Christian morality are free to develop and the people can still be considered Christian not merely in name. Such a State would acknowledge the spiritual authority of the Church as superior to its own; would consider that its primary function is to serve the Christian way of life of its people and consequently would issue no laws or measures that are incompatible with the Church's teaching, *e.g.*, divorce, abolition of the rights of parents.

2. The ideal of the Christian, or rather, of the Christianized[14] State ought to be upheld in spite of there being little prospect of its practical realization. But in no circumstances can the State be absolved from the following duties: i. The goal of the

[14] As we know, the popes are continually appealing for the Christianizing of the world.

State, that is, the total human good, necessarily includes acknowledgement of God, and cannot be achieved without religion, without the worship of God. Religion is the support of civil order, and obedience to human authority derives its conscience forming strength from God alone. ii. Christ authorized his Church to preach his Gospel throughout the whole world. Hence no State has a right to prevent the spread of Christianity or to interfere with the Christian way of life of Christians. We also hold that the State must positively acknowledge Christianity. iii. The State ought to have due consideration for the Christian section of its population. It may not demand what is contrary to the Christian conscience of its subjects.

3. Strictly speaking the country of our birth is a natural and human, and not a supernatural and Christian reality. But Christianity has always highly valued love of our own country and fostered it with care. It has also warned against excessive patriotism.

We are attached to the country of our birth by various links stemming from ancestral lines. The country of our birth is our home in the broader sense, the extension of the parental home (Q. 43). But here we are not so much thinking of the actual land, the soil, as of the people that inhabit this land and till this soil, and to whom we feel related, having certain obligations towards them. In modern times our country is often taken as equivalent to the nation or the State; this is justified as long as regional, or provincial, structures and characters are not suppressed.

Christianity does not merely permit, but commands men to love their own country. This natural love is elevated to the order of supernatural love and given a Christian form (I, Q. 114, No. 4). Hence Christian love of our country in the strict sense is but a supernatural charity towards our own people. Moreover Christian moral teaching enjoins the virtue of piety which enables us to fulfil our duties towards our country. It is our duty to be devoted to our parents and family as also to our native land. Although we may have to put service to our country before the immediate care of our family in certain circumstances, *e.g.*, in a general emergency, yet the family is closer to nature than is our country. Only a perverted patriotism could put the country before the family. Love of country is primarily a matter of the will, not of sentiment, although it does not exclude the vitalizing force of the latter. Thus there is both a human and a Christian duty of patriotic education; there is a genuine patriotism by which we mean a moral attitude remote both from exaggerating or falsely underestimating this sentiment.

65. What are "Christian" politics?

Christian politics are those that are guided by Christian aims and principles.

The modern controversy as to whether there is such a thing as "Christian" politics, and in what it consists, is even more heated than that concerning the Christian State. This dispute is understandable for the reason that even in a non-Christian State at least an attempt can be made to pursue Christian politics, that is, to remain loyal to Christian principles.

The term "politics" (from the Greek *polis;* cf. pp. 179f.) is used today:

i. in a general sense, meaning the (skilful) safeguarding of any interests, whether private or public, for example, club politics, union politics, local politics, etc. Politics in this sense may refer to the State, but not necessarily so. Vocational groups and associations may indulge in politics among themselves; they may also make representations to the State on matters of social policy; but neither the one nor the other is State politics.

ii. "Politics" may be used in a more narrow sense, and denote the proper function and activity of the "political" community and its various divisions, *e.g.*, municipal, State and United Nations politics; national or international politics. This narrower sense is the original one. Henceforth, whenever we speak simply of "politics", the term is used in the second sense. It has various spheres, branches or provinces such as economic, trade, credit, cultural, family and social politics (cf. Lesson 3–5).

1. Thus politics involve the concerns of the political community for the common good and its comprehensive order. Politics require political action and political knowledge inasmuch as this is relevant to practice. Political science is taught in universities. One might say that politics are the management of the affairs of the common good, so far as these come under the care of the State.

i. The two best known and most important spheres of politics are home and foreign affairs. The former concerns the structure of the State in itself, the latter its relations to other States as also to the community of nations and States. Both are closely related and mutually dependent. Strictly speaking home affairs have a "natural" priority; only a sound and well-ordered community can maintain order in foreign affairs. But because of the international situation, at a particular moment foreign affairs may often be more pressing, and sometimes matters of home affairs have to be dealt with in accordance with the foreign political situation, for example, in relation to the European Common Market or to NATO.

ii. Those concerned in politics include the citizen, *e.g.*, through the vote ("political" rights); subordinate State and non-State communities either through their administering a political sphere such as a municipality, an administrative district or a federal State, or through their representing the popular will and making it prevail, or by trying to influence government policy as in the case of trade unions, labour associations, cultural and educational organizations. Above all politics affect the supreme organs of government, which in the strict sense make them: the head of the government (president or primeminister, possibly a monarch), Parliament, Cabinet.

2. The Christian, whether or not he is a politician, ought to be politically conscious from a sense of Christian responsibility. This obligation refers not only to his mental attitude but also to the goals, principles and subject of his activity. Since the Christian cannot possibly disregard his Christian conviction in political life, indeed since he cannot in fact get on without it, we are bound to have "Christian politics" (Q. 64).[15]

EXAMPLES. The "East-West" conflict is clearly one that cannot be decided without taking the Christian standpoint into account. A

[15] Those who reject the term "Christian politics" appeal to the fact that politics deal with temporal aims and functions. Yet political decisions are very often and essentially different according to whether they are guided by a Christian or a non-Christian conscience. We are thus justified in speaking of Christian politics, unless we would maintain that matters that affect the Christian conscience have nothing at all to do with politics. This would mean in effect to reduce politics to a day-to-day pragmatism, the principles of the natural law alone having the force of basic norms; in this connection cf. Q. 102, No. 3. It is sometimes suggested that, for Catholics, Christian politics are in effect politics directed and commanded by Rome. This is not true. The popes proclaim and expound the moral law in so far as it concerns the State and politics. They do not force any particular political decisions on Catholic politicians.

concern for public morality (films, theatre, trashy literature, laws for the protection of youth) cannot leave the demands of the Christian ideal out of account. Ministering to the spiritual needs of those in prisons and reformatories. The controversy concerning the law making termination of pregnancy a punishable offence (abortion). Legalization of euthanasia and sterilization. The observance of Sundays and holidays (cessation of work; bans on public entertainments, say, on Good Friday). The problem of the separation of Church and State.

66. What general principles apply to the work of the State?

1. The norm and standard for the work of the State is the common good which the State has to define according to the historical situation and needs, but which it must promote and safeguard always in conformity with the natural law.
2. The State must acknowledge and protect the rights of the human person and of subordinate societies.
3. The condition of the State must guarantee peaceful co-operation with other States and nations.
4. The State must respect the higher authority of the Church and the conscience of its Christian subjects.

THESE principles summarize the most important conclusions of our first Lesson and serve to introduce the specific questions to be dealt with in the following Lessons.

JOHN XXIII (M. M. 51-55, 60, 88-89, 116-118).
JOHN XXIII (P. i. T. 20-32).

Lesson Two

STATE AUTHORITY AND CONSTITUTION

Sovereignty and Fundamental Law

THE State as an all-inclusive human order, as guardian of the natural law and as guarantor of the common good must have sovereign authority and power (Q. 61). Cf. Matt. 22:15–21 besides parallel passages John 19:11; Rom. 13:1–7; 1 Tim. 2:2; Tit. 3:1; 1 Pet. 2:13–15. The Holy Scriptures leave no room for doubt that secular authority has been vested with sovereign authority by God, and that it commands and punishes in his name. Power is not the essence of the State, but it necessarily results from its essence; it is a necessary consequence, an essential attribute (I, Q. 34).

The power of the State must be so extensive and effective that the State is capable of fulfilling its function. In order to do this, it requires i. in respect of internal affairs the power to command, to compel and to punish; the three aspects or functions of a single power (cf. Q. 68; division of powers); ii. in respect of external affairs the power to protect, that is, the right and the power to repel any injustice threatening it or done to it or its people by foreign powers (cf. Q. 128).

67. What do we mean by the sovereignty of the State?

The sovereignty of the State implies the autonomy (independence) of the State in internal and external affairs.

1. THE State has the fullness of power: i. Internal order is its task and right. It governs and commands (by its own legisla-

tion, system of law) and both individuals and subordinate societies are bound to obey its orders. Thus the autonomy of the State is more extensive and more absolute than the autonomy of vocational groups and the various divisions of the State such as municipalities, administrative districts and provinces. The decisions of the State are final. ii. The State must reject and repel foreign intervention from whatever quarter it may come. States govern within, not without their territory. It is not compatible with their sovereignty for one State to intervene in the internal affairs of another (Exceptions cf. Q. 115). iii. The State is subject to international law, that is, its conduct is governed by international law.[16] But international organizations, too, in international law have this capacity to legislate and act. In spite of its great importance, however, it cannot be put on a par with the sovereignty of the State.

2. Two particular points are to be added:

i. We have the case of a false, that is, assumed sovereignty, when the State claims for itself the unlimited fullness of power and declares itself to be the source of all right. The result is the totalitarian State. It places might above right. Christian teaching concerning the State must uphold the constitutional State. It favours a strong, powerful State, but one which uses its power in the service of Right and Law.[17]

ii. The political developments and complexities of modern times, especially since the two world wars, require inescapably

[16] It may form alliances, establish diplomatic missions and embassies, it has a right to a seat and a voice in the council of the nations and in international and supra-State negotiations etc.

[17] It must be "right" in the true sense, *i.e.,* right that does not contradict the higher norms of natural and divine right.

that States should renounce part of their traditional sovereign rights, that is, transfer them to a higher community and authority. This requirement primarily concerns sovereignty in respect of external affairs, but also in respect of internal affairs (This is dealt with in more detail in Q. 114, No. 4).

68. Is the power of the State divisible?

Basically the power of the State is indivisible; there is only one single power which embraces three functional spheres.

1. Modern political science and practice recognize a threefold power:

i. the *legislative:* the power to make laws and thus to create the actual basis of State order (Qs. 77–81);

ii. the *judicial:* the power to administer justice, that is, to settle legal disputes in a final manner, and to pass judgment (Qs. 82–90);

iii. the *executive:* the power to carry out the decrees of laws and judicial decisions or to supervise and enforce their execution (*ibid.* and Qs. 91–93).

2. The division of power into its functional spheres was already known to the ancient Greeks (Aristotle). However, it was the French scholar Montesquieu (1689–1755) who first laid down that the triple power should be distributed among three separate organs (persons or groups). If by this division the State gets a better government and, especially, if the abuse of power can be prevented by this division, it can be approved of as a suitable, perhaps necessary means. However, we insist that the power of the State forms a unity and cannot be divided into spheres inde-

pendent of one another. The unity of authority must be guaranteed both by the constitution and by a proper co-ordination of the organs of government.[18]

3. The term "government" denotes both the supreme directing functions as well as their organs. It is applied particularly to executive power. To govern (Latin *gubernare,* to guide, to steer) means to direct everything in the proper and effective form towards its end, to make the best choice and arrangement of means in relation to its end and by virtue of that end to make the best choice of means in order to co-ordinate offices and activities in a purposeful manner. To govern means to participate in the divine government of the universe, hence it is a moral function and not merely a technical achievement of organization.[19] Where the term "government" is used without qualification it denotes the supreme direction of the State which may be split between several persons or bodies.

69. Is it necessary to have organs of State power?

Since it is impossible for the people themselves to exercise all powers there must be organs of State power.

1. THE State even more so than any ordinary society (I, Q. 34) is incapable of managing its many important tasks without

[18] In some totalitarian States the division of power is retained in its outward form, but by every kind of trick and use it is done away with by the actual centralization. The lower organs are made submissive by commands, threats and terror so that they decide, judge and carry out whatever is desired by the supreme authority (Qs. 103/104).

[19] Cf. St. Thomas, *e.g.,* I c. G. 1; II c. G. 71; I, 102, 2 and 4; I–II, 87, 1 and 3; II–II, 153, 2.

governing organs. No matter how united and well-disposed the people may be, it cannot lead an orderly existence unless there is "government". This is not changed by the fact that many decisions, often the most important ones, are made by the whole people, in an election or referendum. But the people themselves cannot exercise the entire management of the State.

It is thus in the common interest, that is, based on natural law, that the State has need of special holders of authority. To them is due precedence both in honour and in power. The Catholic Church has always maintained, in conformity with the Scriptures, that every government has its authority from God, thus that State authority also in so far as it is exercised by particular individuals, has its origin in God. Naturally these rulers must obtain their authority in a legitimate manner; wrong cannot come from God (Qs. 109/110).

2. No ruler *is* the State. But each one, whether he be emperor or king, president or head of the government, whether Parliament or Congress, is a true and proper organ of the State and not a mere servant or functionary. We conclude that rulers must be granted that fullness of power which they need in order to rule the State well; and that the holders of authority command and act not only in the name of the people but beyond it – in the name of God. Their laws and decrees are binding of themselves; they do not need to be first accepted and ratified by the people.

3. Every authority is only bestowed for the good and may only be used for the good (I, Q. 40). God vests no one with such extensive powers in order that he may do wrong or protect wrong, but solely in order that he may do right and help right to prevail (Rom. 13). The State ought to govern to the best of its

ability so that God's will be done on earth, that the citizens be able to attain their divinely given goals of life.[20]

70. Does authority derive from the people?

The people determine who is to hold and exercise authority, but God bestows the authority.

JOHN XXIII (P. i. T. 23).

THE question concerning the origin of governmental authority is usually put in this form: Does authority come from the people? Is there such a thing then as genuine sovereignty of the people?

1. Catholic social teaching holds unanimously: i. That political authority has its origin in God, that it is a participation in God's providence and government of the universe. Hence any absolute sovereignty of the people must be definitely rejected (J. J. Rousseau, 1712–78). The claim of the French Revolution (1789–92), that "all authority comes from the people alone", turns the people, or the general will, into the only source and norm of governmental power; ii. that neither an individual nor a ruling family (dynasty) or group (Parliament, Cabinet) ever gains or possesses political authority as their property or as a personal right never to be lost; iii. that the people have the natural right to choose the form of State under which they desire to live (Lesson Five), to accept the constitution (the Fundamental Law) and thereby make it valid (to pass it; Qs. 74–76), as also to designate the person or persons to rule, *i.e.,* to hold and to exercise governmental power. This designation or appointment of the person or persons may be made either by direct or indirect election (the latter, *e.g.,* by elected delegates), by express (select-

[20] St. Thomas, *De reg. princ.* I, 14.

ing a person as one's leader) or tacit agreement, by acknowledgement of a ruling family (hereditary succession) etc.

2. Catholic social teaching is not unanimous on the question whether those who become holders of governmental power by election (appointment, investiture) receive this authority from God or from the people direct. Who is it, we may ask, who transmits authority – God or the people? There are two opposed opinions: i. The first opinion maintains that in its origin (according to the natural law) authority rests not with the people, nor is derived from it, but with God, and is transmitted by him direct to those who according to the will of the people are to govern. The people may only designate these persons but do not bestow authority on them. Hence we speak of a "Theory of Designation"; ii. According to the other opinion, authority originally is with the united people; thus it derives from the people. The people transmit the authority which is their own to those whom they select to rule. Hence the "Theory of Delegation". God has bestowed authority on the people. In transmitting this authority the people act as God's instrument. The people must transfer the authority in such fullness and to such an extent as to guarantee social order. The people themselves actually govern through the government appointed by them. Even after authority has been transmitted it continues, by virtue of its roots, to rest with the people. This theory is nowadays called relative, or moderate, sovereignty of the people. It is a sovereignty of the people because the people are regarded as, by natural law, the first and authoritative sovereign; it is a moderate sovereignty because the people may not be considered the ultimate and only source of authority, and because every form of absolute "democracy" is rejected as false in view of the obligation to transmit authority in a "suitable" form to "suitable" persons.

Catholics may hold either opinion without prejudice to their faith. A "moderate" sovereignty of the people in particular does not conflict with Catholic teaching.

PIUS XII (Address of 2 October 1945).

"If, on the other hand, we consider the main thesis of democracy that the original subject of State authority as derived from God is the people (not the mass) – a thesis upheld by eminent Christian thinkers in all ages – the difference between the Church and the State, even the democratic State, becomes clear."

We can indeed say that the theory of moderate popular sovereignty is well supported by tradition and upheld by many eminent Catholic scholars today. It seems difficult to appeal to St. Thomas[21] or indeed to Leo XIII in support of the moderate form of popular sovereignty. A careful examination of all the statements of Leo XIII shows, however, that this Pope did not intend to condemn moderate popular sovereignty, clearly upheld as it was by some Catholic scholars before and during his reign. On the other hand, we must remember that St. Pius X, quoting his predecessor Leo XIII, expressly condemned the error of the *Sillon* represented by Marc Sangnier. The Sillonists held democracy to be the only justifiable form of government, and regarded the theory that all authority derives from the people as alone corresponding with Catholic teaching; they considered the theory of designation to be contrary to Catholicism.

3. The supporters of moderate forms of popular sovereignty argue that the goals of the State (the common good) and of political power are linked inseparably. Power "follows" the com-

[21] In spite of the much quoted passage in I–II, 90, 4. Cf. No. 3 below.

mon good for which it exists. But the common good is the goal of the people united politically. Therefore the people too are, in natural law, holders of authority, for "a rule or measure is imposed by being applied to those who are to be ruled and measured by it."[22] The people, it is emphasized, governs itself; it exercises authority in various forms such as elections, referenda and protests. Many even describe mere obedience to the law, the paying of taxes and national service as expressions of governmental power.

4. The opponents of moderate forms of popular sovereignty argue their case by saying that the people is incapable of exercising authority since it cannot command itself. The morally and legally binding force of constitutions and laws cannot derive from, or be explained by, the will of the people but solely from the higher authority of God. The organs of government elected by the people are empowered to command and to claim obedience only because of God. If, the argument continues, power derived even instrumentally from the people, and thus only indirectly from God, the people would always be free to accept or reject any enacted law. This would be the end of all true order. It was not without good reason that St. Thomas stated that human laws bind in virtue of the eternal law from which they derive.[23] This decisive thought must be correctly understood. The question is not whether it is possible by virtue of "organization" for the people to make decisions, but rather, who it is who invests these decisions and those made by the Government elected by the people with the force of right and law.

[22] St. Thomas, I–II, 90, 4.
[23] St. Thomas, I–II, 93, 3 esp. ad 2.

5. Weighing the arguments for and against both schools of thought the first seems to be preferable. The people designate who is to govern, God confers authority direct. In this view the fullness of power of secular authority is better explained and is anchored more profoundly. The democratic form of government is not thereby deprived of dignity and force. However, it is difficult in our "democratic" age to find understanding and agreement for this theory, though whether it is true or not should not depend on such acclaim.

71. *What is the government bound to uphold?*

The government is bound to uphold the law of the land or constitution.

1. Every State needs an appropriate order, valid for it in particular, because it should seek to attain the total human good in a manner that will suit its people, their possibilities, historical development and tradition. For this purpose it must be laid down in what form, and according to what guiding principles, the State should be organized, whether, for example, as a monarchy or as a republic, according to a federal or con-federal pattern, with this or that combination of government organs. This basic order is called the constitution because by it the State is constituted and characterized.

2. The constitution is not so much a document as the condition of the State itself, the fundamental order in which the State exists. It may, of course, be set down in a constitutional document but this is not necessary. We distinguish, in fact, between an unwritten constitution realized in the form of Common Law, without being set down in writing (Great Britain), and the written constitution (in most modern States).

72. *May governments exceed their constitutional powers?*

Governments may exceed their constitutional powers only in order to meet extreme national emergencies which cannot otherwise be overcome.

1. OUR answer applies only to the constitutional State. The totalitarian State does not heed the constitution anyway, or only for the sake of appearances. Our answer is based on the principle that what is absolutely necessary for the sake of the common good is by that very fact legitimate. The authority of the State has its *raison d'être* and norm in the common good. The common good is above the constitution and must not be jeopardized by it. It is therefore customary in constitutional States to have certain regulations laid down in their constitutions which invest the head of State or the government with special emergency powers (martial law).

2. The government may go beyond the measures allowed by the constitution under the following three conditions: i. If the common good is seriously threatened, for example, by a sudden invasion, a *coup d'état,* grave internal disorders or extraordinary natural catastrophes. ii. If the constitutional powers and means are insufficient to deal with this emergency effectively, and if there is no time for constitutional procedures. iii. If the measures are only temporary. A democratic constitution usually demands that measures of this kind should be subsequently approved by the people or (and) by parliament. Later disapproval could not be a lawful reason for dismissing the government unless it is obvious that they acted irresponsibly.[24]

[24] Further questions concerning the legality and the removal of a government, concerning revolution and "legal" seizing of power are treated in Qs. 108–111.

73. *What do constitutions contain?*

Constitutions contain only essential fundamental decisions.

1. A CONSTITUTION is not an elaborate statement of all matters that concern the State and come within its competence, but rather a briefly formulated basic norm that is variously supplemented by laws, regulations, orders, etc. It is not possible to give a general rule concerning the complete contents of a constitution, since many, and at times very diverse matters have to be taken into consideration such as the basic beliefs of the people, its composition (classes and grades of society), tradition; cultural level; danger of abuse of power (totalitarian groups and tendencies); international political situation (menaces from outside) etc.

2. Nowadays it is convenient and even necessary for constitutions to regulate:

i. Character and organization of the State community: the form of State, whether monarchy or republic; the organization of the State territory, *e.g.,* into counties, federal States, Cantons, member republics etc.; the sovereign rights both of the whole and of the organic parts in such matters as legislation, its spheres and extent; finance and taxation; police.

ii. Composition, appointment and competence of the government: its chief legislative bodies (Parliament, Chamber, Senate, Privy Council), Members of Parliament and Ministers; elections and electoral system; appointment to office, recall and removal from office; powers of office; passing of laws (which laws need a simple, and which need a "qualified" majority).

iii. Effective preventive and protective measures against the misuse of governmental authority either by the government or by "movements" and political upheavals that endanger the State, by the "legal" seizure of power (state of emergency; constitutional courts).

iv. Fundamental rights of individuals and of subsidiary groupings; they include fundamental political rights (the right to elect and to be elected). Because bad governments or those completely subservient to a political party often pretend to advocate "basic rights" and "basic liberties", it is necessary to define these singly and exactly.

v. The basic norms for an orderly administration of justice: constitution and competence of the courts; independence of judges and magistrates; right of appeal. The legality of justice, one of the greatest goods of free societies, must be firmly anchored in the constitution.

vi. The fundamental relationship of State and Church (rights of religion and denominations). Freedom of religious conviction and worship is one of the fundamental human rights. But the Church is a special kind of society; she is not a subsidiary society of the State. Hence her relation to the State needs to be specially regulated.

Should the name of God be mentioned in the constitution or in its preamble (solemn declaration introducing the constitution)? We answer that a State the majority of whose people consider themselves Christians, should give due expression to this fact in their constitution. Such an appeal to the "Lord of all rulers" (cf. the introduction to the constitution of the Republic of Ireland) will invest the constitution with a special sense of dedication. It is objected that today only a minority of the people professes Christianity or belief in God, and that it would be insincere if a constitution were solemnly to invoke God but to contain regulations irreconcilable with this profession. This latter objection has great force. Surely the name of God ought not to appear in the preamble of a constitution the later contents of which violate the honour and the rights of God.

74. *Who issues the constitution?*

The people of the State have the natural right to give themselves a constitution.

1. THE constitution is the basic order in which the people forming a State live, or should live. Hence it exists not for the government's sake, but for the people. But it is for the people themselves to decide in what form and order they want to live. They exercise this right not only when they form themselves into a State for the first time, but also whenever they are faced with making a new beginning in their life as a State. In the latter case it is usual for a provisional government to be formed which will act until the new constitution comes into force. The principal task of this government is to prepare elections for a constituent Parliament or Assembly. To these bodies the people then transfer the task of giving the State a constitution. This is one possibility. But it may also be that the provisional government or a group appointed by it., *e.g.,* a parliamentary council, draws up a constitution on which the people then vote. In both cases the will of the people is expressed provided there is a real free election or plebiscite.

2. Since the people give themselves their own fundamental order, and since they have the absolute right not to be wrongly ruled or to be subjected to totalitarianism, they may reserve to

themselves certain decisions, *e.g.*, the election of the head of the State, consent to particularly important laws (by referendum). But these must be issues that the people are capable of judging and for which they can take responsibility, and in general it is advisable, in the interest of the people themselves, to make sparing use of their electoral decisions if attendance at the polls is not to suffer.

Every constitution thus depends on the will of the people. But not in the sense of the contract theory which maintains that a constitution comes about through individuals renouncing part of their rights (liberties) which they by "social contract" hand over to the majority or to the government. The constitution is not a contractual agreement, the people cannot conclude a contract with themselves but in voluntary agreement unite and bind themselves to an order whose necessity in natural law they recognize and accept. Naturally this "unity of will" and self-determination constitute agreement about a common order and thus we have something like a contract, and are entitled to speak of a certain "contractual element" in the nature of the State.

3. History shows that only in modern times peoples have given themselves constitutions or have even been asked for their consent. Frequently constitutions were forced upon them, for example when populations were incorporated in other States, when certain territories were ceded or annexed; through the will of the dynasty or a *coup d'état*. But (cf. Q. 115) at times constitutions or constitutional changes of this kind were in fact conditioned by the will of the people with which the government perhaps reluctantly had to comply.

A people may also give its tacit consent by submitting to the constitution and living under it. The constitution becomes an accepted fact, but this may not be done, except in some cases, against the will of the people (cf. Lesson 6 on the right of resistance).

75. *How far does the validity of the constitution extend and to whom does it apply?*

The constitution has validity within the territory of the State and for the people of the State.

1. In order to guarantee order and security a constitution must be valid throughout the State's jurisdiction, that is, throughout the whole territory of the State; and for all who belong to the nation. It follows that the people of the State are obliged actively to acknowledge the just regulations of the constitution. This is both a civil and a moral obligation (obligation in conscience, Q. 80). Hence to undermine the constitution and with it the order of the State, for example by unconstitutional practices, by bringing the constitution into disrepute and incitement to rebellion, is to err in conscience (Qs. 106ff.).

2. To be loyal to the constitution is incumbent upon the organs of government which must govern the State according to the constitution and not contrary to it. Therefore they must know the exact meaning of the articles of the constitution, and in cases of doubt, have them resolved. Loyalty is also expected of the citizens and subordinate societies that are subject to the State's representatives abroad (diplomatic and consular personnel) who must carry out their functions according to the spirit and the letter of the constitution. Those who are merely resident or temporary visitors, who have not acquired the State's nationality, must respect the State's orders. The employment, education or leisure which they enjoy within its territory will oblige them to abstain from disruptive acts against the State,

and to observe those regulations of the constitution applicable to them.

3. It is the function of a Supreme Court (Constitutional Court, Parliament) to ensure the observance and protection of the constitution. Its purpose is: i. To resolve doubts about the meaning and validity of articles of the constitution; ii. to decide whether the servants of the State are not exceeding their powers; iii. to examine whether movements, associations, organizations, etc. might have to be regarded as unconstitutional and hostile to the State, *e.g.*, militant groups; organizations in the service and pay of foreign powers, camouflaged "peace leagues;" formations of a military character, etc. iv. To try actions brought against the State for withholding constitutional rights.

These and similar functions show the great importance of a supreme court which should be absolutely independent in its judgments.

76. *May constitutions be changed?*

Constitutions may, and must, be changed if this is required by the common good; the people have to decide, they may, however, delegate this authority to the government.

1. The constitution should guarantee the State's stability and flexibility. The State is a *societas permanens,* by its nature intended to be permanent, but its order must also take account of historical development. According to natural law the constitution without any doubt may be changed. Natural law invests the State with the powers it needs in order to attain its goal in an orderly manner.

2. The constitution can be changed: i. peacefully or by force (revolution, *coup d'état*.) Here we are concerned with peaceful changes of the constitution; regarding changes by force cf. Qs. 106ff. ii. wholly or in part. Either a completely new constitution is made which may retain some or many elements of its predecessor. There may be changes in the form of the State or government, from monarchy to republic, union with another State. Or individual sections or articles in the existing constitution may be deleted, phrased differently or new ones may be added.

It is basic that constitutional changes may not be made arbitrarily but only in so far as they are required by the common good. The impulse must come from real necessity conditioned by the common good; not just from some wish of the people who may be dissatisfied with the existing constitution, or indeed from the political ambitions of some political movement, party or individual. The constitutional change must be one for the better, *i.e.,* the position of the State, of the common good, must not thereby be jeopardized. Possible serious repercussions on the State's foreign relations or on external relations or international relations in general must be taken into account.

3. Strictly speaking, the competent authority for constitutional changes is the nation as the originator of the constitution. This applies especially if the whole constitution is to be changed, if a new constitution is to be drawn up and adopted. Such changes may endanger the general weal. Hence a corresponding state of national emergency must exist which may be the result of defeat in war or an abortive revolution; or of the evident inadequacy or unpopularity of the existing constitution (Q. 110). Changes within the constitution may be more easily justified,

but, of course, such changes too may be aimed at the ultimate forcible overthrow of the constitution. Most constitutions allow for part changes without the need for a referendum. They empower the legislative bodies (Congress, Parliament) to carry out these changes provided they are decided by a majority, usually of two thirds.

4. Because the welfare of the State depends on the preservation and validity of the constitution the greatest caution is necessary when there is question of "special powers", empowering the government to enact laws on their own authority. By means of these powers the government may change the constitution, but any changes which would touch upon or set aside the basic order of the State are precluded.

Lesson Three

LEGISLATIVE, JUDICIARY, EXECUTIVE

THE constitution guarantees above all the legality of the State. It is the function of the legislative, the judiciary and the executive to develop, implement and protect this legality. Where they function properly by virtue of sound constitutional principles there is every guarantee of a true constitutional State.

The division into legislative, judiciary and executive is not quite the same as the triple powers discussed in Q. 68. For example, executive powers are also exercised in the judiciary (criminal law – execution of justice). There is a certain overlapping of the three spheres,[25] for instance, between civil courts, criminal courts and prison administration.

[25] Cf. E. Barker's *Principles of Social and Political Theory*, Oxford, 1951, pp. 260 ff.

A. THE LEGISLATIVE

77. *What is a law?*

A law is an ordinance of reason promulgated in the interest of the common good by the authority that has care of the community.

1. A LAW [26] is not a request or an advice, but an obligatory norm, a binding directive. A law commands that this or that should or should not be done.[27] Man must obey or be punished. Laws thus impel towards action and, in that respect, affect the will. They derive from the will of the makers of the law, and affect the will of those for whom the law is made.

But basically laws are regulations or ordinances of reason, first, in so far as they communicate, make known something, have content. A law tells us what we must do or refrain from doing, for example, to pay taxes, to do national service, to be married in the presence of the registrar; or: not to tell lies, not to steal, not to commit murder. In the second place, laws are matters of reason because what they command or forbid must be reasonable, that is, in conformity with reason. Reasonable is not just what men *(raison d'état)* "declare" to be useful, but only what conforms with right reason, and thus does not conflict with God's will and commands. We therefore reject what is

[26] The definition given above is taken almost verbally from St. Thomas Aquinas (I–II, 90) and is accepted widely by Catholic political writers. Cf. I, Q. 66.

[27] Hence laws that merely note certain facts as given without expressing an obligation are not actually laws, but statements of fact (declaratory legislation). Regulations laying down certain procedures to be observed, for example, in law courts, may be genuine laws; for they are norms of human conduct for the general weal. However, these laws are more of a "technical" kind.

known as legal positivism which denies the subordination of human reason and legislation to the divine law.

2. Not every society is entitled to issue laws. We speak of State laws, but of the regulations of administrative districts, of club rules, etc. Only a community with genuine powers which apply to the total ordering of human life can make laws: the State or Federal State; supra-national communities (cf. Q. 113).

3. According to St. Thomas Aquinas, four conditions must be met for a law to become effective: i. It must be shown to be necessary from the point of view of the common good, because it expresses demands of the common good in an obligatory form. ii. Hence a law is a general norm that affects not only this or that individual, but all, or at least many, in the community. This is important both for the matter and the scope of laws. Laws must be adapted to the special character of the community and to the capacity of its members. There is no sense in setting the goals of legislation so high that the order it is intended to establish will be jeopardized by the excessive nature of its demands.[28] iii. Laws must be issued by competent authority, that is, by a genuine sovereign authority; for they concern not just the common good of some association or club or social group, but of the "perfect" society (Qs. 60/61). iv. Laws must be published. The citizens have to be informed that they have an obligation, and what it is, for otherwise they are unable to obey. The manner and kind of such publication may vary considerably.

78. Is the State entitled to issue laws?

The State certainly has the right to issue laws.

[28] Cf. St. Thomas Aquinas, I–II, 96, 2; *De reg. princ.* 1, 15.

1. Our reply follows logically from the origin and sovereign authority of the State (Qs. 62, 63, 74). If the State has the right to give itself a constitution, it will be entitled also to issue further norms guaranteeing order on account of the constitution, and these are the laws. The State has from nature the right of legislation; it is given to it by God the Creator and Supreme Lord of nature. Laws may be issued in the first place by the people, by the government or legislative bodies, the form and composition of which are defined by the constitution. Since these act independently as organs of the State-community, the laws issued by them need not be approved of (accepted) by the people (Q. 69).

2. Sound legislation is so important for the nation and the State that it deserves close attention. It matters, for instance, where and how laws are made, whether in one or in several places (Cabinet, House of Commons, House of Lords, Congress), whether in one or in several (usually three) readings, whether sufficiently prepared by experts. Lesgislative organs must carry out their task responsibly and in freedom, but the people must be protected against the abuse of legislation.

As legislation often concerns difficult and complex matters, considerable importance should be attached to the preparation of laws; committees consisting of experts and politicians who ought to inform themselves well, for example, about the ways of thinking and traditions of the nation (education acts), about likely effects (strikes, fall in production), about "reactions" abroad, about the claims of the natural law in matters such as abortion and sterilization.

Modern States have adequate means of publishing their laws in a suitable form such as television, radio, press and poster. But what matters is the official publication, usually in a government publication or gazette.

3. It is the citizens, the people of the realm, who are subject to the laws of the State. But according to its content, the law itself will mention explicitly for whom it is intended.

EXAMPLES. Taxation laws (direct taxation) are intended for those who have a taxable income or capital; national defence laws for those able to bear arms; compulsory education laws for the youth and their parents; electoral laws for those entitled to vote etc. Foreign visitors or temporary residents in the national territory are exempt from those laws which of their nature apply only to nationals, but they may be subject to possible special laws.

79. *What is the concern of the State's legislation?*

Exterior actions only which must be commanded or forbidden in the interest of the common good are the concern of the State's legislation.

1. WITHIN its jurisdiction the State has competence for exterior order.[29] Hence no State law may authorize direct interference in matters of personal conscience.[30] However, State laws indirectly affect the interior life of man.

EXAMPLE. Taxation laws: The State can only order taxes to be paid, but it cannot regulate the frame of mind in which they should be paid. Yet in imposing taxes it confronts its citizens with certain decisions of conscience, for example, whether to pay or to defraud the revenue (Q. 81).

State law refers to arrangements and institutions such as marriage, families, schools, associations, corporations; property and conditions of holding property; divisions of territory: federal States, provinces, counties and municipalities. All this is included in exterior actions, since it is regulated with reference to the actions of men.

[29] Cf. I., Qs. 37, 107, 108.

[30] That the laws of the State bind in conscience is quite a different matter. Cf. Q. 80.

2. The exterior actions of men consist of those that are directly and those that are indirectly related to the common good. The former are concerned with the common good, for example, with government, administration of justice, municipal government, defence and police services. The latter concern virtuous actions that might have a bearing on the common good, *i.e.*, on public order.

EXAMPLES. The State needs revenue, it may demand land for payment of compensation; both are requirements of justice. In times of war, internal disturbances and natural catastrophes the State may order its citizens to face great dangers; it is brave to face such danger. In emergencies (drought, famine, war) laws may be made to ration food and other goods.

St. Thomas Aquinas states as a principle that the law of the State is entitled to command or forbid exterior actions, whether directly or indirectly related to the general good.[31] By virtue of the State's legal prescription of certain actions, these become obligations in justice. Thus in virtue of the law they are legally, or legitimately, due (I, Qs. 58, 105) and concern common justice (*Ibid.* and Qs. 106/108).

80. *What kind of obligation is due to the laws of the State?*

Just laws of the State involve an obligation in conscience, i.e., under God.

JOHN XXIII (P. i. T. 22-23).

1. THIS is a twofold obligation: i. to society (the nation) and to authority (government). It is due to those persons who constitute and govern society;[32] ii. in conscience, that is

[31] I–II, 96, *3*.

[32] For example, a society requires its chairman, secretary, treasurer to report to the annual meeting; members are answerable to the committee if, for instance, they have broken the rules.

before God, since God speaks through conscience. While the former kind of obligation is of a purely legal nature, the second involves moral (religious) responsibilities.

St. Thomas states quite clearly that State laws bind in conscience in virtue of the eternal law from which they derive.[33] This efficacy in conscience of laws is thus not directly due to the State having issued them, but to its authoritative share in the eternal law (Q. 70, No. 4).

2. Of course, only just laws of the State bind in conscience. No human society, not even the State, has the right to demand what is unjust. This is self-evident. But the inevitable question is which laws of the State are just? What conditions must be fulfilled for a law to be considered just? According to St. Thomas a law is just:

i. When it is in keeping with its purpose, that is, when it promotes the common good. But this does not apply to laws which serve the selfish ambitions of governments; which are not at all necessary from the point of view of the common good; and which involve morally reprehensible demands;

ii. When it observes the equality of distributive justice, that is, when it imposes burdens not according to the "standing of persons" but according to their varying capacities (I, Qs. 100, 102). The principle that "all men are equal before the law" is designed to guarantee fundamental rights and to apportion to each that amount of service that is due to him in relation to others. There are laws, especially prohibitions, which apply to all in the same measure, such as those forbidding murder, theft and fraud, and others which must be fulfilled according to the individual's particular ability;

[33] I–II, 96, 4.

EXAMPLES. Taxation laws (graded income tax); national service (physical fitness); criminal laws (sentence according to the nature, gravity and responsibility of the crime).

iii. When it is issued by competent authority. The lawgiver may not exceed his powers, transgress the limits of any human authority. A subordinate authority, for instance, may not without special authorization issue laws that are reserved to superior authority; and no human authority may disregard the commands of God (Acts 4:18, 19; 5:29).

3. The question of unjust laws must be dealt with according to the same principles. Laws are unjust which lack any of the three conditions mentioned; which do not serve the common good or distribute obligations and burdens unjustly or exceed the competence of the lawgiver. It would seem logical to conclude that such laws, because they are unjust, do not bind in conscience. But St. Thomas (I–II, 96, 4) and the majority of Catholic moralists are not of this opinion. For various factors and points of view need here to be taken into account:

i. Who is entitled to judge whether a law is just, that is, fulfils the three conditions? Strictly speaking, the lawgiver himself or his superior authority. Even our worst experiences with unjust laws cannot controvert this answer. Those competent to issue laws will be primarily entitled to judge their validity.

ii. Laws that are bad in themselves and are recognized as such must not be obeyed; they entitle to passive resistance.[34] St. Thomas says that one must not obey laws that offend against the divine good *(bonum divinum)*. This includes all laws that are clearly contrary

[34] Cf. Q. 107, and also I, Qs. 36, 42, 47; and citations from Scripture and popes in these Questions.

to the natural law or to the revealed will of God, for example, those that sanction denial of the faith, apostasy, secession from the Church, divorce from the marriage bond, abortion and sterilization for eugenic reasons.

iii. In the case of laws that are contrary to the human good *(bonum humanum)* only, that is, lack one of the three conditions, without yet sanctioning anything that is bad in itself, St. Thomas makes the following distinction: Considered in itself, the law does not impose an obligation in conscience, because it lacks that which is needed to make it binding in conscience; considered in relation to society, the law may nevertheless bind in conscience, and this when its transgression would cause scandal or disturbance or some other harm *(propter vitandum scandalum vel turbationem . . . maius detrimentum)*.[35] The citizen thus has to ask himself how his conduct is likely to affect order and welfare in the State, whether his refusal to obey or his transgression is likely to cause discord and to stir up resistance. If he foresees such evil consequences he must obey.

4. Even a government that abuses its powers may issue just laws which the people are bound to obey "for the sake of conscience". The individual law in itself will have to be considered. If it demands nothing that is bad in itself citizens will have to obey.

EXAMPLES. If a godless State obliges its citizens to be vaccinated, to contribute to the building of hospitals, to observe traffic regulations, not to kill or deceive or slander anyone; such laws would be just according to their objective, even though they have been issued by an unjust authority.

5. Human laws may need to be altered for two reasons: if the

[35] I–II, 96, 4; *ibid.* ad 2.

law is too narrowly conceived, not clearly formulated or not practical; or if circumstances have changed, if different living or political conditions have caused the demands of the law to become superfluous, obsolete.[36] St. Thomas[37] warns too against frequent changes in laws because they tend to upset the stability of society.

6. As well as positive law there is also common law, or the law of custom, of usage. A custom, or usage, that has existed over a long period of time, that does not conflict with the precepts of God or of the natural law, and that is tolerated by the lawgiver receives the force of law[38]; it may become so deep-rooted as to be almost irrevocable. Many rules of modern international law (Q. 118), for example, are based on custom. Some Catholics advocate so-called "purely penal laws", enforced not on account of guilt (sin) but of punishment only. The individual, according to this view, is not following the commands of God and conscience in obeying these laws, but he has to pay the penalty if he is caught disobeying them. The two different questions, whether in fact such purely penal laws exist, and which they are, exceed the scope of this book. Two kinds are generally mentioned: laws that are expressly defined as purely penal in character and laws commonly considered to be such without any statement to the contrary by the legislative authority, although the latter may be aware of the common opinion (cf. Q. 81).

81. To what extent are tax-laws binding?

Just tax-laws are binding in conscience.

1. THE political community depends upon the revenues that

[36] I–II, 97, 1. [37] I–II, 97, 2. [38] I–II, 97, 3.

are payable to it from the citizens and that are commonly called taxes. It cannot fulfil its function without material goods such as money, buildings, highways. The State's budget has to be covered annually. Thus the State must have the right to levy taxes and to pass tax-laws. No one doubts this right today. The obligation to pay taxes is expressly acknowledged in Rom. 13:5–7: "Wherefore be subject of necessity, not only for wrath but also for conscience sake. For therefore also you pay tribute. Render therefore to all men their dues. Tribute to whom tribute is due." St. Paul refers to the political community as such, that is, any (legitimate) secular authority. Matt. 22:21 is generally regarded as an unambiguous proof from the Scriptures. Christ answers the Pharisees question concerning taxes: "Render therefore to Caesar the things that are Caesar's, and to God, the things that are God's." But we must remember that the question put to Christ was a "catch question". The Pharisees "consulted among themselves how to ensnare him in his speech" (*ibid.* 15). To their question: "Is it lawful to give tribute to Caesar, or not? they wanted a direct answer, a clear yes or no. But to have given any direct answer would have been fatal for our Lord. A negative would have enabled the Pharisees to turn him over to the Romans; an affirmative would have implied the denial of the theocratic claim of the people, a grave religious crime. Our Lord, "knowing their wickedness" (*ibid.* 18), left the question open deliberately, replying quite generally: "Render to Caesar the things that are Caesar's." What these things are, and whether taxes are part of them, he leaves for the "hypocrites" to decide. The meaning of the passage is this: Just as the emperor is entitled to the fulfilment of his claims, so is God to his. Thus, you hypocrites, render to both the things that are due to both. Actually nothing is stated there explicitly concerning tax-laws.

2. Tax-laws, too must be just. They are a burden on the citizens' personal property. The political community may under no circumstances consider itself the owner of its citizens' goods and thus dispose of them as it pleases, not even in times of great emergency. Taxes and tax-laws, and consequently the fiscal policy of the State, should be regarded as just only under the following conditions:

i. The actual scale and nature of the taxes must be required by the common good. At the same time in estimating this we must remember that unexpected situations may put new burdens on the exchequer and that it needs certain reserves to cover any special expenditures. The common good includes a standard of economic well-being for the nation and its existence in human dignity. Hence tax-laws must not endanger the national economy, because the well-being of the people depends upon it. The State may justifiably have to frame its tax-laws with the primary intention of promoting the national economy. In certain circumstances this may be the only way for the State to get the enormous sums needed if it is to fulfil its social obligations.[39]

ii. Taxes should be imposed according to the requirements of distributive justice (Q. 80, No. 211; I, Q. 100). People differ in their ability to pay taxes and accordingly in their obligations.

[39] For example, the possibilities of deductions granted by the exchequer will have to be, perhaps even primarily, considered from the political community's social obligations. On the other hand, it should not be regarded justifiable but as morally wrong for the taxpayers to make unscrupulous use of these possibilities without thought for the social needs of poorer fellow-citizens, and to claim that within the law they can do with their money what they like. It is by no means certain that every action according to a positive law, legitimate as it would be to that extent, is also morally right and morally permissible. Examples: a man may be legally entitled to expand a disreputable business or to spend large sums on luxuries – while social misery abounds around him.

Distributive justice requires a progressive system of taxation, that is, higher rates in cases of higher incomes.

iii. The political community has no right "to drain a man's means by excessive taxation "(Leo XIII, R. N., 35; Pius XI, Q. A., 49). The personal property of citizens also sets limits to the State's right to levy taxes. The State ought to observe the following guiding principles:[40] The people must be able to pay their taxes out of their current incomes without having to draw on their capital. They must be in a position to support themselves from their income (salary, wages, profits, pension) in spite of taxation. "Support" does not mean an existential minimum but a decent livelihood, which should include, for example, a sound education for the children as well as some savings for the future (Q. A., 61, 71, 75). The individual has a natural right through industry and thrift to increase his possessions, thus also to make profits from which he may enlarge his business. The common good and this natural right of the individual forbids the State to increase taxation to such an extent that economic progress is undermined and men see themselves actually penalized for their industry and thrift.

iv. The State must be determined to use the moneys brought in by taxation in the best interest of the people. A "reasonable" use would include economizing wherever possible, for example, by reducing administrative costs, observing simplicity in public buildings; creating tolerable economic and especially social conditions, for example, by promoting housing and settlement schemes, providing public employment in times of economic crisis or unemployment.

[40] We are not speaking here of extraordinary taxes that may be justified under very exceptional circumstances, for example, in the event of war, but of the normal taxes – taxes in the narrower sense.

We may therefore conclude that citizens are bound in conscience to pay taxes that are in accordance with the conditions mentioned. The obligation to pay taxes comes under general, or legal, justice (I, Qs. 104–109). The question whether specific taxes are just or unjust will depend on the general principles underlying the tax legislation. If the legislative authorities are sincerely concerned to "spare" the taxpayer as much as possible, there will be a strong guarantee for just assessments. Mistakes are possible, but apart from the fact that they are difficult to detect, they do not justify defrauding the revenue. On the other hand suitable legal machinery should exist so that mistakes can be rectified and hardship mitigated.

3. In modern taxation the indirect tax has assumed considerable importance, that is, taxes levied on goods before these reach the consumer, for example, taxes on sugar, tobacco and spirits; purchase tax. Most of the indirect taxes can be said to offend against distributive justice, since those with unequal abilities to pay, hence varying obligations, are required to pay the same taxes. They are treated equally but in effect unequally, for a tax on consumer goods is a very different matter when there is a small or a large income, especially in the case of big families. Concerning indirect taxation, the legislature should be induced to reduce these taxes as much as possible instead of increasing them. Taxation of luxury goods may be justified provided it does not deprive ordinary people of basic amenities. On the other hand direct taxation should be increased and simplified.

Thus it may be the moral duty of the State to undertake an extensive and radical reform of taxation although this may be difficult to carry out. Any taxation reform ought to observe certain basic principles: The continued provision of vital goods of "real value" (Pius XI) must be ensured. The economic productivity of the nation in this respect must be maintained. The reform will have to be a social one, that is, it should not make life more difficult for those in poor circumstances and those of small incomes; rather it should relieve their situation as much as possible. An increase in allowances that are at present inadequate may be more urgent than a reduction in income-tax for those who because of their secure and profitable living are better off. Any such reform should be accompanied by extensive reduction of State expenditure; the State is not entitled to exact taxes that could be avoided, for example, by administrative reforms, saving in expenditure.

4. Direct taxes are those that are levied by assessment of property and income. They may be assessed in proportion to paying capacity and make provision for rebates, for example, by reason of the general economic situation, the public benefit conferred (in the cases of educational and charitable institutions) or the necessary expenses of individuals (children, aged and infirm dependents). Thus where there is good will a just system of direct taxation is possible. Nowadays in most countries there are complaints that even direct taxation is much too high; that the State has no right to take twenty, forty per cent, or more in taxes from the honest earnings of its citizens; and that States use a considerable part of their tax revenues for unnecessary, if not for evil purposes, anyhow not for the common good. Such complaints are justified. The modern vast machinery of the State, lack of social-mindedness, rearmament, a general tendency to ostentatious living often lead to superfluous, and in fact questionable, expenses. Nevertheless, before we can deduce from this state of affairs a right to tax evasion (No. 5) we shall have to consider that individual nations are caught up in a general development for which they are only partly responsible. For

example, the State has to take into consideration technical and economic progress and the international situation with its tensions and dangers, and meet these with sometimes very costly measures. The people themselves are not without responsibility for these developments, which might have been prevented by earlier and determined resistance.

Finally we believe that the assertion that taxation destroys the possibility of decent living is simply not true. In spite of taxation, which admittedly may be unjustly high, many people are making profits and are able to meet expenditure which they were quite unable to do in other times.

5. Those who do not pay the taxes for which they are liable deceive the revenue. Tax evasion is often looked upon as a kind of secret self-indemnification. The taxpayer as it were takes back by non-payment of taxes what the State has unjustly taken from him by its unfair assessments. There are many ways and means of at least partly evading taxation. Some are harmless, others are very dubious or wrong: skilful interpretation and exploitation of concessions granted by the law, false returns, "double" bookkeeping by concealing cash amounts, bribing of revenue officials. It is argued that many present-day taxes are clearly unjust, and that no one could be so foolish as to pay taxes to the full amount, for the State made over-assessments from the start in order to acchieve the desired result in spite of the defaulters. Even when due allowance is made for these arguments it cannot be denied that the moral standard in regard to taxes has seriously declined and a return to Christian moral principles is desirable also in this respect.

Evasion of taxes entails the possibility of punishment; the penalties may be considerable according to the sums involved. To evade taxes is to inflict a wrong upon one's fellow men who will eventually have to make up the loss in revenue that has been caused. Wage earners and salaried workers who have their income tax deducted from their earnings, can hardly be expected to stand by and watch others cleverly evading their payments. However, considering the claims and the vast expenditure of modern States, tax offences should, in our view, be judged lightly if the tax demanded is really crushing and the taxpayer is granted no rebate in spite of the evidence he has provided; or if the State is clearly pursuing unjust objectives, or if it is obviously using its revenue in an irresponsible manner. In practice these matters are often so complicated that an expert opinion will have to be sought. Bribery and corrupt practices would also, in our view, reduce the moral strictures on tax evasions. But no matter what opinion is adopted, whether it is the stricter or the more lenient one, a number of subsidiary problems remain unsolved or unsatisfactorily solved. The more lenient opinion given here is held by recognized authorities. I personally can only agree with it with considerable reservations. I am led to this by the circumstance that most tax evasions are based on the "latitude" which some people enjoy because their tax is not deducted at source and they take advantage of their freedom in this respect. In this there is an injustice towards millions of civil servants, employees and workers who often have to pay proportionately higher taxes on smaller incomes and, in addition, are still heavily hit by indirect taxation.

6. The State has to handle its taxation policy firmly but with understanding. Reductions and delayed payments should be granted where these are justified. In this way the State would create quite a different basis for proceeding against the evaders and those who are slow to pay; that is, provided there is a sufficient number of efficient and conscientious revenue officials.

Those who are obliged to pay taxes should have at their disposal suitable legal means for appealing against taxes that they consider unjust. The forms this might take in practice will vary.

7. Tax legislation and the management of public finances are much too centralized in modern States; they do not conform to the principle of subsidiary function which must apply here also. Member communities such as the municipality, administrative district and federal State ought to have restored to them the greatest measure of independence possible in matters of economy and finance; they should be in a position to provide themselves at least the basis of their material resources.

B. THE JUDICIARY

82. What is the State's concern with the law?

The State must provide for the orderly administration of justice, that is, for the security of the law.

PIUS XII (C. B., 1942; C. T. S., pp. 16–7).

"He who would have the star of peace to shine permanently over social life must make every effort towards the restoration of a juridical constitution .... A constitution conformable with the divine will gives man a right to juridical security, and accordingly grants him a sphere of rights immune from all arbitrary attack. The relation of man towards man, of individual towards society, towards authority, and towards civic duties, and the relation of society and authority towards individuals – all these must be based upon a clear juridical foundation and, where necessary, protected by the authority of the courts."
JOHN XXIII (P. i. T. 30).

1. The State is the servant of the law; only as such can it fulfil its function in respect of the common good (Qs. 60/62). It must

guarantee security of the law, and this is only possible in a proper administration of justice. In virtue of its sovereign political authority, the State is entitled to punish injustice, to restore justice that has been outraged, to call transgressors to account and to punish them.

As servant of the law the State is not outside the law. That would be contrary to the nature of the State as part of the order of creation.

2. The order of justice and the security of the law are among the most sacred values of mankind. For this reason the State cannot take seriously enough its obligations as servant of the law.

83. *What are the functions of the State's administration of the law?*

The functions of the State's administration of the law are:

1. to resolve doubts concerning the law;

2. to administer justice (judiciary).

1. LAWS form the objective norm of justice. They indicate and define what is right and what is not right. But doubts may arise as to what the law means and whether a certain matter comes under the law. These doubts must be resolved; otherwise people will not know what they are to do or not to do, and the courts will not know how to pass judgment.

2. Administering justice means pronouncing a person to be in the right or not to be in the right. This judgment is of a judicial (not private) nature and rests on the "judicial" power which is part of the sovereign authority of the State (Q. 68); this judgment must in the last instance be final and legally effective.

84. What norms govern the administration of justice?

The administration of justice is subject to established law, i.e., to the established norms and customs of law.

1. It is for the courts to decide what is just in individual cases, what is due, or is not due, to individuals (or a group, a community), whether it is a matter of material goods, for example, in disputes concerning wages or inheritance, or of punishment. This "justice" which it is the function of the courts to find or determine is to be derived from the object, not from personal wishes and opinions. Occasionally it is difficult to establish "objectively" the borderline between what is just and what is unjust. In order that the courts may be consistent and sure in their judgments the State must create a uniform and sound basis for them. This basis is called established law and is formulated in Britain in a system of judicial precedents, in the United States in periodical "restatements" or elsewhere in written codes, such as the Code Napoléon. The courts (judges, public prosecutor, juries, counsel etc.) are bound by this law. It stands to reason that the facts of a case must be judged in accordance with the laws that are in force at the time of the occurrence, and not according to laws that may be passed subsequently with retrospective validity.

Customs or usages that have developed and become deep-rooted in the course of time may have the force of laws and may play a considerable part in the administration of justice; they are based on long experience and testify to that spirit of equity which is characteristic of a sound administration of justice. Customs of this kind are "umwritten laws".

Pius XII stated briefly in his Christmas broadcast of 1942 (C. T. S., p. 17) the basis of a juridical order and of the administration of justice. i. Principles of law must be unambiguous, that is, clearly defined, and not so nebulous and flexible that anyone can interpret them to suit his own case. ii. They must be such that they "cannot be upset by unwarranted appeals to supposed popular sentiments or by mere expediency". iii. The State too must also recognize the principle that it as well as "its dependent officials and organs are obliged to make restitution and to revoke measures by which the liberty, property, honour, advancement and welfare of individuals, have been harmed."

2. The administration of justice can all the more unhesitatingly abide by legal norms and customs the more the established law respects the natural law. The natural law affects the administration of justice in various ways: i. It regulates the application of laws. An administrator of justice ought to decide on the reasonable degree (on what is right and fair) of applying what is prescribed by established law. For example, the court must establish to what extent the defendant was in ignorance, was provoked or intimidated. ii. It helps to solve conflicting laws. When several laws (legal obligations) contradict one another the question of what here and now is "right", appropriate, just has to be examined and settled. iii. It fills the gaps of established law. A person may commit an offence, even against the community, without breaking the established law, especially if the established law has overlooked certain matters or could not regulate them (Q. 85, No. 315).

85. What is an orderly administration of justice based upon?

An orderly administration of justice is based upon
1. the equality of all persons before the law;
2. the independence of the courts.

1. ALL men are equal before the law; *i.e.,* there is no "respect of persons" before the law. This means: i. All those who are subject to the law enjoy its protection as long as they observe it. ii. Considerations that have no relevance to the case at issue must not be introduced: for example, membership of a political party, political convictions, wealth, personal friendship, kinship and the like are aspects that must not influence the judgment of the courts. iii. All are judged according to the same objective standards and not according to the saying "little thieves are hanged, but great ones escape". iv. Poverty and similar conditions should not render a person defenceless. If an individual cannot afford to pay for his defence, legal aid must be provided for him by the State.

2. The courts (judges, jurors, etc.) must be able to act with a sense of free responsibility. Their independence alone can guarantee a "clean" administration of justice. Judges must be absolutely proof against any undue influence, especially against any kind of open or secret bribery. The State (or the Sovereign), in whose name justice is administered, may not put pressure on the judges. It is entitled to prevent serious professional offences, if necessary by removal from office. A judge who is liable to be taken to task for conscientious decisions loses the mental equilibrium indispensable for the service of justice "in season, out of season" (2 Tim. 4:2).

3. Certain weighty conclusions follow from waht has been said:

i. The State must pay the greatest attention to the professional qualifications and the appointment of judges. An exact and extensive knowledge of the natural law ought to be, but is, alas, not always part of the professional qualifications of judges.

Considered merely from the point of view of natural law, the appointment of judges could be made by the people. But the people are not in fact in a position to judge professional and moral qualifications. For this reason the choice, or the appointment, of judges must be left to the government, (President, Ministry of Justice, Lord Chancellor, the Attorney General). The right to propose candidates and a voice in deciding appointments might be given to vocational organization bodies, to a senate or council.

ii. Directives that present the judge with a prepared judgment and force him to pronounce it under threat of penalization (*e.g.*, removal from office) make a mockery of justice.

iii. It is a much disputed question what a judge should do when the established law demands a decision which conflicts with his conscience. This can happen especially where the established law obviously conflicts with the natural law.

EXAMPLES. Divorce in the sense of dissolution of the marriage bond. Cruel punishment for slight offences. Participation in political trials.

In a civilized State the judge ought to be able to declare his inability to justify certain decisions in conscience, whereupon the cases in question would be handed over for decision by another judge not so inhibited. Since experience shows that the number of such cases is very small in systems of legal justice, the judges will hardly be inhibited in the general exercise of their office. If this course is not open to the judge he could try to avoid the case altogether on the plea of illness or in some other way; or he could merely recognize the civil effects, unless, of course, there is no other alternative for him but to resign from office, if, for example, he should be compelled to pass death sentences which are blatantly unjust.

iv. What is to be done if (new) factors arise that have not been foreseen by the established law?

We can imagine emergencies when people may die of starvation and cold unless they help themselves to food and fuel, while others may shamelessly exploit the need of their fellow men by black market deals.

The case of extreme necessity is also recognized by the law and the courts; to save himself from dying of hunger or cold a person is allowed to take what he requires in order to overcome his extreme need, provided he does not thereby reduce his fellow-man to a similar plight. Legislation must provide as speedy an arrangement as possible for dealing with emergencies of this kind; it could do so by authorizing the courts to examine the circumstances with every consideration for natural equity and to decide accordingly.

It must be possible to prevent and to punish clear and serious injustice even when the case is not covered by the established law, and the courts have not been specially empowered to deal with it. The natural law ranks higher than positive law, and the community must be able to prevent and to punish crimes against humanity even where the established law does not provide any direct means of doing so. Usually the courts will have adequate points of reference in parallel cases of law or of jurisdiction.

86. What is required for a sound administration of justice?

A sound administration of justice requires:
1. that the facts of the case and the degree of responsibility should be proved with certainty;
2. that pressure should not be exercised in giving evidence;
3. that recourse to appeals should be possible.

1. Opinions, conjecture, suspicion and distrust may also have their place in the judiciary, but sentence must be passed on the strength of proven facts. The court must establish the actual facts of the case, what happened, for example, in a motor or railway accident, how the accident came about, whether, for example, a level crossing was left unattended, who did or did not, participate in a case of fraud.

The degree of responsibility depends on the degree of voluntariness. No court has direct insight into the human will. But there are sufficient indications for establishing the degree of voluntariness, even when the person concerned denies it. Obviously the greatest care must be observed to avoid erroneous judgments (miscarriage of justice).

Examples. The court may have to decide whether someone contracted marriage voluntarily or under compulsion; whether or not a person is fully qualified to act and to contract; under what external or internal compelling influences a wrong was committed (intoxication, mental derangement, excitement, threats and blackmail, military obedience); whether the case is one of manslaughter or murder; whether a dismissal from service or from a place of employment was justified on impartial grounds or resulted from personal vindictiveness.

2. The objectiveness and impartiality of the law, the dignity and liberty of the human person, the character of the State as a moral and legal political community demand that the administration of justice should be carried out in an orderly manner, avoiding any kind of disregard for human rights. Therefore:

i. Emergency situations apart, justice must be administered in competent ordinary courts; recourse to legal action in the ordinary way offers the greatest guarantee of reliability and juridical security.

ii. The courts must be authorized and obliged to use all available lawful means in order to establish the facts of a case. Lawful means are, for example, interrogation (cross-examination), testimony of witnesses, documents, letters, newspaper reports, statutory declarations. A court would act wholly illegally if it suppressed or misinterpreted evidence deliberately.

iii. The defendant must have the right to representation of his cause, either through himself or through counsel. Before the court every one must be able to speak freely concerning the facts of the case; he may not be debarred from bringing all the evidence for and against.

iv. The court may require the (accused) parties to answer and give evidence in a decent form. The procedure must not be degraded by threats, intimidation, extortion. English and American criminal law presumes the innocence of the accused until his guilt has been conclusively proved by the prosecution. A civilized country that respects human rights will not allow prisoners to be starved, beaten into submission, tortured. Drugs that have the effect of breaking down the resistance of the will, denial of sleep by continuous cross-examination will be equally shunned.[41]

[41] Both jurisprudence and ethics agree in condemning the employment of "truth drugs" and leucotomy for the purpose of eliciting confessions. "Truth drugs" induce mental stupor; the victim's reflexes become depressed; he can be made to talk and tell his innermost thoughts; he will be unable to distinguish what he himself has done from what others have done. Leucotomy, which is a brain operation (there are other types of what is basically the same thing, and other names for it), means a technical operation on the "centre of personality"; the effects of the operation are irremediable; the two severed parts of the brain cannot grow together again. Some medical authorities recommend this operation in certain cases of serious mental illness; in recent times, however, only in the form of prefrontal lobotomy and no longer in the form of strict leucotomy (I agree with this opinion), but they are opposed to the treatment of healthy persons in this way in order to procure confessions. Various methods of "brainwashing" have been developed under totalitarian regimes.

3. A proper administration of justice requires that the way of appeal should be open to convicted persons or to those who have reason to question the court's decision. Appeal is a kind of self-defence; its necessity is based on human fallibility. It is for the law to determine when, where and in what manner an appeal should be made.

The administration of justice may prescribe legal action in cases when this is required by public order. In cases, however, when the common good does not necessarily require legal action, it ought to be left free to settle matters out of court, by agreement, compromise, voluntary renunciation etc.

Strictly speaking the administration of justice is a "public" matter. The Crown or the people, on whose behalf justice is administered, must be able to see that all due care is devoted to the administration of justice, and that sentences are just. But a court may have to exclude spectators temporarily in the public interest, for instance, in cases of sexual crimes, spy-trials, when there are persistent disturbances in court.

87. *When is the State entitled to use coercion?*

The State may use coercion when this is absolutely required in the interest of public order, especially:
1. in order to safeguard the law and the decisions of the courts;
2. to meet a threat to public safety;
3. to prevent or to punish crime.

WE DISTINGUISH between i. "moral" coercion, which seeks to move the will so that a man may decide himself (commands, prohibitions, admonitions, warnings, fear and threat); and ii. "physical" coercion, which affects the individual externally, constrains or hinders him in his freedom of movement or action.

There are numerous means, such as impounding and confiscation of property, distraint, cordoning off a street and closing it to traffic, arresting and taking into custody, threatening with a weapon, even passport controls, traffic regulations etc.

1. The State depends upon the use of coercion and force for the proper fulfilment of its function (Q. 68). Power of coercion is therefore a consequence and part of the State's exercise of power for the preservation of law and order; it lies in the nature of a constitutional State. It is indeed true that physical coercion conflicts with free will (I, Q. 38, No. 1); man ought to do good and avoid evil on his own impulse. But taking man as he is in reality, and considering the complexities and dangers to which his social life is in fact exposed, we have to admit that the use of even a considerable measure of physical coercion cannot be avoided.

EXAMPLES. Sudden panic caused, for example, by natural catastrophes such as earthquakes, storms, floods, forest fires, volcanic eruptions etc. may bring about wild confusion and riots that make police measures necessary; the inhabitants of entire districts may have to be prevented from entering their homes. Sometimes the danger of an epidemic can only be met by imposing extensive restrictions on the liberty of both sick and healthy.

2. Just laws that are not observed and valid decisions of the courts that are not implemented are useless for the preservation of order. The State therefore must protect itself against transgressions of the law by an appropriate penal code or in some other effective way. If a matter has been decided in the courts, and the persons concerned nevertheless refuse to comply with their judgments (say, to pay, or to make restitution), the State has no other choice but to intervene with coercive measures such as compulsory auction of goods, arrest.

3. It is a difficult and controversial question what kind of coercive measures the State may adopt "in order to meet a threat to public safety" (Reply, No. 2). As guardian of law and order the State cannot tolerate subversive agitation and activity, threats to the public by asocial and criminal elements, the dangers likely to be caused by insane persons or those suffering from infectious diseases. In these and similar cases it is a matter of meeting emergencies to which the State must be entitled. On the other hand we must be conscious of the acts of cruelty that were and are being committed in totalitarian States under the guise of preventive and protective measures, *e.g.*, protective custody and concentration camps; pogroms and ghettos, compulsory labour in mines, in road and canal construction or reclamation of swamp lands; even the genocide of entire races or nations.

The powers of the State must be governed by the principle that preventive measures do not possess a penal character; therefore they must be distinguished according to kind, duration and effects from penal measures. It is regrettable but unavoidable that often considerable hardship has to be inflicted on innocent people for preventive reasons. In such cases the State must endeavour to mitigate hardship as much as possible. i. Concern for the health of the nation, for the fate of displaced persons or of those suffering material loss through natural catastrophes may require compulsory measures and bitter sacrifices, *e.g.*, isolation, compulsory medical examination (for venereal diseases), settlement in camps. ii. In certain circumstances the State may have to introduce compulsory labour, *e.g.*, natural catastrophes, blockade, war. iii. The State may have to protect itself and its citizens in good time against those who clearly show criminal proclivities and who, judged as far as this is humanly possible, may sooner or later turn into criminals (by compulsory confinement, not by imprisonment). iv. It may be necessary for the protection of the State and of public order to ban and to dissolve political groupings (Q. 103), mass demonstrations and political meetings. Even traffic restrictions and suspension of traffic are for various reasons often unavoidable. v. Concerning compulsory restrictions on public communication media such as press, theatre, films and broadcasting and especially the liberty of the sciences and learning, in short, forms of censorship, we should like to state the following by way of general principles (for details see Qs. 95 ff.): The political community cannot possibly be unconcerned in matters likely to have an inciting and corrupting effect on youth and nation. The political community has the unquestionable right to intervene when the common good is seriously threatened and cannot otherwise be protected. The political community must confine itself to stopping abuses; a universal State-control is not justified.

4. Coercive measures by the State such as pursuit, arrest, even the use of weapons, are necessary especially when offenders have to be apprehended. Yet a proper administration of justice requires that any person who has been deprived of his liberty must be brought before the magistrate without delay, and the latter must examine most carefully whether the allegations are justified. Being held for interrogation is not imprisonment; this must be manifest in the manner and duration of the restriction of liberty.

5. The executive organ of State coercion is the police force. It is an institution for the specific purpose of maintaining public order. In emergencies the assistance of the military may be enlisted. The police force must be qualified for its task of main-

taining public order, *i. e.,* it must be well trained, absolutely reliable and sufficiently strong in numbers and equipment. It is customary to maintain a non-uniformed police (Criminal Investigation Department) which operates unrecognized by the public. A "secret" police force of this kind, if subject to severe controls, run by persons of good character, shunning any illegal methods and liable to severe penalties for any abuses can be approved of. The secret political police of totalitarian States must be definitely rejected (Q. 105, No. 3ii.).

88. What is the purpose of the State's right to punish?

The purpose of the State's right to punish is:
1. to restore legality which has been culpably violated;
2. to reform the offender;
3. to deter from further similar crimes.

1. PUNISHMENT is an evil which a person suffers against his will because he has committed a wrong, that is, incurred guilt. i. Punishment causes suffering and is experienced as such regardless of whether man is deprived of or has to renounce something (deprivation of property or of liberty) or whether a heavy and painful sentence is imposed upon him (hard labour, solitary confinement). ii. Punishment presupposes a guilt, a transgression. Guilt derives from the free will, whereas punishment is imposed on the will by another who brings the guilty one to justice and compels him to suffer the evil of punishment. iii. Punishment is not revenge in the ignoble sense, because it may be inflicted from the highest motives. Punishment has a threefold meaning: First, it is retribution, expiation imposed because order has been violated, and its purpose is to restore order; second, it is an incentive and a help for reforms and thus

has an educational purpose; third, it is a means of deterrence both for the offender and for others (society).

2. The State has the right to punish the insubordinate and the offender. And because it is the guardian of law and justice the penalties inflicted by it have also, and often primarily, the character of retribution and expiation. The State punishes wrong as such; it compels man to restore the violated juridical order.

89. When is the punishment inflicted by the State just?

Punishment inflicted by the State is just only:
1. when the offence has been definitely proved;
2. when guilt and punishment are in due proportion;
3. when the rights of God are not violated in the individual.

It is self-evident that the penalty must be just. Unjust penalties are an abuse of power. A person may suffer from no matter what authority only the punishment he deserves.

1. Nothing is more liable to bring law and legal security into disrepute than arbitrary criminal laws and penalties. The branches of the law must remain within the confines of their competence. Three conditions are necessary for a matter to become a punishable offence before the civil courts:

i. It must be an external act or the attempt at or default of such an act. Malicious thoughts that are not "translated" into words or acts do not concern the criminal law.

ii. It must conflict with the established law. The act must be forbidden by law and thus be illegal. We distinguish between:

acts that are of their nature punishable though nevertheless expressly forbidden by the State (for example, robbery, inflicting bodily injury, except in cases of self-defence and of surgical operations, rape, calumny etc.); acts that are permissible in themselves but are prohibited by the law (entering certain streets and localities [curfew; a state of martial law], traffic regulations etc.); acts for which the State prescribes a certain form to be legal (making a will, marriage).

iii. Proof of guilt must be established in accordance with the law; according to the facts of the case, circumstances, foreseen or foreseeable consequences; according to the degree of responsibility (cf. Q. 86):

Before sentence may be imposed the guilt must be established, that is, proved beyond doubt. Judgment remains suspended as long as there is reasonable doubt whether the act really happened or was illegal; fresh evidence may be sought, further witnesses may be called and expert opinion brought in, but the court is not entitled to "condemn" and to punish. The kind and degree of guilt will depend, first of all on the facts of the case, that is, upon what was or was not done, for example whether it was a case of larceny or robbery, bodily injury or defamation of character, fraud or blackmail. Then the circumstances will have to be examined which caused, accompanied or determined the act (rape of a child or adult, violence used). Finally the consequences have to be considered, that is, the effects resulting from the punishable act, for example, a forest fire caused by a camp-fire; the failure of an operation due to the doctor's negligence; a drunkard with previous convictions for drunkenness; a motorist driving at great speed on a road he knows to be dangerous. The extent of guilt also depends on the degree of a man's responsibility at the time of the action. Hence the court must take into account exonerating circumstances like fear and excitement, ignorance, provocation and seduction, physical and mental distress, (unintentional) negligence, poverty, illness, shock, evil habits, education, inexperience. In short, the degree of negligence or deliberation may increase or reduce the guilt and consequently the penalty that is due.

2. The sentence imposed by the civil courts must be just both in regard to the guilt and to the general penal practice. There must be no fear or favour in the administration of the law. What matters is in the first place the punishable offence. Grave guilt deserves severe punishment, but lesser guilt deserves lesser punishment. Also to be taken into account is the character of the offence and the degree of danger to society, for example, whether it is a misdemeanour or a felony, whether human life or health was at stake, whether it is an offence against a person's honour, reputation, property, whether it was directed against defenceless persons, whether deliberate cruelty was involved etc. Special circumstances can so change what in itself may be a trivial offence so that it will have to be punished severely.

EXAMPLES. A soldier who returns to barracks late may be given a light punishment; but if he leaves his post at the front he is liable to be court-martialled. A police officer who aids and abets in a crime, however lightly, incurs severe punishment since he has failed in his professional duty.

It is contrary to justice to exculpate an accused person merely because of who or what he is, because he is related to, or a friend of, the judge. A petty theft is obviously not less harmful because it was committed by some high official; murder remains a grave crime even if ordered by people in authority against their political enemies.

3. The State judges and punishes in the name of justice, that is, in the name of God (Rom. 13:4). But no State has the right to prevent an offender, however heinous his crime, from making his peace with God. The Church has the right to exercise her pastoral office in prisons to enable the prisoners to fulfil their duty to God and their souls. Divine service, preaching and administration of the sacraments on Sundays and holidays of obligation, spiritual care for individual prisoners, especially those awaiting a death sentence.

Is one obliged to tell the truth in court? Or may one omit the truth or deny it? A defendant need not incriminate himself in court; he may even proffer denials, since it is for the prosecution to prove his guilt by external evidence. Witnesses in court must tell the truth conscientiously and to the best of their knowledge, unless they are obliged to remain silent (official secrets, seal of confession) or if they are not allowed by the established law to refuse to give evidence (the husband or wife of an accused person may refuse to give evidence). It is a crime against truthfulness and humanity to commit perjury (The trial of Jesus; staged trials in totalitarian countries).[42]

90. What kind of penalties is the State entitled to impose?

The State may impose penalties proportionate to the guilt; it must, however, take into account the development and prevailing sense of justice.

1. THE political authority of the State is a fully sovereign authority, and the administration of criminal law should serve not only the purposes of correction and deterrence but essentially also the restoration of law outraged. The State is therefore

[42] Confession and testimony in the totalitarian State; cf. Q. 109, iii.

entitled to impose and to carry out that penalty which is proportionate to the guilt. In former centuries teachers of natural law, especially St. Thomas Aquinas, undeterred by opinions to the contrary, acknowledged the right of the State (the political community) to inflict *damna irreparabilia* (irreparable injury and loss) on offenders. They had in mind not only imprisonment for life but also bodily mutilation; for example, thieves, being a menace to society, had their hand chopped off. Other societies may only punish offences confined to their particular provinces; they may not demand satisfaction which would permanently affect the individual or destroy his physical inviolability.

Examples. Parents may chastise disobedient children and confine them to the house for hours or days; clubs and associations may impose moderate fines, punish with expulsion conduct which is contrary to their rules. But they may not punish with imprisonment, condemn members to compulsory labour lasting for years or deprive them of their civil rights. Parents may indeed sometimes punish their children very severely and irreparably, for example by disinheriting them or turning them out of the home. But even this does not mean a "total" forfeiture or constraint since the children can earn their own livelihood or take legal action against their parents.

2. Many types of punishment were formerly considered not inhuman or beneath the dignity of man, but they no longer conform to the modern sense of justice and have been abolished in criminal law. They have been reintroduced, sometimes with even greater cruelty, in totalitarian States. Modern criminal law usually imposes fines, restraint of liberty (imprisonment), deprivation of civil rights (loss of suffrage or of the right to be elected for Parliament, hard labour). In special cases persons may be committed to the care of trustees or guardians or under police supervision; young offenders may be sent to remand

homes or approved schools. The present age, too, recognizes the State's right to impose severe penalties.

3. The way in which sentences are carried out has been humanized considerably. Especially those who support the theory of the "reform" of offenders, that is education as the sole purpose of court sentences, aim at the gradual transformation of prisons into remand schools.

It would be false indulgence to abolish completely the character of punishment. Punishment is and remains painful. It is doing a bad service to law and social order to treat criminals on the same basis as the sick and mentally ill, when honest members of society may have to suffer greater privation than the inmates of prisons. Retribution ought to be combined with reform and the stereotyped execution of sentences ought to be replaced by a more balanced treatment of offenders. In the case of young offenders, however, education ought to be the primary aim.

4. The courts have the right to defer or mitigate sentence by granting probation or reprieves by which latter act penalties may be remitted or commuted. Here also established law and the order of the common good ought to be the touchstone. If the handling of the right to reprieve were to rob the penalty of its gravity and indeed to encourage illegal acts, it would be contrary to the order of the common good. On the other hand, for example, the prisoner's good conduct, changes in the law, may make it seem unjustifiably severe to persevere in the execution of the penalty.

91. Is capital punishment justified?

Capital punishment is justified in expiation of the gravest crimes; the administration of justice must decide whether and in what circumstances it is actually called for.

1. WE SAY that capital punishment may, if at all, be inflicted only for the gravest crimes. For capital punishment takes from man his highest earthly good, which is his life. For this reason St. Thomas Aquinas says that only two kinds of crime may be punished by death, those causing the gravest, irreparable damage to society (to fellowman), and those that are particularly heinous,[43] for example, murder, treason, grave blasphemy, violent rebellion against the legitimate authority of the State. It is self-evident that the capital offence and the offender's full responsibility must be clearly proved, since errors and injustices cannot be corrected once a sentence of capital punishment has been carried out (judicial murder).

2. With few exceptions Catholic moralists have always maintained that capital punishment is justified as atonement for the gravest crimes and that the State (the political community) alone has the right to impose it and have it carried out. At the present time this view is being challenged on the basic ground that no human authority can ever have the right to take human life; God alone is Lord over life and death, for which reason every sentence of death is an encroachment on God's rights as Creator and sovereign Lord.

Catholic moralists base their view on the Scriptures. In the Old Testament the execution of criminals was not only consid-

[43] II–II, 66, 6 ad 2; cf. Q. 64, also III c. *G.* 146.

ered permissible, but was expressly approved and even commanded by God (Lev. 24:17). In the New Testament St. Paul supplies the key passage: "..., for he (the magistrate) beareth not the sword in vain, for he is God's minister, and avenger to execute wrath upon him that doth evil" (Rom. 13:4). The expression "beareth the sword" then signified having authority to execute offenders, to have them beheaded with the sword. In view of the teaching and the attitude of the Church, it is, moreover, out of the question that she would have remained silent for centuries if capital punishment conflicted with the Sacred Scriptures or with the natural law.

PIUS XII (Address of 14 September, 1952; U. A. vol. 2, p. 143).

"Even when there is question of the execution of a condemned man, the State does not dispose of the individual's right to life. In this case it is reserved to the public power to deprive the condemned person of the enjoyment of life in expiation of his crime when, by his crime, he has already forfeited his right to live."

Reason provides a further basis for the Catholic view. By committing the gravest crimes, especially premeditated murder and similar acts of violence, the individual forfeits his right to life because he violates the highest good of his fellowmen and turns into a menace to society. The only proportionate atonement for such a crime is that the good, of which the culprit has quite unlawfully robbed others, namely life, should be taken from himself. Society has no other way of exacting just retribution.[44] Equal to murder are a few other crimes of a grave

[44] Capital punishment cannot be shown to be justified either on the grounds of its reforming purpose which is obvious, or as a deterrent. It can never be permissible to take a person's life in order that others may not commit similar crimes and incur similar punishment (as a deterrent again to others). The only plausible

nature, high treason, the vilest profanation (desecration) of the name of God and his house of worship, systematic extermination of the Christian faith and Christian morality. However, it is not usual nowadays to punish by death such crimes against religion, indeed they are let go unpunished altogether. In these cases, and provided its judgment is just, civil authority acts as God's representative. The objections that are raised against capital punishment in the name of humanity should not be lightly brushed aside. But we must also consider the depravity revealed and the suffering caused by many a crime. Not everything can be excused on grounds of bad hereditary disposition, evil environment etc.

3. Capital punishment has been abolished by a number of modern States, while others have retained it for some particular crimes only, and may often substitute for it a sentence of life-imprisonment. Three principal reasons are mainly given for the abolition of the death penalty: First, that it is ineffective, since it does not lead to a decrease in crime; second, that it is no longer in accord with the modern sense of justice; third, that it is altogether inappropriate as punishment because of the terrible abuses of it in our age.

There is much to be said for and against each of these reasons. The modern sense of justice is by no means uniform. Today many right-thinking people are still in favour of the death penalty. Its abuse is no proof to the contrary, for in a constitutional State such abuse should be ruled out, and the totalitarian

argument in its favour is that based on its expiatory purpose. I agree with the opinion that the principles and text of St. Thomas ultimately and actually have regard to justice and its equity, that is, to crime and just expiation, rather than to social dangers and the needs of protecting society. The latter concern the norm for a rational application of the death penalty.

State is not influenced by such facts and considerations. Today it is sometimes argued that the modern State, even the non-totalitarian, is no longer a constitutional State, based on law and justice. By the great number of wrongs which it is continually committing it has forfeited the right to inflict such penalties. We answer that when St. Paul acknowledged the right of the civil authority to inflict the death penalty he had in mind the Roman Empire of his time which admittedly had a distinctive system of law, but which in many respects was very far from being a constitutional State. There are, moreover, States that strive to be constitutional and to guarantee human rights. Finally, since party political conflicts in many countries are attended by the danger of totalitarian rule, the constitution or the judiciary must effectively preclude the abuse of the death penalty; but this is no reason why it should be abolished.

4. Former, harrowing forms of execution such as stoning a person to death, burning at the stake, crucifixion, quartering etc. are now happily abolished. The usual forms of execution nowadays are by shooting, beheading, electric chair and hanging. But here again certain States form a dreadful exception. It is a particular disgrace in the present age that convicts who have not been sentenced to death are nevertheless done to death by their treatment and by overwork, often resulting in complete exhaustion to the point of death from starvation; by sanitary conditions in the prison camps where medical attention is refused or is completely inadequate when epidemics break out; by the arbitrary attitude of the guards who are allowed to maltreat the prisoners even to the point of death.

It is a callous injustice to refuse the assistance of a priest to a condemned person (Q. 89, No. 3). It is inhuman repeatedly to postpone the date of execution and thus cause the condemned man several agonies of death. The finality of death demands that just death sentences should either be carried out at the appointed time or be repealed by a reprieve.

C. THE EXECUTIVE

It is impossible to discuss here even briefly the wide and varied functional field of modern public administration. We shall confine ourselves to the basic questions.

92. What is the function of public administration?

It is the function of public administration duly to carry out the laws of the State and to issue the necessary supplementary rules of law in the form of regulations and orders.

1. PUBLIC administration serves legislation which it presupposes as its basis. It is necessary because the process from the passing of a law to its application comprises new tasks that may be indicated by the legislator but cannot be carried out by him. The law provides only a general norm which is not always sufficient in practice. For example, the State possesses estates, buildings, roads and rivers, revenues and moneys that have "to be administered".

2. The guiding principle of the administration should be the common good. It is the function of the administration to carry into effect, preserve and promote in its own province the fabric of the common good. The fabric itself is fixed by the law. The work of the administration will always require the issue of special regulations and orders that deal with special conditions. Unexpected events, difficulties that may arise, threats to, and

disturbances of, public order may condition such supplementary regulations and measures.

Examples. Natural catastrophes such as local earthquakes, storms, floods, avalanches etc.; political unrest, public meetings, strikes; railway and aeroplane disasters; maintenance of roads and waterways.

Strictly speaking it is the administration's job, being the executive, merely to carry out the decisions of higher authority (Q. 68); hence it exceeds its competence whenever it goes beyond the regulations and measures of execution. This is often the case today; a development in the wrong direction which ought to be halted.

3. Modern States have their own legal system of administration which lays down the norms both for the administration as a whole and for its various branches and functions. Some also have courts of administration in which complaints of abuse in government administration can be lodged.

93. What are the elements of public administration?

Public administration is based upon areas and functional departments.

That the administration of the modern State has assumed such proportions is due to the increasing complexity of social life in general and the tendency of the State to extend its competence. Public administration is particularly prone to be victimized by bureaucracy.

1. There are administrative areas such as parish, borough, county, province, canton, department, state. In these we distinguish between local and central administration. The former is the

proper concern of each administrative area, carried out on its own responsibility. The latter is carried out on behalf of the government and under its direction.

2. Functional departments may deal not only with the State's finances, traffic and police, but also – an indication of the State's inroads into the concerns of human society – with schools, labour, trade and social welfare administration.

3. The principle of subsidiary function ought to inspire both the area divisions and functional departments. By this we mean that the "social" spheres ought to come under the autonomous administration of the vocational groups (Q. 52). The principle of subsidiary function also implies that what can be done by lesser authorities should not be taken from them by the greater ones (Q. A. 80). There are no hard and fast limits; the obligations of greater and lesser corporations will also be determined by changing circumstances (Q. A., 79).

94. What is the special need of public administration?

The public administration especially needs competent officials with integrity of character who know how to combine loyalty to the law with consideration for individual men and circumstances.

THE civil servant has been defined by Professor Nell-Breuning, as "one who must be close to the people, of cheerful disposition, keen to make decisions and to take on responsibility. He ought not to stick too closely to the letter of the regulations and hide behind them. But he must adhere all the more firmly to the great precepts of the divine moral law. He ought to be free from selfish interests, mental and physical laziness; he ought not to be open to any form of improper influence and especially of bribery, following only his better judgment and his conscience, and using all his energy for the good of his fellow-citizens whom he should not treat as his subordinates, recognizing rather that he is their servant. An imperturbable impartiality supported by expert knowledge of his special concerns, enobled by readiness to help and by sincere goodwill – these are the virtues of the civil servant."

Lesson Four

CULTURE AND PUBLIC WELFARE AS FUNCTIONS OF THE STATE

CATHOLIC ethics maintains that the State must concern itself with law, culture and public welfare as its three principal functions.

By "culture" we understand the cultivation of intellectual and moral values; by public welfare "that sufficient amount of material goods which is necessary for a life of virtue" (St. Thomas Aquinas). "Culture" embraces science, education, art, public morality (and the institutions relating to it), customs, language and tradition.

95. *How far are cultural concerns the State's business?*

The State has to protect and, in various ways, to promote cultural concerns but it may not seek to dominate them.

1. ANY State monopoly of culture must be rejected. Culture is a concern of the nation or of particular institutions, a social rather than a political activity.

2. The State fulfils a primary and eminently cultural "mission" by protecting and safeguarding the nation's cultural concerns not by hampering these or forcing them to conform to particular ideologies. Accordingly there are two things that the political community must do: i. It must respect the aims and activities of the cultural institutions and allow these to develop in their own particular way. Culture is partly a matter of "growing", partly of creation by men with particular talents and inclinations. Cultural achievements are not made to order. It is precisely in the cultural concerns that the principle of subsidiary function has particular validity. Inasmuch as cultural institutions are capable of fulfilling their functions independently they must be guaranteed full liberty. ii. The political community ought to protect the cultural concerns from the various threats to their existence and development. Many activities are nowadays disguised as "cultural" which are anything but that.

3. The political community ought to promote genuine culture through material assistance, provided this will not entail an undignified dependence on the State of the recipients; and through directly and indirectly influencing the public (cf. Q. 96).

4. The State's concern with cultural matters should be of a general co-ordinating kind, having the character of guidance, rather than of centralized direction. Its activity should be of a complementary nature; it should do the sort of things which the institutional groupings in the nation are unable to do on their own. It will, for instance, try to bring about uniform standards in primary, secondary and university education. The different cultural spheres ought, with the State's help, to be able to complement and promote one another as much as possible.

5. Whether the State may and should impose any restrictions on scientific research and publications is a controversial question. Some Catholics have opposed any State interference with the freedom of the sciences and the universities.[45] We believe that:

i. science and learning must be guided by an unconditional striving after truth. It is absurd to want to prescribe scientific method and results of research, as has been done in totalitarian States. Errors in science are overcome by convincing counter-arguments, not by State prohibitions; ii. the most effective means of facilitating science and learning in their service to truth is generous support for scientific research, for example by the establishment of chairs and scholarships, of funds for institutes and graduate research, travelling scholarships, by subsidizing scientific publications etc.; iii. the State is not obliged, indeed not entitled, to tolerate scientific teaching which is downright corruptive in the ideological or the civic sense. After all, all fields of culture, inasmuch as they directly affect the common good, come under the competence of society as a whole. The best solution would be for learning to establish its own defence against abuses.

96. What ought the State to do for public morality?

The State ought to promote public morality effectively and possibly raise its level.

THE morally good, or virtuous, life is pre-eminent among human values and therefore also in society.

1. Since the State is responsible for external order, it is directly

[45] Leo XIII opposed a false idea of liberty of teaching; cf. *Lib. praest.*, Image Bk. pp. 73ff.; *The Liberty of Thought and the Separation of Powers.* The Zaharoff Lecture for 1948 by Charles Morgan (Oxford, 1948).

concerned with public morality. The term "public" denotes first of all whatever is open and accessible to everyone (Radio, TV., theatre, films, newspapers, magazines) what is displayed in bookshops, waiting-rooms, etc. But much happens "in private" that concerns and influences the public (clubs and night clubs). The best protection of public morality is the innate moral attitude of the nation. For this reason the State ought to encourage those efforts and institutions that cultivate moral living — the Church, religious denominations, family, school and educational institutions.

2. The constitutional State ought not to tolerate circumstances in which virtue and vice, decency and depravity, right and wrong are allowed equal latitude. It would be desirable that gross offences against basic morality ought to be forbidden by law and the offenders prosecuted. In practice, today in civilized countries not even the grossest dangers and transgressions by which public morality is threatened are proscribed, for the State has to tolerate many evils in order to avoid worse ones. This is recognized expressly by St. Augustine, St. Thomas Aquinas and Catholic social teaching. But the State is, of course, not entitled to command, permit or assist what is intrinsically evil. We must remember that the resources of the State are limited; it ought to, as St. Thomas Aquinas said, follow the example of God's government of the world which also permits much evil so that good may come about and prevail. It is for political prudence which includes a right sense of moral action to bring about what will best serve the common weal. In many cases it will be up to individual societies by their own efforts, if possible with support from the State, to overcome, or to correct the evil.

3. To what extent is State censorship of press, radio, theatre

and films justified and necessary? i. Undoubtedly these forms of public opinion ought to build up rather than to tear down. Hence they ought to be truthful in their reporting (no deliberate misrepresentation, concealment or suppression even of uncomfortable facts); they ought to treat with respect those things that deserve respect (the name and word of God, conjugal love and fidelity, divine worship, undeserved poverty and distress, human life); they ought to champion just causes; sincere endeavour to promote internal and external political peace. ii. The State is not entitled to run these mass media though it may exercise vigilance over them to ensure that they will not endanger the legal or moral order. However, even a State-guided press or State-guided broadcasting system conflicts with the freedom that is man's birthright. iii. Hence any legislation concerned with the press, broadcasting and film ought to aim at preventing influences that are harmful to society; and enabling systems of responsible self-management and self-control. Self-management and self-control of the relevant cultural bodies are the best and most direct means of protecting the nation and its youth. But these bodies will render fruitful service only if they are properly constituted and if their decisions are respected in practice. Not only film producers, distributors and audiences, but also Church and school as well the State as guardian of public morality ought to participate. iv. In some countries film and theatre can only exist through State subsidies. These subsidies ought to be social in their entire purpose, since they are drawn from the national income. TV., film and theatre performances that endanger public morality are clearly socially damaging and ought not to be subsidized from public funds.

97. *What is the State's concern in social welfare?*

Social welfare covers:

1. laws, institutions and measures that guarantee the nation an orderly condition of material well-being;

2. additional assistance contingent on existing economic conditions;

3. measures to meet special emergencies.

JOHN XXIII (M. M. 52-55; P. i. T. 27-28).

THE entire economic and social policy inasmuch as it involves the State (thus not merely what is called "public welfare") forms part of the State's concern in social welfare.

1. A full human life is impossible without a proper order in property and economic conditions. Morality and cultural pursuits need an adequate material basis; the State as well as all other societies depend upon material goods. Poverty as such is an evil, and when it affects wide sections of the nation it is harmful to society. Hence the State, which on its own territory should enable man to lead a full human life, is undoubtedly entitled and obliged to concern itself with his material welfare. It will seek to secure to its people an adequate and proper standard of living above the minimum requirements (Q. A., 75). The State is not an economic association; to procure and to distribute material goods is not the State's direct responsibility, but that of industry and commerce. However, modern large-scale economics, coupled with the progressive dependence upon each other of national economies require a greater measure of the State's concern with economic affairs than formerly. Inasmuch as a nation's economy is capable, on its own, of meeting its material needs the State ought not to interfere (principle of subsidiary function; Q. A., 71). Regulation of existing economic and property conditions will also come under the law. By appro-

priate laws and other measures the State has to help in establishing a basis of genuine material well-being for the entire nation. Particular forms of property and economic functions are nowadays, and with good reason, controlled by public authority, for example, roads and communications (railways, post, telephone and telegraph); economic agreements are concluded with other countries (commercial treaties); nationalization of certain industries with the object of preventing abuses injurious to the common weal (Q. A., 114).

The State's economic policy ought to be concerned with large-scale planning in regard to the total requirements and the total order of the national economy. It belongs to the function of trades and industrial organizations to prepare decisions of this kind and to propose them in a suitable form (Q. 56).

PIUS XII (Address of 5 July, 1952).

"In order to raise production of goods, as it is in duty bound to do, and to be able wisely to adapt it to human needs and human dignity, the State must within the framework of the general management of the national economy give first place to the control of such production. Without putting its oppressive omnipotence in the place of the legitimate autonomy of private enterprise public authority has here an indisputable task of co-ordination, the urgency of which is increased by the complicated social conditions of the present time."

Certain international developments or dangers may entail supranational or international economic associations that can only be brought about by agreement with, or with the consent of, governments, *e.g.*, the European Economic Community, and thus are subject to State economic policy and legislation. Ratification usually takes the form, or at any rate has the effectiveness, of a law.

2. Modern industrial economy and/or modern private capitalism have increasingly forced the State to adopt extensive national and social policies. Such policies have the character of additional aid measures which presuppose social policy in "society", for instance in industry and in the trades. These embrace regulations, institutions and measures that concern partly the individual person, partly economic life and partly the labour of those in need of help and protection. The Welfare State has undoubtedly brought many blessings. But we must not overlook the dangers also, of which we mention only two: i. There is the danger that personal responsibility of individuals and groups may be weakened, if not altogether destroyed. Men tend to rely upon the help, for example, of social insurance. ii. There is the danger that a necessary social reform may be obscured, delayed or even prevented; for example, necessary reform of the social and economic order.

3. Circumstances may come about in every State, for which the government and the people may, or may not, be to blame, which will affect either the whole country or certain areas, and which can only be overcome by special State aid.

Examples. Natural catastrophes: earthquakes, forest fires, hurricanes, flooding of large and perhaps very fertile areas, famine, epidemics, poverty and destitution resulting from war and "scorched earth" policies; dislocation of communications, destruction of industries, care for the victims of war; movement of population resulting from flight and expulsion, camps for evacuees and refugees.

The State must, if in a position to do so, repair such "exceptional" damages out of its normal revenues, and without resorting to a special levy on the people. However, there is also a natural obligation on the part of those belonging to the same community and sharing the same fate. In great emergencies all citizens, and especially those who by good fortune have suffered little or no loss, are naturally obliged to contribute what falls to their share according to distributive justice, and the State has the right to demand this share.

Lesson Five

FORMS OF STATE

Democracy and Totalitarian State

STATES differ not only according to the position and size of their territory, or according to the numbers and structure of their population, but also according to their type as States. The nature of their political order will have fundamental differences, as a monarchy differs basically from a republic; a Western from an Eastern democracy. We refer to these differences when we speak of the forms of State. States may change these forms in the course of history; monarchies may turn into republics, totalitarian into democratic States or vice versa.

1. From the point of view of natural law there is no obligation to adopt one or another form of State; for the common good may be achieved in various ways. Hence men are free to choose that form of State that is the most suitable one for them. The Catholic Church has always upheld this freedom and has only demanded that the form of State should meet the requirements of the common good.

PIUS XII (C. B., 1944; N. C. W. C., p. 3).

"It is scarcely necessary to recall that, according to the teaching of the

Church, 'it is not forbidden to prefer temperate, popular forms of government, without prejudice, however, to Catholic teaching on the origin and use of authority', and that 'the Church does not disapprove of any of the various forms of government, provided they be per se capable of securing the good of the citizens' (Leo XIII: Encyclical 'Libertas', June 20, 1888)."

2. As derived from the political science of antiquity three basic types of just political rule are usually mentioned:[46] i. Rule of one man (monarchy): the highest authority resides in one person (king, prince, emperor); monarchy may be either hereditary or elective according to the manner of legal succession. ii. Rule of the best men (aristocracy): A few, but the most virtuous and the most capable, govern. iii. Rule of the people (democracy): Government is exercised by the people, or in accordance with the will of the people.[47]

All three types may degenerate. Therefore opposed to them are three basic forms of unjust rule, namely: tyranny, which is despotic rule by one person; oligarchy, which is despotic rule by a few, a clique; ochlocracy, which is rule by the masses, mob-rule. All basic types of just as well as of unjust rule may have a number of subdivisions. Sometimes the actual type of State cannot be recognized from its self-styled forms. Totalitarian tyrannies may call themselves democracies. In parliamen-

[46] Cf. St. Thomas Aquinas, De reg. princ. I, 1. The terms used especially to signify the third basic form were not always identical. Aristotle and also St. Thomas referred to *politeia* rather than democracy; what today is termed ochlocracy that is, rule of the "plebs" they called democracy. It is necessary to bear this in mind in order to understand why these and other thinkers of ancient times had such a low opinion of democracy.

[47] Every State that is not a monarchy is called a republic. According to the amount of power held by the single ruler, a monarchy may in fact be republican in its constitution and government.

tary monarchies the State's guidance may derive from popular representation (Parliament), rather than from the monarch. The freely elected president of a republic may have powers far surpassing those of most monarchs.

3. In practice the best type of State is that which fulfils the following conditions: i. which guarantees most effectively both the liberty of the people in relation to the government and of the government as against the people; ii. which best conforms to the political maturity and the will of the people. For the people themselves have the right to determine the type of State, and government must be supported by the popular will; iii. which most readily enables the people to fulfil its historical function within the community of nations. Every nation is obliged to co-operate harmoniously with the other nations.

If we consider these conditions and the political situation of our time, then surely the most fitting type of State and of political rule is "true and genuine democracy" (Pius XII).

A. DEMOCRACY

98. Which State is a democracy?

That State is a democracy in which government is exercised in accordance with the political will of the people.

OUR answer refers to "genuine" democracy.[48] Strictly speaking

[48] The term "democracy" is used to denote very different kinds of social structure; we speak of social democracy and of economic democracy; there are secular and religious associations that are democratic in constitution and government. All these structures have this in common that the holders of authority

"democracy" denotes a certain type of State or government, but a natural type, not its abuse in "ochlocracy", or mob-rule. Understood in this sense, democracy implies right goals, norms and means.

1. Government in a democracy is based on the political will of the people. This means firstly that the people must have a considerable share in the government of the country. When a nation is dominated and, at most, called upon to confirm the policy of their government in sham referendums, democracy is a mere pretence as in Russia, China and their satellite States. This means, secondly, that the government is formed in accordance with the political will of the people, thus according to the order that has been accepted freely by the people.

2. The order within a democracy must be such that it will guarantee the common good. This condition applies to every type of State. But it is particularly important for modern democracy, for there is the danger that the people may make a wrong decision (contrary to its own welfare) and accordingly be wrongly governed. The result is a purely "formal" democracy. Democratic rules appear to be accepted, since the people were able to decide in free elections but "materially" there is disorder. The aims and norms of the natural law are being discarded, and the common good is misinterpreted to the detriment of the people.

EXAMPLES. A political party that has won free elections then proceeds to override the Constitution and to govern one-sidedly in its own interest.

are not nominated or put into office, but elected, and that all members, or partners, have an equal voice in decisions and an equal share in responsibility. Here the term "democracy" is used in its political sense; this is the original sense from which the other meanings were derived.

Abortive elections: Because of political immaturity (Q. 100) the people vote for parties and candidates opposed to the natural law and thus to the true goals of the State.

PIUS XII (Address of 2 October, 1945).

"Because a democracy is without agreement of outlook at least in the fundamental principles of life, particularly in what concerns the rights of God and the dignity of the human person, respect for honourable personal activity and liberty also in political matters, such a democracy would be defective and lacking in stability."

In the larger democratic States usually only the most important issues, such as the election of the head of State and of the popular representatives are left to the decision of the whole people. Most important is the people's consent to the constitution. Because of the multiplicity and import of modern governmental functions and of political issues, most decisions can only be made indirectly by the entire people; the organs elected by the people decide directly.

3. It is rare that the people are unanimous in supporting one single political opinion. Almost everywhere government is by the will of the majority, the majority form the government, and the minority are in opposition. The principle of majority rule can be dangerously strained, if everything were to be estimated and decided quantitatively rather than qualitatively, on the merit of candidates for political office. There is then the danger of democracy degenerating into "mass" democracy.

PIUS XII (C. B., 1944; N. C. W. C., p. 5).

"... the masses ... are the capital enemy of true democracy and of its ideal of liberty and equality ..."

99. *What ought to be the special concern of the democratic form of government?*

A democracy ought to be concerned particularly:
1. that subsidiary groupings retain their special character and have an effective voice in the political sphere as a whole;
2. that any abuse of power is forestalled.

THE nation is not a mere sum total of individuals, but an "organic and organizing unity" (Pius XII, C. B., C. T. S., 22). We distinguish between: i. political organization into territorial units (administrative districts, municipalities, counties, member States etc.); ii. social organization, cf. Q. 47.

1. The territorial political groupings have a natural right to a life of their own and to independence in the exercise of their own functions. But they must also have a part in the government of the country through their co-determining influence on political affairs in general. It is, of course, possible only in the smaller States to grant every commune or administrative district a seat and a voice in the supreme institutions (Parliament, Senate, Chamber); in larger States only the greater groupings can be directly represented.

The danger of a democracy lapsing into a kind of political machine can be effectively prevented by giving trades and professional groupings, that is to say, the real social institutions, a share in political responsibility (cf. Q. 56).

2. The protection of democracy against the abuse of power is a principal duty of democracy. The extent and means of this protection depend upon a variety of circumstances, *e.g.*, on the character, political maturity and sense of tradition of the people, on the danger of infiltration of foreign influences, on

current political ideas, on the forms of political conflict. Accordingly the control of power will be regulated differently in different States. We are above all familiar with: i. The system of two or more chambers. Legislative and executive powers are divided between two or more corporations, none of which can circumvent the other; ii. a court of special jurisdiction, the function of which it is to give a binding interpretation of the constitution in cases of doubt, to decide constitutional issues, to establish the constitutionality of laws etc. (Supreme Court); iii. the responsibility of ministers. Ministers are answerable to Parliament. The opposition has the constitutional position and function of an organ of control; iv. means of forbidding and disbanding unconstitutional political parties, while allowing them the protection of the courts; v. plenary powers of the head of the State (in Britain: the Queen in, not above, Parliament) that enable it to take emergency measures in times when the welfare of the country is at stake, for example by dissolution of Parliament, ordering new elections, declaring a state of national emergency.

3. A union between two or more States in which each retains its autonomy is called a federation. The member States are politically autonomous; they have their own government, their own legislature and executive (administration, police, education, social services etc.). Not only democracies like the U. S. A. or Australia, but also monarchies may be federal in their constitution and organization, *e.g.,* the former German Empire, the Austro-Hungarian Monarchy. Federalism is a requirement of the natural law in the sense that every State, no matter what form it may have, must tend towards federalism.

The term "federal" is also used in a social sense. It means that the lesser social units such as the family, vocational organizations, voluntary associations etc. enjoy their own natural rights in accordance with the principle of subsidiary function. A State that does not embrace subsidiary states may yet be able to preserve and promote the individual life and responsibility of its territorial, political, social and cultural entities; thus it may well be federal.

A centralized State is one that plans and regulates everything centrally, tolerating no genuine independence and individual responsibility, and subjecting the entire social order to "reason of State". Centralization may penetrate into every type of State. "Separatism" denotes those tendencies that aim at severing a district (a member State, a province) from the existing State in order to set it up as an independent State or to incorporate it in another State. Such a separation may be justified and even necessary (Q. 115). In practice we usually speak of separatism in connection with a splitting off which forcibly separates natural and historical bonds.

100. What are the rights of the people in democratic States?

The rights of the people in a democratic State are to live in freedom, to co-operate in making decisions and to accept them.

PIUS XII (C. B., 1944; N. C. W. C., pp. 4, 5).

"To express his own views of the duties and sacrifices that are imposed on him; not compelled to obey without being heard – these are two rights of the citizen which in democracy, as its name implies, find their expression. ... that before the State, everyone has the right to live honorably his own personal life in the place and under the conditions in which the designs and dispositions of Providence have placed him."

JOHN XXIII (P. i. T. 31).

As WE know, the French Revolution of 1789 fought for the rights of the people under the slogan of "Liberty, Equality and Fraternity". Each of these concepts has often been misinterpreted, but can be understood in its valid sense.

PIUS XII (C. B., 1944; N. C. W. C., p. 5).

"In a people worthy of the name, the citizen feels within him the consciousness of his personality, of his duties and rights, of his own freedom joined to respect for the freedom and dignity of others. In a people worthy of the name all inequalities based not on him but on the nature of things, inequalities of culture, possessions, social standing – without, of course, prejudice to justice and mutual charity – do not constitute any obstacle to the existence and the prevalence of a true spirit of union and brotherhood."

1. Democracy presupposes a morally and politically mature nation, for it is the people who make the most responsible and the weightiest decisions (in elections and referenda). Hence those entitled to vote must possess at least as much sense of responsibility as will enable them to cast their vote to the good of the common weal and not to its detriment. This requires integrity and political sense, since a number of factors have to be considered, *e.g.*, the suitability of the candidate; his views and programme, trustworthiness of the political parties (their candidates, speakers, press, publications etc.); the (demagogic) influence of political catch words, promises, mass meetings; the effect on relations with neighbouring countries.

Modern democracy is the political expression or form, of the modern consciousness of, and striving after, freedom; hence we speak of "democratic freedom".

2. It follows from what has been said that the education of

citizens to become free and responsible members and supporters of democracy is a chief requirement in every democratic State. The so-called "mass-man" is not a real democrat, but rather an entirely undemocratic type. A growing "mass-mentality" within the nation is likely to lead to the decline of democracy and its transformation into a collectivist, totalitarian system.

3. Pius XII named two basic rights that must be granted to the people in a true and genuine democracy (cf. the text last cited): i. The right to the free expression of opinion, thus, above all, freedom of speech and freedom of the press. By this the pope did not mean unrestricted liberty to say and to write whatever one may think regardless of whether it is true or false, honest or dishonest, likely to promote the common good or to damage it, but rather the right to discuss openly and freely matters that are controversial from a political point of view or that are being demanded of the people. A democracy may not order the people to discharge their duties or make their sacrifices without the right to form their own views, giving honest expression to these views and asserting them in a manner compatible with the common good. ii. The right "not to be compelled to obey without first being heard". This clearly refers to the practice in totalitarian states for the people's representatives merely to express agreement with the government by "acclamation".

101. What are the basic duties of democratic governments?

Democratic governments must:

1. possess true and effective authority;

2. be equal to their task;

3. always be conscious of the fact that they are the representatives of the whole people.

PIUS XII (C. B., 1944; N. C. W. C., pp. 6, 7).

"The democratic State, whether it be monarchical or republican should, like any other form of government, be entrusted with the power to command with real and effective authority.

The deep sense of the principles underlying a political and social order that is sound and conforms to the norms of right and justice is of special importance in those who in any kind of democratic régime have, as the people's delegates, in whole or part, the power to legislate.

To secure effective action, to win esteem and trust, every legislative body should – as experience shows beyond doubt – gather within it a group of select men, spiritually eminent and of strong character, who shall look upon themselves as the representatives of the entire people and not the mandatories of a mob, whose interests are often unfortunately made to prevail over the true needs of the common good . . ."

1. DEMOCRACY is a form of the constitutional State. Therefore those who hold authority, especially government and parliament, must possess adequate authority and power in order to preserve, develop and protect the system in accordance with the basic norms of the constitution. In practice this may give rise to considerable difficulties caused in countries with several political parties.

2. A parliamentary candidate's "suitability" is not simply established in that he is properly nominated by his party. A clear appreciation of the purposes assigned by God to every human society, and moral integrity, experience and intellectual ability are required. It follows that those responsible for proposing and nominating candidates are bound to consider the suitability of the candidates. In a Christian society suitability must also include a genuinely tolerant attitude towards Christianity. Those lacking these qualifications ought not to be elected.

Usually a person gains experience and responsibility in dealing with greater issues by beginning with smaller matters and progressing by stages. This shows the importance of getting as many as possible in the lesser spheres (parish, municipality) to participate in responsible local government and thence learning to judge matters concerning the political life of the nation.

3. Authority must be exercised in the interest of the people. Hence each holder of authority is a representative, trustee and servant of the entire nation, unconditionally obliged so to decide and to act as the common good demands.

But it cannot be taken for granted that the principles, aims and tendencies of a particular political group or party really aim at the common good or will benefit the nation as a whole. The lust for power of individuals or groups (party, opposition) is the worst enemy of the common good.

102. How is popular representation achieved?

Popular representation is nowadays usually achieved on the basis of free, general, direct, equal and secret elections.

1. The representation of the people (parliament) is the supreme authority in a democracy. The government (cabinet and ministries) is formed from those representatives, and it must enjoy their confidence. (Thus in parliament we may have a motion of nonconfidence, or a vote of confidence).

Strength and weakness of democracies thus depend largely on the character and composition of parliament. In order to ensure a good popular representation the constitution or electoral acts must contain appropriate regulations, *e.g.*, concerning the franchise and the competence of parliament, and these regulations must be strictly carried out.

2. In modern democracies the representatives are mostly elected. Accordingly the franchise is guaranteed constitutionally to the people, or to individuals. We distinguish between active suffrage, which is the right to cast a vote, and passive suffrage, the right to be elected, as prescribed by law or constitution. Usually more is demanded for the exercise of the passive than for the active right, *e.g.*, higher age, special qualification etc.

An election, to be meaningful, must produce a result that faithfully reflects the real situation. This result must give expression to the opinion of the electorate. Election results that are settled beforehand, or forcibly arrived at, are obviously a sham.

3. Partly in virtue of the natural law (i), partly in the light of developments, experience and political considerations (ii–v) elections in almost all modern constitutional States are prescribed to be:

i. Free, *i. e.*, without compulsion and hindrance. The electors decide to whom they will give their votes, without detriment to themselves from their decision. Political parties, governments, police forces are not entitled to bring pressure to bear on the electorate. The parties may solicit votes through the spoken or written word and they may present their candidates to the voters. The abuse of the written and spoken word is also contrary to true freedom of election, since it influences the electorate unjustly. It misleads the judgment and may intimidate to such an extent that the intimidated electorate may vote for particular policies or candidates.

ii. General: Every citizen has the right to vote who has reached a certain age and has not been barred because of mental illness or the loss of civil rights. Almost everywhere today both men and women have the franchise. The voting age differs in different countries.

iii. Direct: The members of the first chamber (*e.g.*, the House of Commons) are elected by direct ballot in very many States today, and in many States (where there is a second chamber) also the members of the second chamber. The result of the election is a certain number of members, or deputies. In virtue of their election these are representatives of the people, and not of a party.

iv. Equal: No matter to what class or profession the elector may belong, or how good or bad his political judgment, each has but one vote, and all votes are of equal value. The votes are counted, not weighed. The unequal (graded) franchise is now almost a thing of the past. Only individuals, and not groups, are entitled to vote. The basic political rights are accorded to all without distinction.

v. Secret: Only the voter himself knows the one for whom he has voted. No one else has a right or a possibility of finding this out, unless of course the voter tells him. Voting is done in private, in polling booths. Actually an election need not be secret in order to be "objective", if the voter could, and would, dare to express his conviction publicly. But the secret ballot is necessary in order to ensure freedom of elections.

4. It is a controversial matter which is the best electoral system. This is not just a technical question; there is also a moral aspect. The point at issue is to find that system of voting and of distributing votes which will be just both to the electors and to the

nation. Elections in modern democracies should reflect the political will of the people; they should produce a popular representation that is capable of action. The latter is undoubtedly more important than the former. Hence the principle that that system of election is right which more surely and more effectively guarantees a popular representation that is capable of action. There are two principal systems of election:

i. Election by simple majority in single-seat constituencies. There are only one-seat constituencies, corresponding in number to the number of members (representatives) to be elected. In each constituency any number of candidates may contest the seat, but only one is elected, that is, he who obtains a simple majority of the votes. The advantages of this system are: Clear majorities are obtained; the relation of the elected candidate to his constituency is closer and more personal; the sense of responsibility grows on both sides, since each candidate has to win his seat in personal contest with the others; this system prevents the multiplying of parties, which is a very important matter, because the smaller parties (splinter parties) have little or no prospect of winning seats. The disadvantages are: Considerable sections of the electorate remain without representation; since the government is formed exclusively from the party that wins a majority of the electors, possibly a very large minority has no part in it.

ii. Proportional representation, or the system of lists by single transferable vote or by party list systems which are common in continental Europe. The whole electorate is divided into large constituencies or districts. A definite quota is fixed which must be attained by a candidate if he is to be directly elected. All the "remainder" votes are then collected and credited to the parties on a total list. The candidates on the lists are thus indirectly elected. It is possible for a number of candidates to be directly elected in a single constituency. Parties (lists) are elected, not personalities as such. The advantages of this system are: the popular will is numerically covered, since smaller parties also have prospects of election successes; government (more often than not a coalition) corresponds more to the situation of the popular will. Disadvantages: danger of splinter parties; difficulty and instability of coalition governments, as exemplified in the past in France; little contact between electors and members (representatives); a weakening of the sense of responsibility.

Both systems have their disadvantages, but the system of election by simple majority in single-seat constituencies is to be preferred. In many States there is a combination of both systems that is often quite complicated and not very convincing. Perhaps the system of election most to be preferred is that in which 80–90 per cent of the members are directly elected, and the remaining 10–20 per cent are indirectly elected by way of lists. In this way the parties have the possibility, at least through the main lists, of getting a number of experts elected, who are needed in parliamentary work. If there is a condition to the effect that no party may have more candidates elected by way of the lists than by direct election, then splinter parties are effectively prevented, since their prospects in direct election are very slight.

5. The right to vote brings with it a corresponding duty[49] to vote which is sometimes a serious obligation in conscience. In this connection the following points should be noted:

i. No one may give his vote to those who support a policy that is harmful to the people and the State, and no Christian may vote for those who are hostile to Christianity and to the Church.

[49] In some countries the law makes it obligatory to vote. Cf. Titus Cranny, *The Moral Obligation of Voting* (Catholic University of America Press, 1952).

ii. In many countries Parliament decides matters that must be definitely considered matters of conscience for the electors, for example, education and marriage laws, relation of Church and State (Concordat), recognition or rejection of the principle of private ownership involving such questions as nationalization of land, state control of industry. No person with a sense of responsibility can vote for parties and candidates that disregard his conscience in such matters.

iii. If an election is likely to bring parties to power that do not guarantee basic human and (or) Christian rights, then there is a serious obligation in conscience to take part in the election, and not to vote for such parties, but for others.[50] This is the case for example where there is a possibility of totalitarian, atheistic and militarist parties gaining a majority.

iv. Finally there is a veritable conflict of conscience when the elector is convinced that no party satisfies what must necessarily be demanded of it. On the other hand, he sees clearly that the political situation obliges him to take part in the election. How is the conflict to be resolved? The person in doubt would do well, and is obliged, to obtain the advice of those who are both conscientious and competent to judge. He should consider what would be the effect of abstention. In political matters it is sometimes very difficult to judge, since so many, partly hidden, circumstances are involved.

[50] This principle takes severely to task those who for convenience's sake or through thoughtlessness, because of annoyance or obstinacy, religious indifference or ignorance, class egotism or business considerations and the like, abstain from voting or throw the responsibility on to others and thereby incur the blame for election of the wrong people. Political indifference often is the decisive cause of an election result having disastrous consequences for Church and nation.

103. What is the purpose of political parties?

Political parties in a democracy should:
1. form and express the political will of the people;
2. take a decisive part in the formation and the functions of the organs of government;
3. educate the people to take a responsible part in political life.

1. DERIVED from the Latin *pars,* meaning a part, the very name "party" shows that it is never an end in itself, but must always serve the whole. In spite of their great importance, political parties are not direct organs (parts) of the State, but of the people; they belong to the social sphere. The term "party" also implies, since a part is never the whole, that there must be two or more parties. Thus parties are groups of citizens joined together for political reasons and differing from other similar groupings by their political outlook and aims.

2. Parties are necessary in every genuine democracy, even if the entire nation should acknowledge the moral bases of politics. For political issues to a large extent concern questions of expediency and discretion, on which there may very well be differences of opinion in spite of agreement on basic principles.

EXAMPLES. Basic order of the State: Whether it should have a federal character as in Switzerland, Western Germany, U. S. A., or should consist of a single political unit as in France, Spain, Norway; composition and powers of the organs of Government; whether a policy of alliances or neutrality is to be preferred; national service; relation of Capital and Labour (co-management, nationalization); system of taxation etc.

Rarely do we find a single standard of values and order commonly accepted by a whole nation. Hence it is not surprising that almost everywhere political groups are formed that represent very different political views.

The people in a democracy have the natural right to organize themselves into political parties in order thereby to form and express their political will. Strictly speaking no citizen who is entitled to vote may be denied the right to establish a party. But the State can prevent an unwarranted multiplying of parties, *e.g.*, by its system of election. It is in the nature of political parties that they should recruit members and supporters and seek to canvass as many votes as possible for their candidates in elections. Normally the number of party supporters, that is, those who vote for the party, is considerably greater than the number of inscribed party members.

3. Political parties should fulfil certain basic requirements: i. Their programme and activities should be determined by the needs of the whole society, that is, of the common good of the State; their policies should benefit the nation and not merely the party. ii. It stands to reason that parties must have a positive attitude towards the constitutional basis of the political community. They may seek by constitutional means to remedy deficiencies in the constitution, but a policy of opposition for the mere sake of opposition is to be deprecated. iii. All politics are bound by the principles and precepts of the natural law, directly by those that directly concern political life, and indirectly by those that concern all other forms of life in society. Party programmes and aims ought not to contradict the natural law.

4. The political character of political parties brings us to the question of what are called "ideological"[51] parties among which

[51] By "ideology" we mean a basic outlook or conviction regarding the origin, meaning, dignity and duties of human life, as well as of the political life of the

we include Christian parties, of which there are many in European countries.

i. Strictly speaking "ideological" questions do not lie within the scope of the functions of political parties; rather they are a matter for the conscience of the individual, for religious societies (such as the Church) with a faith and a moral code.

ii. Yet party politics cannot disregard ideologies in so far as political issues ultimately rest on basic ideological convictions, and are necessarily decided in accordance with them. This dependence is greater or less according to the character of the particular issue. For example, the separation of Church and State, nationalization of land and industries, measures of collectivization, will have to be decided in accordance with the parties' views on property, religion and the Church, natural law etc.

iii. The more tradition and the political maturity of the nation enable the political parties to disregard ideological questions and to devote themselves to specifically political questions, that is, the actual requirements and needs of the common good, the better it is.[52]

iv. In countries like Western Germany, Netherlands, Belgium, where political parties used to be orientated by ideologies, it was expedient and even necessary to have parties that were based

nation. The individual derives his conduct from some basic views, and, in accordance with these, decides the nature and degree of his political responsibility and obligation; these basic views will also determine his idea of the functions and limits of the State and of State authority.

[52] For example, where the question of denominational schools, a typical ideological and not a political issue, is well regulated by tradition and custom there is no need for a conflict between denominational and State interests. The same is true regarding the position of man and wife within the marriage and family community.

on a uniform religious faith. Such denominational or "confessional" parties nevertheless were political rather than religious in character. Naturally they were and are guided by the principles of their denomination, but they act neither in the name, nor according to directives, of the Church, but rather on their own political judgment and responsibility, from purely political considerations.

v. Christian parties of an interdenominational character have in many respects to contend with considerable difficulties although at times they may be necessary. Often their rise was due, as in Germany in 1945, after the end of the "Third Reich", to a situation in which Christianity as such was attacked by the (Nazi) State and Christians, who had been persecuted in common, afterwards joined for common political action in the "Christian Democratic Union" (C. D. U.). The fundamental differences that exist between the Christian denominations cannot be ignored; there is no such thing as "general Christianity" (Q. 65). But it should also be recognized how much the Christian denominations have in common.

5. We can now proceed to consider briefly the three points of our answer:

i. Political parties reveal and decide the political thinking and will of the nation; at the same time, they will endeavour to exercise as effective an influence as possible on politics, perhaps in the form of an opposition party. Whether the parties do really reflect the political opinion of the people depends on how far the people are in a position to vote freely.

ii. Since the parties manifest the political will of the people, they have the right to form the popular representation and the Cabinet.

iii. The parties also have an obligation to foster political understanding and responsibility in the country, and to stimulate a greater participation of the people in the affairs of the nation. But more important still than political education is the formation of political sense, and vision in a general sense.

iv. Political parties ought to devote particular care to preparing young people for playing their part in the politics of the future. They ought to train them to look beyond their own country, beyond nationalist concepts, and to try to understand the supra- and international aspects of much in modern politics. They ought to preserve youth from the danger of the herd mentality, the bureaucratic spirit and party egotism. Small discussion groups should be encouraged; also independent tasks suitable for those more advanced in years. It would be desirable to prepare youth gradually to assume political office and functions, and in this way to preserve the party from the domination of the older generation. This will also involve granting material aid for the party's work for youth.

6. The formation of a real political will is only possible when there are several, or at least two, parties. The honest clash between argument and counter-argument leads to the solution of tensions. There are three variants of party composition:

i. The one-party State. Only one single party exists (or is allowed) which thereby loses the character of a genuine party. In some countries, for example in the Soviet Zone of Germany, the other parties are not actually banned, but they are so completely dominated by the one party that they only have a shadowy existence.

ii. The two-party system. Normally only one party will form the government, and the other keeps a strict watch over it.

This system has its obvious advantages, precisely by reason of the mutual control. The governing party knows that it will lose the support of the people if they are disappointed with its methods of running the country (Britain and U. S. A. are typical examples). In this way the political community is more easily protected against government crises than when there are several parties resulting in weak and often short lived government coalitions.

iii. The multiple party system, as it exists in many European democracies. Several political parties contend for power. The nation is divided into many political groups, and it is rare that any one party succeeds in gaining an absolute majority in the elections enabling it to form a government from among its own members. Coalition governments are formed from two or more parties. In many States this is the only way – one might say, the way out – but it has obvious disadvantages: There is the danger of the splinter parties; an evil that has proved disastrous for many a democracy (there were 32 parties in the Weimar Republic). The formation, work and duration of governments are jeopardized on account of the different mentality and the egotism of the parties. Frequent cabinet crises, delay of decisions through long debates in parliament are the results.

7. Some concluding observations on: i. Compromise: political aims are generally the subject of "deals", until finally a result is achieved which has the general consent. Modern democracy cannot get along without compromise; but not every compromise need be a dishonourable betrayal. A genuine compromise is often possible without the surrender of basic political views; and sometimes a tactical compromise may be necessary, when a "lesser evil" is chosen for the time being in order to avoid greater evils. ii. Party discipline: nowadays all parties decide

on a particular position or attitude and oblige their members to support it (by the party whips). It is a matter of necessity that political parties should act as a solid block in seeking to carry through their views and demands. But there are matters that of their nature are not suitable to come under party discipline, for instance matters of conscience for which each individual must give an account to God. iii. Party membership and support: it is not morally lawful, nor is it permissible for reasons of expediency, to belong to a political party that is obviously hostile to religion or to the State, or to support it by voting for its candidates or by material assistance.

B. THE TOTALITARIAN (AND AUTHORITARIAN) STATE

104. *What is a totalitarian State?*

A totalitarian State is one which arrogates to itself unrestricted authority over men, society and all its spheres.

1. THERE have always been exaggerated forms of political power and authority. But their aberrations and claims in the past rarely went as far as denying any higher authority or any binding order of values. The totalitarian State claims an authority without any limitation. This is its primary and most frightful claim. It deliberately and unconditionally places might before right. It is true that totalitarian States base their actions on carefully devised codes of law, which themselves, however, are the result of ideologies that turn the law into an instrument of power and in fact completely ignore the people and their most sacred beliefs. The totalitarian State claims presumptuously to decide what constitutes the only valid goal of life for man. It determines

the norms and means by which this goal is to be attained. It prescribes what men must do or not do without consideration for superior rights and authorities.

2. The totalitarian State degrades man and deprives him of his rights as a person, since it completely subordinates him to its goals and endeavours. The eternal destiny of the individual is repudiated. The totalitarian ideology is altogether secular in character, the individual is a temporal being who exists solely for the purpose of procuring prestige, well-being and expansion for the people. Basically the individual person as such has no rights, since all rights are conferred by the State and at the discretion of its leaders. The power of the State extends beyond external order and reaches into the personal, private life of its citizens. The State may prescribe a particular mental attitude and ideology, regulate the spiritual life of its citizens and order them to abandon their religious beliefs. The individual must form and use his conscience according to what the State thinks and prescribes. The State seeks by every means to enforce its orders. The individual must obey without questioning the lawfulness of what is ordered. In this way the State provides against every independent judgment and every true criticism, against every frustration and delay of its plans and against every intrusion of a higher obligation in conscience.

3. In the totalitarian State the independence of various spheres of interest is increasingly restricted and finally abolished altogether. The principle of subsidiary function is abolished. Centralization grows and finally dominates everything. Local government, *e.g.*, in municipalities, administrative districts, provinces etc. is completely subject to centralized directives. The media of public opinion are either nationalized or placed under the control of

State-censorship. In the totalitarian State there is only one "legitimate" opinion, that of the State or of the party. The national economy must be developed and arranged as the State prescribes. The State has possibilities enough to gain control of industry even without nationalization: through credit loans, armament contracts, subscriptions for State and party purposes etc. Science and learning are not immune from the State's interference; grants may be given only for certain fields of research; university lecturers and their teaching are made to conform.

4. The totalitarian State deprives all independent corporations of their rights, and forces them into its service. Either it intervenes directly in these corporations or it puts pressure on their members, or it pretends to help and to protect these communities. Family life in accordance with natural or Christian claims is rejected. Much is done for the family in totalitarian States that is unfortunately often neglected in other countries, for example, allowances for young married couples and large families; health services; free holidays; free schooling for talented children etc. But all this is done for political reasons, for the sake of the State and not of the family. The totalitarian State considers all education from the kindergarten to the university as its exclusive domain. The goal of its education is a generation subservient to the State, of the same ideological and political bent. Religious societies, the Christian denominations, the Catholic Church above all, are hated by every totalitarian State. The totalitarian State is essentially unchristian and unbelieving, indeed hostile to religion and the Church. No outward profession of Christianity, no treaties with the Church such as were concluded by Fascist Italy, and Nazi Germany can hide this fact. The religious policy of the totalitarian State for tactical reasons often chooses the way of perfidious deception.

5. The totalitarian State has up to now appeared in three forms in history. These three forms differ considerably from one another in respect of their ideology, of their political order and of the power attained by them:[53]

i. Bolshevism (the Soviet Union). It is striving to establish Communism in its most complete form. Lenin and Stalin have in many respects given a new interpretation to Marxism, but they have retained its basic materialistic, atheistic and collectivist ideas (I, Q. 9). The last phase which began during the Second World War is characterized by a pronounced nationalism which nonetheless sticks to the aim of world domination (world imperialism).

ii. National Socialism (Germany). It raised the nation, on a racial and biological basis, to be the all-determining value ("Blood and Soil").

iii. Fascism. It declares the State itself and its government to be the ultimate basic law. Fascism was least given to the excesses of totalitarian power. This was in no small measure due to the undaunted firmness of Pius XI.

105. What are the means used by the totalitarian State?

The totalitarian State unscrupulously uses any means that it deems suitable for its purposes.

1. At the head of the totalitarian State is one omnipotent individual or body. This makes the totalitarian State superior to every democratic State in technique and organization, in so far as uniformity, speed and accuracy of action are concerned.

[53] The totalitarian regimes that have arisen since the second world war have been set up under orders and pressure from Moscow, or at least under its intellectual and political leadership.

2. The totalitarian State is a single-party State. All other parties are either banned or rendered powerless. Party and nation are synonymous entities. The ruling party is regarded as the only valid expression of the popular will; the "irrefutable" proof of this is furnished by compulsory elections and falsified election results. The popular assembly (Parliament) has but to consent to government declarations. The party, hierarchical in structure, is the instrument of the rulers and the government who are not elected, but appointed. The higher party positions are reserved for a carefully selected élite which is supposed to comprise the "best" of the nation. Party education, strict party discipline, party courts and purges are parts of this apparatus. Larger units are formed which are affiliated and subordinated to the party, for example, youth organizations, labour and para-military formations. In this way the party to an ever greater extent intervenes in the life of the people. Membership of the party or party formations as well as political reliability are indispensable conditions for academic careers, professional training and employment.

3. The totalitarian State operates above all by means of propaganda and terror:

i. Propaganda dominates all the channels of communication (Radio, TV, press, films, public meetings) but also individual contacts of the population. The aim is so to control public opinion that finally the people believe only what they are told. Such propaganda deliberately makes use of unworthy and immoral means (open and concealed lying, distortion and falsification of facts, calumny, public confessions of guilt, etc.).

ii. Terror, as applied to the totalitarian State, means the systematic measures of suppression and liquidation that, either by order or with the knowledge of the responsible government, concern any person who is considered dangerous, difficult, unreliable, undesirable etc. Terrorist actions of this kind are possible only under a regime which shamelessly disregards law, morality and decency, despises man as a human person, fears for its own power and future, and has enough followers at its disposal who, from ambition or lust for power, from fear or foolishness, allow themselves to be misused.

A comprehensive system of spying is needed, the function of which is to establish or invent offences and charges of political unreliability. In the end nobody knows any longer who has to denounce whom. For these purposes a secret political police as the principal organ of control and execution is necessary. It operates in secret and according to secret orders, and it possesses almost unlimited powers. Brainwashing, torture, blackmail are used in interrogations, executions are ordered without legal trial. In Russia this secret police force was called successively the Tcheka, OGPU, NKVD, MVD. Nazi Germany had the "Gestapo". Other forms of political terror are concentration camps, "protective custody" which can be worse than a term of imprisonment, since there is no time limit and no legal way of reducing the time or of proving the innocence of the person concerned.

For obvious reasons the totalitarian State restricts the competence of ordinary courts, and transfers certain "crimes" which are considered particularly harmful to the community, to the jurisdiction of special courts, conducted by loyal party followers. The procedure of these courts and their severe sentences for sometimes trivial offences are an affront to any proper administration of justice.

106. What is the result of totalitarian rule?

Totalitarianism is a terrible scourge for any nation and a threat to international peace.

1. The nation is deprived of its most sacred rights and exposed to the fundamental evil of general lawlessness. Law is turned into an instrument of political power; the administration of justice forfeits its independence and is tied to the executive. Freedom is enslaved by the combined pressure of propaganda, spying, party and police rule etc. The general political control of life means that the individual is robbed of doing practically anything without constraint and fear. Education of youth and of the nation is misdirected since the institution of the family is undermined and the whole system of schooling made to conform. The sense of truthfulness, reverence and authority gradually disappears. Whole categories of values are denied or falsified. The nation is subject to an artificial re-grouping of society that does not correspond to its natural and traditional course of development. There is a new upper class recruited especially from the higher party functionaries. In Soviet Russia, where this process was most radically carried out, as also in some of the satellite States and in China, the former classes of the intelligentsia and peasantry were brutally exterminated.

2. International life is constantly threatened by totalitarian States, since they constitute an abiding danger to peace among the nations. This is primarily due to imperialism, that is, the urge to ever greater expansions of power, conquest of the world or at least of whole continents. The totalitarian State is imperialist in principle, either by reason of its ideology aiming at world revolution, or from a presumptuous sense of mission to reform the world. It aims not at peaceful penetration but at the conquest

and enslavement of the nations, economic exploitation, intellectual and ideological subjugation. As a result of this imperialism there are attempts at the open and secret undermining of foreign nations by means of agents, spies, press, radio; remote control of totalitarian parties, etc. Rearmament is accentuated, ostensibly for defence. Imperialist policies hold the world in a state of permanent unrest, and compel other nations to rearm.

The totalitarian State knows no fidelity to treaties. It considers and concludes treaties from a purely utilitarian point of view; they are regarded as no longer binding once they have ceased to suit it (Q. 119).

In its attitude to other nations the totalitarian State uses, when able to do so, methods of violence similar to those employed towards its own people. In occupied countries the results are: measures of extermination, shooting of hostages, transportation to labour and concentration camps, exploitation, collectivization of industry and agriculture, censorship of press and radio; science, learning and education have to conform to the ideology and purposes of the occupying power. Neighbouring States are turned into satellites with similar or identical aims and methods.

3. We refer to "totalitarian" as well as to "authoritarian" States. Often this is a matter of two terms for the same thing. There are those who can see no difference between a totalitarian and an authoritarian State. They say that what is nowadays considered an authoritarian (non-totalitarian) State is merely a new form of dictatorship,[54] or usurpation (Q. 108). It seems to us that there

[54] There are certain false notions about dictatorship. One defines every form of despotic rule, and especially every totalitarian State, as a dictatorship; another attaches to every dictatorship the stigma of illegality, of usurpation of power. Dictatorship is government by emergency rules, or an extension of governmental powers conditioned by an emergency situation, and hence of a tempo-

are in fact States, for example, Spain and more clearly Portugal, that are so new that a new term should be applied to them, and this new term might be "authoritarian" State in contrast to "totalitarian" State. The authoritarian State has two characteristics:

i. It is governed by authoritarian methods. The powers of government are controlled by a single person who wins power either by free elections or by (physical or moral) force. This sole ruler exercises authority according to his own personal judgment and through his own personal decisions. He determines policy; he appoints the ministers who are in the narrower sense his assistants; he commands the police and military forces.

This situation leads to the people being compelled to renounce a part of their political rights. The authoritarian State is necessarily supported by a single authoritarian party; the political formation of the popular will and the people's participation in the government are either impossible or denied, since no genuine functions of government are left to parliament. Political minorities cannot actively engage in politics (neither in the government nor in an opposition which does not exist). There is great danger of an abuse of power because the head of the State[55] by reason of his extensive powers may easily act harshly and oppressively, but also because in spite of the most conscientious exercise of power wrong decisions and serious blunders are more easily brought about.

rary nature; as soon as the emergency is over it ceases to be just (which it may well be by reason of, and during, the emergency). Unless the dictator relinquishes his power, or has it approved by the people, his rule will be subject to other laws that are discussed in Qs. 109–110.

[55] In the sense of political science the authoritarian ruler is not a monarch (king, prince, duke). Therefore, he calls himself Head of the State, President, Prime Minister etc.

ii. The authoritarian State recognizes and respects a higher power and higher rights, the authority and validity of which it may guarantee (authority and rights of God, Church, community of nations). Because, and in so far as it does this it is not totalitarian, for the essence of the totalitarian State consists in this, that it refuses to acknowledge authorities and laws above its own. This subordination to a superior power or to superior rights can only be genuine if the inalienable fundamental rights of the individual and of institutions are preserved and protected (freedom of conscience, right to work and property, family rights).

Lesson Six

RESISTANCE TO THE AUTHORITY OF THE STATE

1. THE question concerning the right and the duty of resistance to the authority of the State is one of the most delicate in ethics.

2. The distinction between "legal" and "legitimate" is important in this issue of resistance. Both terms, which are not always used in the same sense, derive from the Latin *lex,* meaning law; hence both signify "lawful", and, since law is the norm of right, "rightful". We use these terms in the following sense: Legal is that which accords with positive law and with its letter; accordingly illegal is that which departs from the positive law. Positive law comprises both written and unwritten human laws, that is, those laws that are issued by men in virtue of their own authority (Qs. 79/80; I, Qs. 27 and 106). Legitimate is that which is demanded by, or is in accordance with, the natural law. Order, existence and development of the common good rank

higher than the positive law. Accordingly that is legitimate which is necessary for preserving the basic order of the common good even though this may be contrary to the positive law, even though it may be "illegal"; on the other hand illegitimate is that which conflicts with this fundamental order even though it may be legal according to positive law. A "legal" seizure or exercise of power may be quite illegitimate.

3. Resistance to the authority of the State may be passive, when the citizen refuses obedience, or active, when the citizen positively acts against the holders of authority, uses methods that hinder or even overthrow authority. It suffices that the resistance is carried out with moral means.

4. The Catholic Church does not, as is often alleged, reject any resistance against State authority. Witness the encyclical of Pius XI (of March 28th, 1937) on the situation of the Catholic Church in Mexico. The Pope laid down the following principles:

i. Citizens may be entitled and obliged not only to refuse to obey (passive resistance), but "to band together in order to protect themselves and to preserve the State *(nationem)*", which clearly means active resistance. However, it is clear from the context that Pius XI was speaking of active resistance for reasons of self-defence only; thus, in order to be permissible, active resistance may not have the character of direct aggression *(resistentia activa defensiva,* not *aggressiva)*.[56] Thus action is necessary in just self-defence; just self-defence presupposes on the other side, in this case on the government's, an unjust attack or unjust acts of violence.

[56] This was confirmed by the address of Pius XI (14–9–36) to Spanish refugees.

ii. (Catholic) citizens are actually entitled to resist if the legitimate government (this was the case at that time) abuses its power in order "to attack the innate liberties of religion and civil order".

iii. The struggle may not be an end in itself, nor may means evil in themselves be used. Thus through their resistance citizens ought to pursue higher goals. It is now for ethics to establish what actions must be considered "in themselves evil". The pope was unable to lay down a general rule, as the intrinsic rightness or wrongness of an action depends also on the existing circumstances.

iv. The damage caused "to the community and to justice" by resistance must not exceed that which has to be overcome or removed, and the whole undertaking must have prospects of success (Q. 109).

5. Many of those who reject as (morally) unlawful all resistance to State authority base their arguments on the Sacred Scriptures, especially on the words of our Lord in the Sermon on the Mount ... "Resist not evil" (Matt. 5:39), on Christ's own example in offering no resistance, allowing himself to be unjustly arrested, condemned and crucified, and also on St. Paul's admonition, "Thus the man who opposes authority is a rebel against the ordinance of God" (Rom. 13:2). We offer the following comment:

The Old Testament distinguishes between resistance movements that were not in accordance with God's will, for example, those against which the prophet Jeremiah had to fight, and those that were clearly in accordance with God's will; the latter are explicitly praised in the books of Moses, Judges and Machabees.

Regarding the New Testament, it is in almost all cases a very doubtful procedure to attempt to derive the whole wisdom of the Sacred Scriptures from single words and sayings of our Lord. In particular, the New Testament quite clearly commands the individual Christian to obey the rulers of this world (Rom. 13:1ff.; Tit. 3:1; 1 Pet., 2:13ff.). This obedience can only extend to matters in accordance with the natural law and with the revealed will of God, and in which the State is competent. "Render then to Caesar the things that are Caesar's"; clearly not all things are Caesar's. Hence the New Testament indicates that the individual may be obliged to refuse obedience to secular authority (Acts 4:13; 5:29). Our Lord's words: "Resist ye not evil" must be considered within the context of all his sayings. There may be cases when the Christian, for the sake of Christ, should give way to unjust oppressors, handing over his coat and offering the other cheek. But what the individual may be able to do, perhaps be obliged to do, cannot be regarded as a general norm, since this would make an orderly community life quite impossible. The reason why Christ in his passion did not offer resistance to the civil authority was undoubtedly that he willed his passion in order to make amends to the Father for the sins of the world and to redeem men; he freely accepted the chalice which the Father offered him through men. No matter how long the world may last and how the history of mankind may develop, this situation in which Christ was placed by God remains unique; what alone may be compared with it is the vicarious suffering of expiation which someone may take upon himself on account of his belief in Christ and in his imitation. Moreover, we must not forget that Christ did not offer the other cheek to the servant of the High Priest who struck him, but countered with the question of justice: "If there was harm in what I said, tell us what was harmful in it; if not, why dost thou strike me?" St. Paul derived the order of nature and creation from God. Because all authority is from God, secular authority too is from God. This proposition is valid for secular authority as such, but not for every demand of this or that authority. God's will is higher than the will of men, and when men command something that conflicts with God's will, we must refuse to obey. St. Paul himself proved this by his example. The famous passage in Rom. 13:1 ff. was written in order to prevent misunderstandings that might arise among Christians. The Christians, as those "called forth from this world", might think that they were obliged by reason of their election and their faith to obey God and Christ only, but not the secular authority. As against this St. Paul stressed that the Christian has to acknowledge all legitimate authority because it is from God and commands in his name, provided that it does not command anything that is inimical to God.

Since the Sacred Scriptures, in their references to secular authority, are obviously concerned with conditions prevailing at the time, we ought to be very careful in applying these references to our time. The modern problem is of a very different character; it cannot be answered direct from the Sacred Scriptures. It would certainly be going too far to interpret the New Testament to the effect that any active resistance, even armed resistance, to the authority of the State is contrary to the will of God as revealed to us in Christ.[57]

[57] The passage in the Apocalypse 13:1–10, which we cannot discuss here for reasons of space, must also be explained from the context of the Apocalypse as a whole. This book intends to describe how God himself will create order in the final struggles that precede the end of the world. The chief figure of this is God. The question how man as a secondary cause must intervene in the course of world history does not arise, hence it cannot be directly answered from there.

107. When is passive resistance required?

Passive resistance is always required if the State makes demands that are bad in themselves; it is permitted or required under certain conditions if public order is gravely threatened by the State.

I. Bad Laws

1. "Bad in themselves" means objectively, intrinsically bad. There is no ground that could make such an action good and honourable. Certainly the individual's appraisal matters considerably. He must be himself convinced that he may not, under any circumstances, do a certain action and this conviction will be influenced by his beliefs or information or lack of them. However, there are certain factors of general validity: there are crimes that are so heinous that ignorance never excuses them, for example, murder, *i.e.,* the deliberate, direct killing of an innocent person. Even when the worst is to be feared one may not obey if one sees clearly that the order is bad in itself. The ability to foresee possible consequences cannot remove responsibility; yet it may, if coupled with great fear, cloud judgments and considerably lessen voluntary consent, and thus the measure of guilt.

2. It is justifiable and necessary to appreciate all the excusing reasons that may exculpate man in general (I, Q. 19) and modern man in particular. But not everything that is done on the orders of a given authority can be excused. We cannot apply to Christian nations standards that may be proper for nations that have never come in contact with Christianity and with Western civilization. Men cannot expect to be released from their

dilemma simply by passing on responsibility for crimes and atrocities to those who order them and not to those who execute them.

EXAMPLES. Issuing and executing orders to kill; extorted confessions concerning crimes that were never committed; spying for the purpose of denunciation; blasphemy. To Catholics, in addition, would apply: denial of the faith, blaspheming Christ, the Cross, and the Sacraments; divorce of the marriage bond; abortion; education of children in unbelief.

II. Serious Threat to Public Order

Civil authority exists to preserve order. Where it fails to do this, although in a position to do it, it offends against the common good; it abuses its powers and commits an injustice which is the more serious the more it infringes or destroys public order. The citizens are often justified in parrying or overcoming such injustice by passive resistance, and may even be obliged to do so. They are responsible for their common good and may not suffer serious damage to be done to the common good. According to Catholic teaching, passive resistance is permissible under these conditions:

1. The welfare of the community must be endangered considerably; not every inappropriate and even unjust measure of the government makes passive resistance permissible.

EXAMPLES. Gross defects or delay in legislation; completely inadequate economic and social policy; a foreign policy that endangers the State; using the danger of war irresponsibly as a means of policy.

2. The people must first of all try to remedy the evil in a constitutional way. Passive resistance is a kind of revolt that is only

permissible when constitutional means are exhausted or cannot be employed because the government terrorizes the people or rejects negotiations, complaints, proposals etc.

3. There must be human certainty that the outcome will be successful. If it is certain that the only result will be new and greater setbacks for the common good, there is no point in resisting; for example, if terror is intensified, if innocent people are endangered, if vital supplies for the people are rendered impossible, as might happen in a general strike.

The question as to when resistance is permissible and necessary cannot be resolved like a mathematical equation. The matter must first be weighed very conscientiously. Resistance demands a sense of responsibility and courage. Although passive resistance does not oppose force to force, but remains "passive", it may, nevertheless, be effective and even achieve considerable success. Passive resistance often inevitably takes on the form of active resistance, if only because it has to be organized in order to be effective. The best example is the strike. But the strike must be prepared, directed, perhaps even enforced and protected; here we have the active element (cf. Q. 109).

108. How are citizens in a totalitarian State to conduct themselves?

Because of the totalitarian State's terrible and constant abuse of power, its subjects must very carefully consider when, and to what extent, they may obey.

A TOTALITARIAN State pursues evil goals and brooks no opposition. This leads to the serious question whether the individual ought to desist from any kind of co-operation. Ultimately, everything that is done for the totalitarian State is abused, and every kind of co-operation down to the paying of taxes, the "voluntary" contribution, the indispensible subscription to the party newspapers, contributes towards supporting it. Yet those who do not go along with the others or even resist, endanger their own livelihood, bring the greatest dangers on themselves and on their families, are considered "dangerous elements", "enemies of peace"; they will be persecuted with loss of position and income; concentration camps, torture, and frequently loss of life are their fate.

I. Basic Considerations

1. Strong spiritual and moral ties bind the individual to his people and his native land. For this reason it is both an honourable and sacred duty for one who loves his country to co-operate to the best of his ability so that adverse and unworthy conditions may cause as little harm as possible.

2. The God-given goals of the State remain in force even when a government betrays them and establishes a despotic rule of terror. There are plenty of jobs that simply must be done in the interest of the common good, and that do not lose the true and good meaning they have in themselves even when the authorities make them serve wrong purposes.

3. The people are obliged to observe the just laws of the State (Q. 80). Only a small part of the people can emigrate when conditions are odious. The rest must needs do many things that may well be abused, but which in the first instance contribute to the preservation of the nation and the State. The citizens may do these things with the sole intention of serving order and the common good.

4. We must not forget the intricate, indeed hopeless position of individuals as well as of the people as a whole. Who has the right to demand that everyone oppressed by an ungodly State *must* expose himself to disaster? The situation differs considerably, i. according to the stage which the totalitarian State has reached; ii. according to the possibility of recognizing the true aims of such a State; iii. according to the state of mind of the people, due to terror and propaganda and possibly also to the attitudes of foreign powers.

5. Undoubtedly everyone must co-operate in preserving the nation and youth from the harmful spirit and the wrong decisions of the totalitarian State. But this will mostly have to be done in secret, "underground". It is easier to withdraw completely from public life and to leave this dangerous underground agitation to others. But the question is, what is right? It is often presumptuous to condemn "collaboration", especially if one happens to do so from the safety of another country. The virtue of prudence (I, Q. 40) which combines realism with courage and responsibility will have to dictate what is right in each individual case.

II. Some Detailed Considerations

1. It can hardly be right to join the supreme organs of a totalitarian State. In accepting high office one would have to identify oneself completely with its aims. It is sometimes argued that, for instance, ministerial appointments could be held if the person concerned has the courage uncompromisingly to voice his objections and to enlighten the public, and if he firmly refuses any participation in harmful decisions, and makes use of his position to work for a change in the situation or indeed for the overthrow

of the regime. But it is questionable whether such intentions can be realized in the totalitarian State.

2. No one may engage in an activity that will necessarily lead to evil actions. How easily this can happen is shown by the following.

EXAMPLES. Those in charge of camps may find themselves responsible for the carrying out of severe penalties. Doctors in Nazi Germany, who were in leading positions as heads of hospitals and clinics, had to carry out laws of euthanasia, to destroy "worthless lives", in other words, to commit murder. German judges had to pass sentences "according to instructions" and to extort confessions by inhuman methods. There are writers and scientists prepared to place their intellectual gifts at the disposal of a criminal regime.

3. Those whose profession continually puts them in danger of having to betray their conscience will have to take up another occupation. There are circumstances in which this may not be feasible, and in such a case the person may continue in his profession as long as he is able to evade instructions that clearly conflict with his conscience. But if every way out is blocked he will have to give up his profession and bear the consequences with heroic resignation.

EXAMPLES. Teachers compelled to educate youth in a sense hostile to God and to Christ. Doctors who cannot avoid having to perform operations or give treatment that are not permissible on any grounds, for example, the killing of prenascent life or of the mentally deranged; giving injections and drugs that deprive the individual of any will of his own for the purpose of putting him completely at the mercy of the courts. Judges and magistrates who are no longer able to hold out against having to give obviously unjust decisions.

109. When is active resistance permissible against the State?

In very grave national emergencies that cannot be overcome either by constitutional means or by passive resistance, active resistance is permissible if:

1. there is a prospect of success;

2. the common good will not suffer still greater harm.

1. THERE are natural rights and natural norms of order that always remain valid even when they are infringed or denied. The people must resist when against all natural and divine right they are deprived of their most basic rights. A people, too, may find itself in a position when action in just self-defence is necessary.

2. Only extreme emergencies of the common good can entitle to active resistance. It is the ultimate means of self-defence.
3. Active resistance is permissible only when there would seem to be a prospect of success. But success cannot be calculated; it can be predicted only with more or less probability. Active resistance is thus always a definite risk, but it should never be a foolhardy rash action.

4. Active resistance is not permissible if the situation would not thereby be improved but would be worsened. For in any case it will be accompanied by grave disturbances and sacrifices.

5. Catholic ethics unanimously teaches that a moderate despotic government can be tolerated, and that against it the only permissible form of rebellion is a passive or active resistance by moral means. In view of the terrible actions of modern totali-

tarian States, many Catholic moralists would support active armed resistance in the last resort.

They argue that no holder of authority, which may even be a constitutional and legitimate authority, is above the law. There is a higher law to which all men are subject, and there are the claims of truth, humanity and justice that cannot be rejected. An authority that criminally destroys these values and this order of the common good ceases to be legitimate. It turns into an unjust aggressor against whom the nation may revolt. But it must be clear beyond all doubt that the government without any consideration or scruple are driving the people to moral or physical ruin. An example is the continuation of the last war by the Nazi leaders for the sake of prolonging their own power.

6. Who has a duty to active resistance? Strictly speaking, the nation, for it is its deliverance or preservation, well-being and future that are at stake. But the nation needs leadership, since of itself it is not capable of united action. Besides the nation is often enough divided in itself. Hence it is almost always necessary for individuals or groups to take up the cause of the common good, *i. e.*, of the whole nation. The person who by reason of a responsible position and of (military) power which he can marshal possesses the better insight and the greater possibilities of action must consider himself – before others – to be thus called upon.

7. Active resistance that employs merely moral means can more readily be permitted than armed resistance, since there are usually fewer risks involved.

EXAMPLES. Organizing mass demonstrations and protests, when irresponsible government action appears to lead to war; when the duty of providing for impoverished classes or sections of the people is obviously being grossly neglected; when there is only inadequate government action against the spread of public immorality; when the economic policy of the government is clearly destroying instead of ensuring the well-being of the nation; when the State disregards parental rights and refuses denominational schools although the parents, having the right to educate, demand it (school strike).[58]

8. The people are entitled to reject a government that is completely incompetent or that gravely abuses its power, and those holding authority are in duty bound to resign. Should a dictator refuse to resign, the people cannot be denied the right to compel his resignation even by force. Both complete incompetence to govern as well as the grave abuse of powers are cases of extraordinary emergency. If the abuse of power gives rise to an endless negation of rights, an extreme situation will have come about, which entitles the nation as well as individuals to cause to be done or to do, what is indispensably necessary, to remedy the affliction.

EXAMPLES. Incurable mental derangement of a king; complete indifference to warnings that the welfare of the State is at stake.

9. The people may defend themselves with armed force against individuals or groups that are about to usurp power illegally and thus to gain control of the State. The usurping body has no legal grounds for claiming power; nor is there an extreme

[58] The question of strikes on political grounds has been much discussed recently. On the Catholic as on the non-Catholic side, it is maintained by many that such a strike is always immoral and unlawful. But I fail to see why the political strike should be morally wrong in itself, *i.e.,* in every case, why it should conflict with the natural law. After all, it is conceivable, for example, that a government may be pursuing a completely unsocial economic policy, or denying fundamental rights and that a change cannot be brought about through Parliament; or that a government may pursue an insane war policy, and that it may be possible, by means of a general strike, to prevent the achievement of its aim.

national emergency that would justify such a rebellion (Q. 110). The usurping body is solely concerned with the attainment of power. It disregards the supreme political right of the nation to decide itself under what form of rule it wishes to live and who should rule over it. For this reason such an usurpation has the character of an unjust aggression. Any individual in the nation may prevent it, and in doing so may kill the attacker if necessary.

110. Is revolution justifiable?

A revolution is justifiable only as the ultimate means of just self-defence.

EVEN in this qualified form the opinion represented here can not be described as *the* Catholic teaching. Even today many Catholic moralists completely reject revolution as a permissible form of just self-defence. They regard passive resistance or patient endurance and trust in divine providence to be the only attitude that a Christian may adopt even under extreme duress. However, our opinion has the support of, among others, Cardinal Ottaviani who wrote: "National leaders and nations that possess the certainty that their governments are aiming at war and thus preparing the bloody ruin of the nation may, and must, overthrow the government by just means."[59]

1. We cannot here examine the unhappy or happy consequences of various revolutions in history. We can only discuss in principle whether, and on what conditions, a revolution is permissible. There are several forms of revolution:

i. Violent revolution when the government is overthrown by armed force, and usually a new form of State is introduced,

[59] A. Ottaviani: *Institutiones iuris publici Ecclesiastici,* Rome, vol. 1. p. 155.

thus, for example, a republic instead of a monarchy. The entire political order is forcibly changed; a new State arises. (French Revolution, 1789; the Russian Revolution, 1917; Spain, 1935).

ii. Revolution by non-violent means, nowadays also described as assumption or seizure of power, national rising. The existing government is replaced by a new one in a "legal" (constitutional) way. A political party, or a coalition of parties, comes to power and utilizes this situation in order to dominate the State and to change it so radically that in fact a completely different political order of State is brought about; for example a republic may be changed into a dictatorship. Often the former name is retained as in the case of Russia which retains the name USSR (Union of Socialist Soviet Republics) although there is no longer any democratic self-government.

iii. The word "revolution" continues to be used also in a social sense, as opposed to "reaction" or mere "restoration" movements. This implies a transformation of the entire social and economic, not just of the political order. History shows that most revolutions have been followed by grave disturbances and civil wars, with considerable physical and material sacrifices. Even revolutions by peaceful means often lead to bloodshed. An extremely grave responsibility rests on those who instigate and lead revolutions.

2. It can obviously never be justifiable to unleash a bloody revolution from frivolous or selfish motives. This would be a crime against the nation, the common good. Lust for power, the mere rejection, in principle, of particular forms of government (for instance, of monarchy or democracy), personal feelings of dissatisfaction, the mere conviction that another government might be preferable – such motives can never justify vio-

lent revolution. In all these cases the primary and most important condition is lacking, which is, that "the rulers evidently oppose truth and justice to such an extent that they undermine the very foundations of authority" (Pius XI). In such cases the subjects would not be fighting to maintain sacred rights that were being withheld or taken from them.

3. An assumption of power would be "legal" if it comes about in a constitutional manner and adheres to the constitution in the exercise of authority. Such an assumption of power could only come to be "legitimate" if thereby the common good and basic political rights in particular were to be guaranteed, and if there was no violation of the Constitution. But the case is very different if the new government, elected democratically, immediately proceeds by dishonest means to subdue Parliament and extort from it unlimited powers that could never have been obtained by honest means. Such a government could hardly ever become legitimate and what may well appear to be constitutional in the government's way to power can be wrong from the point of view of the natural law.

4. Only if the well-being of the State is actually threatened by complete ruin or has already been destroyed, and provided there are no other possibilities, can it be justified, we believe, to aim at, and to effect, a change of government, and, if absolutely necessary, a change in the form of State, by violent revolutionary means. It is thus a question of ultimate possibilities of just self-defence in case of extreme necessity.

111. Can murder be permitted for political reasons?

Murder can never be permitted, not even for political reasons or in order to remove a tyrant.

1. This raises the old controversial question whether tyrannicide is permissible.[60] This issue has again become topical through totalitarian regimes in our time. Our problem is whether individuals or groups, without being expressly empowered by competent authority, may consider themselves justified in killing a tyrant on their own responsibility. Can a despot commit such grave crimes against his people that anyone may be entitled, in conscience, to rid the nation of him? We assume that the murder is not motivated by personal revenge or enmity, but solely by the desire to help the nation in extreme necessity.

2. Most Catholic moralists reject as not permissible and as immoral in itself such a "private" homicide of a despot. They hold that this is murder, irrespective of the criminality of the regime, its threat to peace within and without the country.[61]

They base their opinion on four principal arguments:

[60] For the distinction between murder, which is always wicked, and permissible homicide, cf. Qs. 42 and 90.

[61] There are Catholic moralists who would defend the opinion that in present-day circumstances it is quite possible for somebody to be tacitly deputed to carry out an act of self-defence to which the nation is entitled, but of which it is incapable through terror. They argue that there are modern dictators who are deliberately driving their State and nation to ruin. What they are doing is obvious to all who can use their eyes to see. Such dictators have forfeited their lives a thousand times over, and the nation is without any doubt entitled to have them condemned and executed. But the nation is powerless; it cannot repel the criminal attack on itself. These dictators may no longer be considered lawful holders of State authority. They have, through their own fault, forfeited the right to govern. But since the nation cannot save itself, anyone who is in a position to do so may take over its deliverance, that is, as executor of the national will he may lawfully and justly kill the ruler, provided i. there is no other way out; ii. that the matter will not entail still greater sacrifices. An improvement of the situation must be foreseeable. There is thus a distinction between the murder of a despot, which can never be justifiable, and the killing of a despot, which may be permissible on the conditions mentioned.

i. The right over life and death belongs to God alone; from him this right is handed on to the legitimate authority of which he is the direct author, and which alone may impose the death sentence. No one may assume a tacit commission, since this would merely be the presumption of an authority to which he has no right. The abuse of authority alone by one who lawfully possesses it does not deprive him of the authority itself. Consequently such a tyrant must be tolerated in the common interest.

ii. Even the nation as a whole has not the right to kill a legitimate despotic ruler. Hence no one can appeal to a commission from the people; because a people can neither expressly nor tacitly transfer a right which it does not itself possess.

iii. If the private killing of a tyrant were permissible no one could foresee the possible consequences which might well be worse than the evil it was intended to remove. There would be no check on political passion and arbitrariness, and public order and security which will always depend upon men who are not perfect men would *a priori* become impossible.

iv. The nation is always at least partly to blame for its being oppressed and tortured by a tyranny. It must therefore accept its fate in some way as God's punishment for its fault.

Part Four

The International Political Order

The Community of Nations and States

1. NATIONS and national groups, States and State structures throughout the world are becoming increasingly inter-dependent. With this in mind we must ask whether the political order that exists within the individual States is sufficient or whether a higher political order to which all States and nations are responsible is necessary? What ought this structure to look like?

2. International life is exposed to numerous and diverse, often evil and disastrous tensions, complications and conflicts. They may be due to national honour or jealousy, lust for territorial aggrandisement, economic rivalry and envy, claims to world domination, breaches of treaty and political murder. We have only to think of modern warfare (Q. 130) in order to realize that a comprehensive and stable order that would guarantee peace to the world is absolutely necessary (Q. 113).

3. Cf. the important addresses of Pius XII on "Coexistence"; C. B., 1954; 8th Oct. 1955; C. B., 1956.

Lesson One

THE COMMUNITY OF NATIONS AND INTERNATIONAL LAW

112. *What are the nations in relation to one another?*

According to God's plan the nations of the world constitute one large single family whose goal is the "good of all nations".

PIUS XII (S. P.; C. T. S., p. 29).

"Mankind, by a divinely appointed law, is divided into a variety of classes; by the same law, it is divided into a variety of peoples and States. These do not depend on one another, so far as the ordering of their internal affairs is concerned. But they are bound by mutual obligations in law and in moral right; they form a vast community of nations, which is designed to promote the general good of the race. They are governed by special rules, which preserve unity amongst them and advance, from day to day, their happiness."

PIUS XII (C. B., 1942; C. T. S., p. 4).

"God is the First Cause and ultimate ground, the Creator of the first married pair, which is the source from which all society – the family, the nation, and the association of nations – takes its rise."

PIUS XII (C. B., 1948; U. A. vol. 1, p. 93).

"The Catholic doctrine on the State and civil society has always been based on the principle that, in keeping with the will of God, the nations form together a community with a common aim and common duties."

1. NATIONS, States, may agree among themselves to form a definite community (Q. 113). But prior to such unions established by men there is the natural community of nations, the "family of nations" in the divine plan. All mankind share the same origin, it derives from God. Human nature is common to all men (I, Q. 12); all have the same ultimate natural and supernatural goal, namely, to perfect themselves in tending towards God and to find their eternal happiness in God (I, Qs.15 and 18).

2. The goal of this family of nations is "the good of all nations".[1] This implies that i. every nation has its place and its rights within the family of nations (Q. 115); ii. that a natural solidarity exists among the nations from which results the natural duty to complement and to help each other; iii. that the good of all nations is attained by each nation making its own quest for humanity, and all together in sincere and unselfish co-operation providing that which the single nation lacks or cannot accomplish by its own energy.

113. What is man's present international obligation?

Man's present international obligation is to bring about as soon as possible the creation of an ordered community of nations empowered and strong enough to ensure international well-being and peace.

IN OTHER words an "organized" community of nations must be established as soon as possible, that is to say, the existing one must be further developed and consolidated.[2]

[1] The community of nations established by men and organized in a specific form also has the good of all nations for its natural goal and function (Q. 113).

[2] In order to avoid repetition and misunderstanding the term "community of nations" will henceforth be used in the sense of *organized* community of

PIUS XII (C. B., 1944; N. C. W. C., p. 12).

" . . . all things considered, there is only one way of getting out of the meshes in which war and hate have wrapped the world, namely a return to the solidarity, too long forgotten, a solidarity not restricted to these or those peoples, but universal, founded on the intimate connection of their destiny and rights which belong equally to both."

PIUS XII (C. B., 1951; U. A. vol. I, p. 121).

"And here we have in mind primarily the family and the State, as well as the society of States, since the common good, the essential purpose of every State, cannot be attained or even imagined without this intrinsic relation of the States to the human race as a whole. Under this aspect the indissoluble union of States is demanded by nature."

JOHN XXIII (P. i. T. 47-52).

1. That this obligation exists is clear from the following three reasons:

i. The *natural* community of nations compels the nations to give an appropriate practical form to their mutual relations and fellowship; for this natural community is too indefinite to be capable of action.

ii. Modern progress has made the world "smaller" and brought the nations closer. Population problems, the mass media of modern communication and information, cultural dependence have contributed to the "one world".

iii. The rise and growing strength of big powers that clearly aim at world domination, and the terrible threat of nuclear war require an organized community that will guarantee peace and protect man from himself.

nations; where the term is employed to denote the *natural* community of nations this will be expressly stated.

PIUS XII (Address of 6 April, 1951; U. A. vol. I, p. 250).

"Your movement dedicates itself to realizing an effective political organization of the world. . . . It is necessary therefore to arrive at an organization of this kind, if for no other reason than to put a stop to the armament race in which, for decades past, the peoples have been ruining themselves and draining their resources to no effect."

2. The form (organization, constitution) of such a community of nations is not defined by nature; it must be found and freely agreed upon by men themselves. That form is right which most effectively guarantees the well-being and the peace of the world, as also the basic liberties both of individuals and of States:

i. For various reasons a world State (with a world Parliament) must be rejected as a suitable form. The great number and diversity of nations, political views, cultures, living standards and ways of life do not seem to favour it. The demand for a world State cannot be inferred from the specific unity of human nature, because the individual differences and difficulties must also be taken into account.

ii. The hypothesis of one single major power assuming world domination, *i.e.*, subjugating all nations and imposing its will on them is to be condemned completely. No nation on earth has a right to this (Qs. 114/115).

iii. There remains some kind of federation or confederation of nations to which individual States can belong without losing their independence and individuality.

PIUS XII (Address of 6 April, 1951; U. A. vol. I, p. 250).

"You are of the opinion that this world political organization, in order to be effective, must be federal in form. If by this you understand

that it should not be enmeshed in an artificial uniformity, again you are in harmony with the principles of social and political life so firmly founded and sustained by the Church. Indeed, no organization of the world could live if it were not harmonized with the whole complex of natural relations, with that normal organic order which rules the particular relations between men and men, between different peoples. If it does not do that, then, no matter what its structure may be, it will not be able to stand up and endure."

3. What matters is that an organized community of nations must possess the necessary authority and means to fulfil its function. It has a natural right to this:

i. Whatever exceeds the competence of individual nations (States), and whatever has to be done so that order may prevail among the nations, necessarily falls within the functional orbit of this community; thus the preservation of world peace, the protection of human rights, the promotion of international co-operation in the economic (commercial) and cultural fields.
ii. The organized community of nations, described by Pius XII as a "world authority", ought to enjoy not just formal, but genuine sovereignty of a legislative, juridical and executive kind (Q. 68).

4. This means:

i. The community of nations has the right to its own constitution, but also to issue laws and decrees to be obeyed by its own members and in fact by all States throughout the world. These laws would be a basis of genuine international law (Q. 118).

ii. Order and peace cannot be achieved without jurisdiction. There must be a body authorized by the community of nations to give judgments that have to be obeyed as being legally valid and that, if necessary, must be imposed by force. Such an international court of justice (or whatever it might be called) has to settle disputes (court of arbitration), hear charges concerning the infringment of human rights, and clear up doubts concerning the laws issued. It, or another body, would decide when and where sanctions (reprisals) or "police action" should be employed against this or that power in order to prevent, or to end, armed conflict.

iii. World peace will never be made secure without an international armed force. If this force is to serve its purpose it must be sufficiently strong and mobile to be employed anywhere and at any time. But this requires the nations to disarm, that is, to content themselves with small security forces sufficient to preserve internal order and to defend the country against an attack from without until the international armed forces can intervene. The international armed forces would then merely need to have the character and the strength of a police force for the preservation of international order; there would be no need for huge armies with tank divisions, bombing squadrons and nuclear missiles.

5. It is not inconsistent with the community of nations for States to form alliances among themselves, or for States that are closely related to form groups, or blocks, *i.e.*, associations on a larger scale, confederations of States that are closely linked by geographical position, by common traditions and cultural development, by similar political ideals (democracy), and that are able to help one another to promote their common interests. But all contracts and alliances (pacts, confederations) of this kind are only admissible so far as they are consistent with the goals, principles and existing state of the community of nations. Here we might distinguish two stages of development:

i. As long as mankind is but groping for an organized community of nations, pacts or alliances of this kind may be necessary and unavoidable (NATO).

ii. Once the community of nations has been fully established, all alliances of a military nature will become superfluous; agreements and associations would then be entered into exclusively for peaceful purposes.

6. In the concluding part of his Christmas broadcast (1940) on conditions for a new world order Pope Pius XII spoke of a five-fold victory as an indispensable basis for a world order of peace:

i. "victory over the hatred which divides the nations today";

ii. "victory over suspicion which . . . causes breaches of international agreements" (Q. 117); iii. "victory over the disastrous principle that . . . might can create right"; iv. "victory over those potential conflicts arising out of the imbalance of the world economy" (Q. 117); v. "victory over the kind of egoism which, relying on its own power, aims at impairing the honour and liberty of individuals."

7. In the twentieth century, principally as a result of the two world wars, two big efforts have been made to establish a comprehensive community of nations; in 1919 the League of Nations, in 1945 the United Nations Organization (UNO) were founded.

i. The League of Nations, whose constitution comprised 29 articles, and in which several international organizations *(e.g.,* the International Labour Office) were incorporated, foundered because there was no firm conception of law, no genuine and effective authority, and because the leading nations participated insufficiently.

ii. The United Nations Organization represents an important step forward, yet it is far from being the ideal community of nations. Its principal organ is the Security Council, the decisions of which are considerably restricted by the veto which each of the major powers represented on it possesses; in this way any one major power can thwart and frustrate all its decisions.

114. *Who belongs to the community of nations?*

The community of nations is formed from independent States which are its members with equal rights.

PIUS XII (C. B., 1948; U. A. vol. I, p. 93).

"The Catholic Christian, persuaded that every man is his neighbour and that every nation is a member, with equal rights, of the family of nations . . ."

PIUS XII (Address of 6 April, 1951; U. A. vol. I, p. 251).

" . . . so also it will enjoy effective authority only in so far as it safeguards and encourages everywhere the life that is proper to a healthy human community, to a society in which all the members co-operate together for the well-being of the whole of humanity."

1. For nations to become States they must be in possession of a legal and political structure (Q. 63). As organized political units they constitute the actual members of the community of nations; for the latter is nothing other than a supra-national, political structure. Hence it would be more proper to speak of a community of States. The establishment of the organized community of nations is the duty of all the States, but particularly of those States that by reason of their vision, prestige and power are in a

position to undertake it. Every State that recognizes the necessity must seek ways and means of having the "constituent assembly" convoked as soon as possible.

2. Once it is established every State in the world is obliged: i. to join the community of nations as a member; ii. to accept and to carry out its rules, aims and decisions;[3] iii. to co-operate in preparing the community of nations for its world-wide tasks.

This obligation is based on the natural solidarity of the nations (Q. 112). Every State is obliged to help in promoting the common good of the human family. The community of nations itself is obliged to grant membership to all States that have given sufficient proof of their aptitude and willingness for sincere co-operation. Defeated nations ought not to be refused admission, while "victor" nations that are continually causing grave unrest in the world and frustrating every decision by their veto play a leading role in the community of nations.

Smaller States have a special importance; as they often are genuinely interested in peace and averse to imperialism of any kind, they can do much in the way of mediation and balancing of interests.

3. The community of nations is based on the equality of States. In other words, States are members of the community of nations with equal rights. This does not mean that all have the same importance, that all States are entitled to the same number of seats and votes, for example, that every State, whether great or small, should have one seat and one vote, as is the case in UNO. Proportions of size and power should be expressed and made

[3] We are assuming that our community of nations would recognize the natural law (Q. 118) and would not unduly restrict the sovereignity of the States (Qs. 114/115).

effective in a manner which would serve the common good of the community of nations. By equal is implied:

i. All members are entitled to the recognition, preservation and protection of those fundamental rights which are essential to a sovereign State, for example the right to exist and to develop, to manage its own affairs, and to be unrestricted in peaceful relations with the community of nations (Q. 115).

ii. All States have a claim to be recognized as full members of the community of nations. There may be mandatory territories and colonies, that is, dependent political units, that cannot acquire full membership (Q. 10). But independent States ought to have more than a consultative voice.

iii. Powers ought to be so balanced that a genuine community can develop and the decisions taken will really be the decisions of the community, and not the extortions, impositions and claims of particular States or groups of States.

iv. There must be no preference. The interpretation and application of established law must not be made dependent on whether it was a great or a small power that has broken treaties, infringed human rights, sown dissension among the nations, rearmed in contravention of agreements and laws, threatened war or actually begun a war of aggression.

4. Pius XII stressed that the "real and effective authority" of the community of nations in relation to member States must be such that "each of them retain an equal right to its relative sovereignty" (C. B. 1944, N. C. W. C., p. 9). This implies that each State must renounce part of its sovereignty.[4] This demand

[4] On the concept of sovereignty cf. Q. 67.

is obvious; for if the member States should continue to determine everything independently – even within the framework of international law – there could be no community "with real and effective authority". On the other hand member States must not become mere parts or members of one all-embracing State claiming all sovereign rights. States ought therefore to renounce those sovereign rights which, if the peace and welfare of the world are to be secured, should belong to the community of nations alone. An exact list of these rights cannot be drawn up, but we can say, nevertheless, that member States should not be entitled: i. to decide on war or peace, or to determine by their own choice the strength and equipment of their armed forces. Manufacture and delivery of war weapons should be subject to the regulations and the control of the community of nations (Q. 125); ii. to make pacts and alliances among themselves which in the judgment of the community of nations endanger world order and peace; iii. to hinder their subjects and member States from bringing complaints, concerning, for example, the infringement of human rights, before the community of nations; iv. to object when the community of nations itself sends a delegation to direct, control or examine some particular issue, *e.g.*, elections or complaints, whether some territory has developed sufficiently to become a sovereign State; control of atomic weapons.

The community of nations should in a new and higher form fulfil the conditions for the political, *i. e.*, the "perfect", community (Q. 60). It should be the all-inclusive political order. At the same time it should be related to its member States in a truly subsidiary capacity (I, Q. 52). It should only take over those functions that directly and properly concern the well-being and the peace of the world, and hence that transcend the domain of individual States.

5. Concerning the pope's position in international law we note that Christ has appointed him supreme head of his Church and invested him with full spiritual authority over the Church; it is his duty to interpret the natural law which must form the basis for any genuine international law (Q. 117, No. 4). The pope is thus not an organ of international law or of the community of nations, but rather an organ of God in the service of international law; he is "above" the community of nations.

As a universal religious community the Catholic Church derives her existence not only from divine institution, but also from the common human right of free association; hence she has a natural claim to be a subject of international law. This claim also belongs to the pope, independent of his being sovereign head of a State. The pope is thus a subject of international law in a double capacity, as temporal sovereign, and as supreme head of the universal Catholic Church.

115. What is the right of national self-determination?

The right of national self-determination means:
1. that the population of a territory may itself determine whether it wishes to form a State of its own, or to belong to another State;
2. that no State has a right to interfere unduly in the affairs of another State (non-intervention).

WE ARE now concerned with the former definition. The right of national self-determination was one of the 27 points of the American President Wilson, of essential importance both for the League of Nations and the United Nations Organization.

PIUS XII (C. B., 1941; C. T. S., pp. 9, 10).

"Within the framework of a new order based upon moral principles,

there is no room for the violation of the freedom, integrity, and security of other nations, whatever be their territorial extent or their capacity for defence. ... there is no room for the suppression, be it open or covert, of the cultural and linguistic traditions of national minorities; for the obstruction or restriction of their economic capacity; or for the limitation or the destruction of their natural resources. The more conscientiously the competent authority of the State respects the rights of minorities, the more confidently and effectually will it be able to demand from their members the loyal discharge of those civic duties which they have in common with the other citizens."

JOHN XXIII (P. i. T. 36-38).

1. If the popular will is decisive for the origin and existence of the State (Q. 74), it logically follows that racial groups or parts of the population that wish to form an independent State of their own have, strictly speaking, the right to do so. Hence they should not be prevented either from remaining part of the State in which they have hitherto been incorporated, or from separating from it as they wish and intend.[5] However, this demand which may be inferred from natural principles, needs supplementing, because political independence may only be granted on three conditions: i. The racial or national group ought to fulfil the conditions necessary for independence; it must possess the economic, social, cultural and political forces that will enable it to exist as an independent State. ii. The political independence desired ought not to result in disadvantages either for the new or for the old State. The favourable development of both States must be taken into account (cf. Q. 99, No. 3 on separatism).

[5] Both after the First and after the Second World War nations and national groups have clearly expressed this wish, but in spite of the solemn declaration of the right of self-determination these aspirations have largely been frustrated. The matter has nowadays assumed a new importance in connection with the colonial question. (Q. 121).

iii. The international situation must also be considered, *e.g.*, the danger of war, perhaps of world war.

2. Every State has the duty to protect its minorities, and to guarantee them their own proper life within the framework of the common good. This duty applies to national, racial and religious minorities so long as these are prepared to observe the just laws of the State and to co-operate in accordance with their own proper character in the running of the State. Unity and order are quite compatible with a rich diversity, and it is as short-sighted as it is unjust for the State to seek to mould everyone and everything to a single pattern.

It follows from what has been said that racial minorities have no absolute right to become independent States, not even when the population gives clear expression to this desire. The good of the whole is superior to the good of the parts, and from the point of view of the whole there may well be reasons that forbid (at least for the time being) any further division, thus that demand a (temporary) renunciation of the claim to political independence.

3. Self-determination implies that others must not interfere in the internal affairs of the State. This brings us to the difficult questions of intervention and non-intervention. Is it possible that a State may have a right or a duty to intervene to establish order in another State? Or is this in every case an unjust encroachment?[6]

[6] We are not here dealing with questions that may arise as a result of a state of war or of a peace treaty, but with intervention in time of peace (with regard to the "cold war" cf. Q. 133, No. 4). The difficulty is due to the essential characteristic of sovereignty. Does the State possess within its own territory and over its own citizens a sovereignty that makes every intervention unjust? Or are there limitations of sovereignty which may not be exceeded, and which, if this should happen, could justify intervention?

i. The Catholic standpoint in political science is based roughly on the following considerations. No human sovereignty is absolute, that is, entitled to do whatever it pleases. There is a natural solidarity of nations and States. There are the higher rights of God, of the individual person and of member communities. It must be of the greatest concern to all mankind that these rights should not be trampled under foot. Disorder and abuse of power in any State may assume unbearable proportions.

ii. Once the community of nations has been established it will clearly be its duty to intervene (Q. 113).

iii. Some Catholic moralists hold that, until such a community of nations has been established, it may be permissible and even necessary for one or several States to intervene in the internal affairs of another. Five frequently mentioned examples are, first, if a State has to defend or demand its own or its citizens' rights when these have been obviously and culpably infringed; second, if a State cannot of its own strength defend itself against an unjust attack or an imminent act of aggression (Q. 134); third, if through the intrigues of another State internal order or obedience to law and authority are being undermined ("fifth column"; movements aiming at the overthrow of civil authority; parties in the pay of foreign powers); fourth, if rights that are a matter of concern to all mankind are gravely disregarded and violated; fifth, if a State fails to restore its own internal order and peace, so that the nation will be ruined unless help is provided from outside.

A State need not intervene if it would run the risk of ruining itself in the process or if intervention would involve unduly great sacrifices; it may not intervene if it would cause a world war. Some means of intervention are, for example, breaking-off diplomatic relations, economic blockade, legal action before a higher court of justice such as the Hague Tribunal, UNO Security Council.

4. Since the Second World War a new type of State, the satellite State, has arisen from which the right to develop its own internal order and independence has been taken either by brute force or by pressure and guile. In international law it is a sovereign State, and in some cases it is a voting member of the United Nations Organization; but in fact it has become completely subservient to a foreign power. Its home and foreign policy is directed from outside. The foreign power prescribes how it must vote in international organizations and bodies, what agreements and alliances it may, and must, conclude, what social and political doctrine is to be taught in schools and universities, how one must vote and who is to be elected etc. The future community of nations ought to abolish States of this kind.

116. Which freedom is essential for the life of nations?

Freedom of the mind is essential for individuals and societies at large in the life of nations.

1. INTELLECTUAL, cultural and moral values constitute that "perfection which the great family of mankind should attain in common" (Pius XII, C. B. 1949, I. U. A., p. 104; cf. Q. 112). The State and the community of States exist in order to facilitate and encourage the perfection of man. Hence they must cater for the steady intellectual and cultural development of their people.

2. The freedom that is due to individuals and to subsidiary communities is derived from man's natural right to perfect himself

intellectually and culturally. No individual and no nation can exhaust the intellectual and cultural possibilities. It is only when the nations complement each other that the divinely appointed goals can be achieved. Intellectual and cultural values are meant to be common property; innumerable individuals and institutions may share in them without their being used up or dissipated.

3. It necessarily follows that freedom of intellectual and cultural co-operation and exchange should be guaranteed everywhere throughout the world, and limited only to such extent as is required by the common good of individuals and of the human family (No. 4). However, this presupposes that individual States must consider themselves "open" communities, that is, they must not close but rather open their frontiers to citizens of other States, for example by the abolition of passport controls, currency restrictions etc. Moreover, at least a secure, simple state of economic and material well-being is necessary for even a modest intellectual and cultural life (Q. 117).

4. States have, of course, the right to demand that the freedom thus granted will not be abused for the purpose of doing them harm. Hence they are entitled to take precautions that influences dangerous to the State will not be disguised as cultural collaboration, as it is by certain educational and cultural societies, various "Peace" movements and societies subservient to certain foreign powers. Sometimes also protective measures may be necessary against moral corruption, say, through certain films, books and magazines.

117. *What must be done in the economic and social sphere?*

The nations are obliged jointly and in mutual assistance to create an economic and social order that will offer to all conditions in accordance with human dignity.

PIUS XII (C. B., 1940; U. A. vol. I, p. 14).

"Therefore, a new economic order was to be gradually evolved which gives all nations the means to secure for their citizens an appropriate standard of life."

PIUS XII (C. B., 1941; for text, see Q. 123, III).

PIUS XII (Address of 1 June, 1947; U. A. vol. I, p. 220).

"But the prosperity of nations cannot be safe and secure if all do not share in it."

JOHN XXIII (M. M. 157-177; P. i. T. 39, 44-45).

1. THE riches of the earth exist for all. God has furnished the world with goods and forces so that all men and all nations may be able to live in it. Property thus has a social aspect, also in international relations. The nations of the earth are very diversely endowed both with the gifts of nature and with human labour, for example there are lands that possess an abundance, and others that are largely deficient of the gifts of nature; there are diversities of talents, climates, traditional habits, capacity for work. This diversity requires of the nations a sense of solidarity in complementing and assisting each other.

2. Undoubtedly a sincere desire for mutual collaboration and aid ought to dominate the economic life of nations, as it alone will guarantee their well-being. A state of reasonable

equality is impossible of attainment if individual economic areas isolate themselves from the others; if one underbids the others to such an extent that genuine competition is no longer possible, or if tariff barriers practically paralyse mutual trading; if areas in want are refused the necessary assistance, for example in raw materials, power and labour services (technicians, engineers and skilled workers), or in the means of developing industry and agriculture, trade and commerce (machinery, roads; credit and loans etc.).

3. The most natural and direct way of complementing one another is undoubtedly the free exchange of goods and services. Yet the unrestricted freedom of imports and exports cannot result in an ordered world economic situation; in this respect also the judgment of Pius XI holds good that "free competition, though within certain limits right and productive of good results, cannot be the guiding principle of economic life" (Q. A., 88). At the same time one may without hesitation agree with the demand that the restrictions imposed on the free exchange of goods should be kept to a minimum.

4. The desired goals might be attained, above all, by i. international agreements (economic agreements, trade pacts etc.). They would be particularly effective and successful if the struggle for world markets could be moderated by international agreement; ii. the creation of greater economic units in order to raise by mutual assistance the economic productive capacity of the individual countries and to secure favourable outlets and marketing conditions for all; iii. favourable distribution of raw materials. "Within the framework of a new order based upon moral principles there is no room for that narrow and calculating egoism which tends to monopolize economic sources and

materials of common use, to the exclusion of nations less favoured" (Pius XII, C. B., C. T. S., p. 10).[7]

The organized community of nations would have at its disposal a wide range of ways and means of giving effective help. The League of Nations and UNO have already done much in the economic and social fields. The community of nations would establish special bodies with the function of studying developments everywhere, arranging for labour, granting loans (it must have its own World Bank for financial needs), wisely directing the circulation of goods, opening up markets etc.[8]

118. What do we mean by international law?

By international law we understand the whole body of legal norms which regulate the order within the community of nations, especially the relations of the States to one another and the community of nations.

PIUS XII (S. P.; C. T. S., pp. 29–30).

"Nothing less is demanded by any international understanding which is to be properly guaranteed and reasonably secure of permanence, nothing less is demanded by the need for fruitful alliances, than a due recognition of the basic principles of international law, and a determination to abide by them. And these principles enjoin that each nation shall be allowed to keep its own liberties intact, shall have the right to its own life and economic development; further they enjoin that any pact which has been solemnly ratified in accordance with the rights of nations shall persist, unimpaired and inviolable."

[7] Cf. *Proceedings of the United Nations Scientific Conference on the Conservation and Utilization of Resources,* New York, 1950–3.

[8] Cf. Arthur McCormack, *People, Space, Food,* London, 1960.

PIUS XII (C. B., 1941; C. T. S., p. 9).

"The new order which all peoples desire to see established after the trials and devastation of this war must be founded upon the immovable and immutable rock of the moral law, that law which the Creator himself has made known by means of the natural order and which He has engraved in indelible characters on the hearts of men. The observance of this law must be inculcated and promoted by the public opinion of all Nations and all States with such unanimity of voice and emphasis that none will dare to question it or to attenuate its binding force."

JOHN XXIII (P. i. T. 32-36).

MODERN international law comprises a copious body of norms, declarations, agreements, sanctions, customs etc.; they relate to all the many questions that have an importance for the life of nations and States, and for life within the nations and States. Modern international law is, however, not to be identified with the *jus gentium* that we find frequently mentioned in ancient and medieval history, especially by St. Thomas Aquinas. Although *jus gentium* literally means "law of the nations", in order to avoid confusion, it is better to translate it by "established law as valid among all nations". Originally it meant the law that was valid for all nations subjugated by Rome, in contrast to Roman law which was valid in Rome, that is, for Roman citizens. Later it came to mean generally those rights that were so natural and obvious as to be known and recognized everywhere, or almost everywhere. For this reason the *jus gentium* was often called simply "common human right". It embraces those norms that are inferred from the first principles of the natural law (I, Q. 72); common experience shows that without them no social order can exist, that is, among men burdened with original sin. Thus the legal norms of the *jus gentium* relate not only to relations between nations and States, but to the human social order in general; for example, private ownership as a necessary basis of social life comes under the *jus gentium*. For our purposes it is sufficient to distinguish between positive international law and natural law which is its basis.

1. Definite and obligatory legal norms are necessary for order in international life. The principles of the natural law, though necessary (No. 3), have to be explained, complemented and variously applied. In other words, there is need of human (positive or statutory) law the norms of which are precisely defined.

2. This "law of the nations" may be of two kinds:

i. Inter-State or international law. It may arise through agreements made, or entered into, by the majority of States, or through customs that have become firmly established in international life and are regarded by the world at large as having the force of law. Existing international law is to a great extent of this kind.[9]

ii. Supra-State, or supra-national law, created by the "world authority" of the organized community of nations. Its obligatory character is much clearer and more absolute, precisely because the community of nations is vested with genuine and even supreme ruling authority; thus its laws and ordinances are not agreements between equal partners, but the expressions of the will of a superior authority. This is the present development which ought to continue.

[9] It is important to remember this. Modern international law claims to be purely positive law. It does not recognize its basis in natural law, *i. e.*, the latter means nothing to it, international law is not based on it, but on positive legislation by the States.

3. The meaning and function of international law undoubtedly lies in guaranteeing order within the community of nations. Hence it comprises the entire body of legal norms that are necessary for this purpose: i. In the first place the relations of States to one another and to the community of nations must be regulated; because the peace and prosperity of the world largely depend on the concord and collaboration of the nations.

ii. Since the end of the last war we have realized that non-State member communities such as international organizations, and especially the individual person, are also subjects of international law, *i. e.,* subjects of rights and obligations in accordance with international law. International law is, and should be, a law for the defence of the human rights of all, that is, a law by which the individual citizen regains his status as a human person beyond the limits of his State. Since the right of free association is also among these human rights, the person belonging to any kind of organization is also a subject of international law without being in need of the mediation of the State.

iii. Thus to be a subject of international law is not the same thing as being a member of the community of nations. The direct and proper members of the community of nations are the States (Q. 114); on the other hand subjects of international law are all those whose conduct is directly regulated by international law.

4. Natural law is the indispensable basis of international law (I, Qs. 61–77). International law, like all human law, is not self-evident, nor can it claim to be valid purely of itself. The agreed will of the nations or the authority of the community of nations may lend it great prestige; but the real and profound reason for its binding character lies, also in this case, in the fact that it is

rooted in the natural law, is a participation in the eternal law of God, and thus the source of its binding force lies in the authority of God. For this reason international law must recognize and protect the rights of nature, not attack and deny them; its laws and customs must be in agreement with the natural law.

EXAMPLES. No international law may permit murder (genocide), the complete or partial extermination of nations, races, members of religious denominations; neither may it permit deceit and calumny, breach of contract (Q. 118), enslavement of conscience; the imposition of one ideology on all; unjust aggression; the appropriation of lawfully owned property.

While the norms of the natural law are valid everywhere, the norms of positive law are valid only for those who agree to them or who expressly accept them, and for those who are subject to the legislative authority which issues the laws. So long as there is no genuine world authority one can only appeal to the agreed will of the States that accept a declaration or an agreement. If the majority of States does this, then one may and must see in it an expression of the common consciousness of what is right. Even before it has actually been established the community of nations already exists potentially; therefore declarations and agreements that are made conjointly by a large number of States and that obviously serve the good of the nations also bind other States.

EXAMPLES. Legal conventions governing the conduct of land, sea and air war; banned weapons, occupation rights, treatment of wounded and prisoners, internment of civilians. The various forms in which contracts and other legal transactions become valid.

119. *Which principle is most important in international life?*

The principle that pacts entered into are sacred and must be faithfully observed.

PIUS XII (C. B., 1940; U. A. vol. I, p. 14).

"Return to the loyalty for treaties without which the secure co-operation of nations, and especially the living side by side of strong and weak nations, are inconceivable."

PIUS XII (C. B., 1941; p. II).

". . . to ensure to the axiom 'Pacts must be observed' that vital moral function which belongs to it in juridical relations between States."

PIUS XII (S. P.; C. T. S., pp. 30–31).

"In the course of time new situations may arise, which were not foreseen and perhaps could not be foreseen at the time when the pact was made. In that case, either the whole agreement or some part of it may have become, or may seem to have become, unjust to one of the contracting parties; or there may be undertakings which now would bear too hardly upon that party, or be impossible of fulfilment. In such a case, the obvious expedient is to take refuge as soon as possible in a full and frank discussion of the difficulty, so that the old pact can be suitably altered, or a new pact substituted for it. It is quite a different thing, to regard all signed pacts as written in water, assuming to oneself the tacit right of breaking them at one's own discretion, whenever self-interest demands it, without consulting or without having any regard for the other contracting party. Such behaviour can only deprive nations of the spirit of confidence which ought to exist between them, it is utterly subversive of the natural order, and leaves nations and peoples severed from one another by deep rivers of distrust."

1. ACCORDING to natural law pacts entered into are binding. States must fulfil honourably and exactly, and in the spirit of the concluded agreements, what they have agreed and promised among themselves (cf. Pius XII, Sum. Pont., C. T. S., p. 30). The worst enemy of fidelity to pacts is political expediency of any kind. It replaces the "sacredness of pacts" with the "sacredness of interests". It proceeds from the pernicious principle that pacts are only valid to the extent and for so long as they prove useful. Moreover, the State concluding the agreement presumes itself to be the judge of whether or not it is still profitable to abide by it.

2. For an agreement to be binding three conditions are necessary which are here directly applied to international life:

i. The agreement must be concluded by the competent lawful State authority or its representatives. Nowadays agreements are nearly always thoroughly prepared over a long period and then solemnly accepted (ratified) (cf. No. 6 below).

EXAMPLES. Unilateral or multilateral agreements concluded between States: trade and economic agreements, non-aggression pacts, defensive alliances, restriction of armaments; peace treaties; agreements on the cession of colonies; use of traffic ways such as waterways, railways etc.

ii. The contents, or object, of the pact must be lawful; neither an individual person nor a community may bind itself by contract to something that is bad and cannot be justified before God. If this should, nevertheless, happen, then the agreement is null and void. The following are a few examples of unlawful agreement between States: Slave trade, white slave traffic; limitation of population on the basis of birth-control; war on religion and the Church; education of the nation and youth to a materialist philosophy of life; offensive alliances; economic blockade against peace-loving States; compulsory deportation or abduction of innocent persons.

iii. The agreement must be voluntarily concluded by all parties. Agreements that are unjustly extorted from a State are not binding.

Strictly speaking agreements must be fulfilled exactly according to the letter. Since agreements between States are very often intended to last a long time they should be flexible. It is best that States should agree immediately on some particular court of arbitration for the settlement of possible differences, for example, an international court of justice; both sides should be ready to submit to its judgment and to renounce any further legal measures.

3. Agreements between States cease to be effective i. when notice of termination is given by both, or all, parties, thus by mutual agreement; ii. when the period for which the pact was concluded comes to an end; iii. when the commitments mentioned have been fulfilled.

4. When has a State the right unilaterally to denounce an agreement entered into? When does it cease, even without previous denunciation, to be bound by the agreement? These are difficult questions. Catholic social teaching suggests that if one side breaks the agreement, then the other side is no longer bound to observe it. It is another matter if, from motives of magnanimity, it remains faithful to the obligations it has taken on.

There is a special case when a State may withdraw or unilaterally denounce a pact, that is, when the situation has in the meantime so radically changed that, had it known or foreseen this, it would under no circumstances have concluded the agreement.[10] The statement needs to be explained:

A State can reasonably promise or agree only to what could have been foreseen. Accordingly if the situation is such that it would never have agreed to the pact, then it has undoubtedly been gravely mistaken; it never wanted the pact in this form and under these conditions. Therefore it does nothing wrong if it withdraws from it; it may even be obliged to do so. Every pact is concluded on the tacit condition, *rebus sic stantibus,* that is, if the situation is not completely otherwise, or does not completely change. Depending on the matter in question and how matters stand, the State that wishes to free itself of a burden that has become intolerable will first of all have to make a sincere attempt to meet its obligations, and by way of agreement (of a new or a supplementary agreement) to save the pact or to arrive at a denunciation by both parties. Unilateral denunciation is undoubtedly a risk, and would, if often repeated, have a disquieting effect on the life of nations. Therefore it must remain the exception.

EXAMPLES. A State sees that the partner with whom it has a defensive alliance is preparing for a war of aggression in which it would be involved. A State has under favourable economic conditions committed itself to certain deliveries which would, in the very bad economic situation that has meanwhile arisen, completely ruin it. A State has declared its intention of remaining neutral under all circumstances, but now it is unjustly attacked – or it sees itself bound in duty to come to the assistance of a neighbouring State in extreme need that has been invaded (Q. 135).

5. Pacts concluded between States and the Catholic Church have a special character (Concordats etc.). In view of the Church's

[10] Cf. St. Thomas Aquinas, II–II 40, 3; 110 ad 5; 140, 2 ad 2.

general principles we may well hold that a State can never have a just cause to denounce such pacts without previous consultation or concluding a new agreement, and negotiations will always prove successful if the State shows good will and does not expect from the Church what she cannot grant without doing violence to herself.

120. How should the world solve the population problem?

The world population problem can only be solved by constantly improving food production and by relieving over-populated areas by means of emigration and immigration respectively.

PIUS XII (Address of 18 October 1951).

"We need not tell you that the Catholic Church feels herself in the highest degree obliged to interest herself in the matter of emigration. It is a question of relieving great distress; the lack of space and the lack of means of existence because the mother country can no longer support all its children and overpopulation forces these to emigrate. It is a question of the misery of refugees who in their millions are forced to abandon their native country now lost to them and to seek to build up a new home in distant lands."

1. INDIVIDUALS and families certainly possess the right to emigrate from their homeland and to immigrate somewhere else. If the common good suffers no substantial disadvantages States cannot oppose this freedom of movement and settlement; such disadvantages would be, for example, the too great number of emigrants or immigrants, proved crimes, hereditary illnesses, arrears in payment of taxes.

2. As in the case of national population policy (Q. 41), the

Catholic Church also definitely rejects modern birth-control as a suitable and lawful way for international population policy. Lawful birth-control, *i.e.,* total or periodical marital continence cannot be considered an effective means, for only a very small fraction of mankind today could summon up the moral strength for it.

3. Fears are expressed that healthy races and nations with a high birth-rate may become a danger to the others. Reply: If these "other" nations do not renew their moral and biological strength, then the danger cannot be averted. It is also claimed that the earth will no longer be able to nourish the increasing world population. In reply we would suggest: i. The increase in population cannot be predicted at a time when the social order is in such a state of restless movement; it is by no means certain that the increase will continue as in the last 150 years when, as we know, the world population trebled itself. ii. The earth's soil is far from being fully utilized (so far only ten per cent of the fifty per cent cultivable land). iii. Production could be considerably raised by means of better use and new methods. iv. Whole nations and territories could well be satisfied with a more modest way of living; instead of this, ever higher demands are made. v. "God does not abandon His own". He has given the earth and its riches to men for their habitation and sustenance; God-fearing men may trust in him and in his help.

4. There is no general rule to assess a country's over-population, for this depends both on the nature and resources of the country as also on support from abroad, for example, the extent of arable land and agricultural development; possibilities of work in industry; exportable surpluses; inhabitants' disposition towards work; colonies; favourable loans and contracts. Each country

also has the duty first of all to settle its population problem by its own efforts. Only if these efforts are unavailing the problem of what to do with its surplus population, either by resettlement or by emigration, will have to be tackled.

5. According to the natural law there is an obligation on the part of the countries concerned to allow their surplus population to emigrate, and countries that are in a position to take these emigrants are obliged to do so. These obligations derive from man's right to live as well as from natural solidarity of nations.

In point of fact, natural antipathies and economic self-interests have nearly always closed the frontiers against distress of this kind, and continue to do so today. One of the most important tasks of a genuine community of nations would be to deal with this matter. Many experts have demanded the establishment of an international emigration and resettlement office the function of which it would be to ascertain both the distressed areas and the ability to help of the various countries; to inspect and possibly to determine areas suitable for settling immigrants; to make provision, in co-operation with the country of residence and the country of adoption, for suitable resettlement.

6. The homeland, the country of origin, is bound to find for its emigrating people a decent form of resettlement and to permit them to take their rightful property with them, or to compensate them for what they are forced to leave behind.

The country of reception cannot be criticized for profiting from immigration; but it must look on the immigrants as human persons rather than as cheap labour. The change of country would fail in its purpose unless adequate living conditions, opportunities of work and earning are thereby obtained.

121. What of the colonial territories today?

The right of national self-determination and world peace demand that colonies should as soon as possible become members with equal rights within the community of nations.

JOHN XXIII (M. M. 171–174).

1. The question whether, and on what grounds, civilized States are at all justified in acquiring colonies need scarcely be asked today; for those parts of the world that are suitable for colonial purposes are "disposed of", that is, they already belong to colonial powers or have meanwhile become independent.

The intellectual and cultural education of "savage and primitive peoples" who by themselves are incapable of attaining morality, true humanity and culture is often used as an argument to justify colonization, as is also the opening up and exploitation of economic resources. Left to themselves the native peoples would be incapable of, and in most cases not even interested, in this. But God has given the riches of nature to the whole of mankind.

2. Christ has given his Church the mission and the right to preach his gospel throughout the world, "to all nations". The nations are obliged by him and his command to listen to the gospel of his kingdom and to accept it. Hence any colonial policy must serve the cause of Christianization to the extent of creating the material and cultural conditions for it. The conversion of pagan peoples was often the justification for a policy of colonization. Unfortunately, the claim was in many cases a mere pretext for depriving these peoples of their rights and exploiting them. No State can claim a right to colonies, for no State is absolutely dependent on them. There are other ways and means of fulfilling the tasks of the State and of making up for the lack of colonies.

3. With regard to just administration and development, the *Semaine Sociale de France* held in Lyons in 1948 laid down as a guiding principle the good of the human community as a whole. Colonial powers should regard their part as that of counsellors and educators acting on behalf of the international community, their work coming to an end with independence. The colonial power is entitled to exercise sovereign rights and to make use of colonies for its own economic and military purposes. But its power is not unlimited and must serve the welfare of the colonies. The native population must not be looked on as serfs or convicts and retain the right: i. to be treated with human dignity (human rights), and to live decently from the produce of their country; ii. to appeal to the community of nations or to some other protective power when these rights are infringed; iii. to continue to develop its own proper life and culture so far as they do not involve objectionable practices and traditions. It is quite compatible with this for the colonizing country to introduce a superior culture into the colony; iv. to a gradually increasing measure of self-government. The colonial powers are obliged to assist the country towards an appreciation of the possibilities of its own culture. The principle of subsidiary function (I, Q. 52) must be observed in the relation of the colonizing country to the colonies.

4. The goal of this work of education and formation is political independence, and in the form and fullness enjoyed by all other States within the community of nations. Concerning this the following points must be mentioned: i. The colony ought to have reached the necessary maturity for this stage in its development. ii. Colonies ought to be obliged to choose a time for the attainment of independence at which separation will be a less painful and less grave matter for the colonizing country. iii. If

there is reason to fear that colonies on becoming independent would fall a prey to, or be brought into, the sphere of influence of a big power which is clearly aiming at the enslavement of the world, then both the welfare of the colonies and the weal of nations forbid the granting of political independence.

5. Again the eventual organized community of nations would have the function of watching over the colonial powers in order to ensure that both the interests of the colonial peoples and the common good of the nations are catered for. It would have to concern itself with all questions relating to colonial policy; with economic, social and cultural development of colonial territories, the gradual process of independence, their peaceful integration in the community of nations.

Lesson Two

SECURING WORLD PEACE

The condition in the world and among the nations that is willed by God and worth striving for is not war but peace. "One thing, however, is certain, peace is the concern of the law of God. Its purpose is the protection of human values, in so far as they are gifts of the Creator" (Pius XII, C. B., I. U. A., p. 96).

122. *In what does world peace consist?*

World peace consists in this, that the nations live together in concord and are concerned to respect and to help one another.

PIUS XII (C. B., 1951; U. A. vol. I, p. 121).

"As human experience teaches then, the State and the society of States with its external organization, in spite of all their defects, are naturally, given the social nature of man, forms of union and order, that 'tranquillitas ordinis' which St. Augustine gives as a definition of peace. These societies of their very essence exist for peace."

1. Peace does not mean that all nations would have attained the same standard of prosperity, or that all tensions have ceased (cf. Pius XII, C. B., 1942) but that the nations respect one another in spite of their differences and peculiarities, that they recognize their responsibility for one and all in a higher goal which is the common good, that they benefit from tensions without resorting to war.

PIUS XII (Address of 1 June 1947, I. U. A., p. 223).

"For those who see things in the light of the supernatural, there is no doubt that even in the most serious conflicts of human and national interest there is always room for a peaceful settlement."

2. Peace among the nations ought to be i. sincere and just. It must be without guile and duplicity; based on the principles of divine and human law, and not on arbitrariness and force (Q. 123); ii. secure and lasting, not continually endangered and threatened; iii. indivisible and complete; internal and external peace condition and complement each other.

PIUS XII (C. B., 1940; U. A. vol. I, p. 12).

" . . . of a peace built on justice, equity and honour, which could, therefore, be lasting."

PIUS XII (C. B., 1942; C. T. S., p. 3).

"No State, in fact, can present a firmly and consistently peaceful front to its neighbours without an internally peaceful condition which will inspire confidence. Therefore it is only by striving for this complete peace, peace within and peace without, that it will be possible to deliver peoples from the cruel nightmare of war . . ."

PIUS XII (Address of 1 January 1948).

"We will not cease to implore those concerned not to lose sight of this indivisibility of peace and never to forget that the internal peace of the nations and their external peace with other nations is such a precious good that even very great sacrifices must not be considered too high a price to pay for it."

3. World peace presupposes the internal peace of the nations:

PIUS XII (C. B., 1942; C. T. S., p. 3).

"International relations and national order are intimately connected, for the balance and concord of one nation with another depends upon the balance of each nation in itself and upon the stage of internal development which it has reached in the material, social, and intellectual spheres."

The internal difficulties and troubles of a nation that is divided in itself easily cause quarrels with other nations. There are types of national unity (for instance, in totalitarian States) that are extremely dangerous to world peace. Nations ought to strive after the right form of unity, which consists in loyalty to the divinely appointed goals and values, claims and obligations (cf. I, Qs. 45–47 and 123; also the papal text quoted there).

123. What are the foundations of world peace?

The foundations of world peace are:
1. Return to the moral order;
2. Recognition and preservation of inalienable fundamental rights;
3. Social justice among the nations;
4. General disarmament and international safeguards for peace;
5. Responsible government everywhere;
6. Freedom of religion and the Church.

JOHN XXIII (P. i. T. 59–60).

THESE six points contain the demands which Pius XII defined as the foundations of a "just and lasting peace".

I. THE MORAL ORDER

PIUS XII (C. B., 1941; C. T. S., p. 9).

"The new order which all peoples desire to see established after the trials and devastation of this war must be founded upon the immovable and immutable rock of the moral law, that law which the Creator himself has made known by means of the natural order and which He has engraved in indelible characters on the hearts of men. The observance of this law must be inculcated and promoted by the public opinion of all Nations and all States with such unanimity of voice and emphasis that none will dare to question it or to attenuate its binding force."

PIUS XII (C. B., 1951; U. A. vol. I, p. 121).

"If men, obeying the Divine Will, will use that sure way of salvation, a perfect Christian order in the world, they will soon see the possibility of even a just war practically disappear. For there will be no

reason for such a war, once the activity of the society of States, as a genuine organization for peace, is made secure."

1. The basic forces of society, also of international society, are truth, charity and justice in that form and fulness which God has given men in Christ. Christ is the "Prince of peace" who bequeathed his peace to the world (John 14:27). In him the Father has given order to the world; Christ has redeemed and repaired fallen nature (I, Qs. 18/19); he has overcome the forces that deny or destroy the internal and external peace of men: hate and envy, lust for riches and pleasure-seeking, the intoxication of power and bloodshed. In him all men are one, and it is his will that understanding and peace should reign in his kingdom rather than discord and strife. "His sublime mission is to establish peace between each man and God, between men themselves and between nations" (Pius XII, C. B. 1951, I. U. A., p. 119).

2. The present danger of war has a spiritual and moral character (Pius XII, C. B., 1951). The nations stand opposed to each other under the compulsion of their respective ideologies: liberty and human rights against bondage and the denial of human rights. Unfortunately the fight for liberty is often fought with the "weapons of hate, greed and of the overweening desire for prestige". This also leads to the fact that "the simultaneous and reciprocal reduction of armaments . . . is an unstable guarantee of lasting peace" (Pius XII, *ibid.*).

3. Only in God and Christ will men find the way to those unshakable principles of morality without which human conduct degenerates into unreason and disorder, arbitrariness and violence, and to that ultimate responsibility which fears to

infringe God's order and to thwart God's "thoughts of peace" (Jer. 29:11).

PIUS XII (C. B., 1951; U. A. vol. I, p. 123).

"If the desire to prevent war is to be truly efficacious, above all a remedy must be sought for the spiritual anaemia of nations, for the ignorance of individual responsibility before God and man, and for the want of a Christian order which alone is able to guarantee peace."

II. Inalienable Fundamental Rights

PIUS XII (C. B., 1939; U. A. vol. I, p. 7).

"The fundamental condition of a just and honourable peace is to assure the right to life and independence of all nations, large, small, strong, or weak."

PIUS XII (C. B., 1941; C. T. S., pp. 9, 10).

"Within the framework of a new order based upon moral principles, there is no room for the violation of the freedom, integrity, and security of other Nations, whatever be their territorial extent or their capacity for defence. . . . there is no room for the suppression, be it open or covert, of the cultural and linguistic traditions of national minorities; for the obstruction or restriction of their economic capacity."

JOHN XXIII (P. i. T. 50).

1. Both the absolutist and the collectivist State ignore the fundamental rights of the human person (I, Qs. 71 and 84/85). The "striking power" of totalitarian States rests precisely on the contempt and suppression of human liberty. Unrestricted power of command and obligation of obedience linked with a system of planned agitation give them dangerous tactical advantages over the democracies.

2. The nations, whether great or small, armed or unarmed, whatever their political structure, possess the fundamental right to exist, to rule themselves and to be recognized in the community of nations (cf. Q. 114). National minorities, whether territorially united or divided, have the fundamental right to live their own life and to develop in accordance with their own particular character within the framework of the common weal. Indeed, often enough the home and foreign policy of States ignores these fundamental rights. If such practices prevail there is an end to any international order of law.

III. Social Justice

1. It is precisely with regard to world peace that Pius XII demanded a "just distribution of goods"; suitable possibilities must be left or opened up to every nation to procure that measure of economic prosperity which will guarantee it a reasonably dignified social order (Q. 117).

PIUS XII (C. B., 1941; C. T. S., p. 10).

"Within the framework of a new order based upon moral principles, there is no room for that narrow and calculating egoism which tends to monopolize economic sources and materials of common use, to the exclusion of Nations less naturally favoured."

2. International life can only be ordered if the nations are conscious of their solidarity. National self-seeking based on false nationalism is one of the worst threats to world peace.

PIUS XII (C. B., 1947; U. A. vol. I, p. 86).

"The human race, then, will be powerless to emerge from the present

crisis and desolation and to go forward to a more harmonious future unless it restrains and controls the forces of division and discord by means of a sincere spirit of brotherhood uniting all classes, all races and all nations with the one bond of love."

PIUS XII (C. B., 1950; U. A. vol. I, p. 114).

"We have at heart the good of all nations. We believe that the close union of all peoples who are masters of their own destiny, and who are united by sentiments of reciprocal trust and mutual assistance, is the sole means for the defence of peace and the best guarantee of its reestablishment."

IV. Disarmament

Pius XII repeatedly combined two demands: disarmament and loyalty to agreements, because international agreements are intended to replace untrammeled rearmament and thus to banish total war, and because effective disarmament presupposes confidence in international agreements. A fuller treatment of disarmament is given in Q. 125 and of the validity of pacts in Q. 119; papal citations are given in the respective places.

V. Responsible Government

PIUS XII (C. B., 1939; U. A. vol. I, p. 8).

"But even better and more complete settlements will be imperfect and condemned to ultimate failure, if those who guide the destinies of peoples, and the peoples themselves, refuse to permit themselves to be penetrated ever more by that spirit which alone can give living authority and obligation to the dead letter of articles in international agree-

ments – by that spirit, namely, of intimate, acute responsibility that measures and weighs human statutes according to the holy, unshakable rules of Divine Law."

States have often enough deliberately caused war. Every people has the grave responsibility of entrusting the government of the country only to men who will guarantee a genuine policy of peace. They ought responsibly to consolidate the nation's will for peace, foster relations with other nations that will serve peace, and make every effort to have war banned as a means of politics. Totalitarian governments are unsuitable for such a policy of peace; hence every effort must be made to prevent the rise of totalitarian States.

VI. Freedom for Religion and the Church

PIUS XII (C. B., 151; U. A. vol. I, p. 120).
"That world talks nothing but peace; but it has no peace. It claims for itself all possible and impossible legal titles to establish peace, yet does not know or does not recognize the mission of peacemaker that comes directly from God, the mission of peace deriving from the religious authority of the Church."

The rejection or suppression of religion inevitably leads to the weakening of the very forces that alone guarantee peace; ordinary human considerations and reasoning can avail little (cf. Eph. 3:18), least of all resolve grave tensions, and, where there is a clash of just claims, cannot renounce and conciliate in generous charity.

1. Pius XII (C. B., 1948, I. U. A., pp. 94–95) defined the Christian will for peace as being i. of divine origin, that is, it

"comes from God" who "has created the world as an abode of peace"; ii. easily recognizable, because it quite definitely abhors war and rejects as justifiable causes those very reasons that usually lead to war, for example, national honour and prestige, territorial aggrandisement etc.; iii. practical and realistic. Its immediate aim is to remove, or at least to mitigate the causes of tension which mostly lead to war. He exhorts especially to social justice; iv. as strong as steel, that is, in no wise cowardly and weak. It does not simply capitulate to brute force, but rather recognizes the right and the duty to defend man's most sacred goods against unjust attacks even at the cost of the greatest sacrifices (cf. Q. 133).

2. Church and popes do not advocate "peace at any price". They do not say that a people that has been unjustly attacked, may not defend itself, nor that it may betray and sell those human values which are gifts of the Creator in order to preserve peace for themselves. There are values that are even greater than peace.

124. What do we mean by "pacifism"?

By pacifism we mean that large movement which systematically endeavours to preserve peace for the world.

1. The term pacifism derives from the Latin *pacem facere,* meaning to make, to work for, not merely to love and to desire, peace. Present-day pacifism is not a uniform movement. It is divided into various trends and groupings, all of which have a common goal, to abolish war and replace it by peaceful solutions. Every thinking person must agree with this aim. Two

main groups[11] are i. Extreme pacifists. They believe in the possibility of permanent peace on earth. This obvious delusion rests on a false notion of man (denial of original sin), and is more likely to endanger world peace than to safeguard it. The extreme pacifists uphold complete and unilateral disarmament, and condemn even just wars of defence (Q. 133); ii. moderate pacifists: moderate, not because they are less eager in their fight for peace, but because in their ideals and efforts they are guided by right reason or by supernatural faith, and therefore prudently weigh the pros and cons, right and wrong.

2. Essential for every form of pacifism is the choice of means by which world peace is to be achieved. Naturally the means must be suited to the situation and to the dangers that threaten. But these means have to be morally unexceptionable. Bad means, for instance, would be birth-control and abortion for the purpose of preventing a rapid increase in the population and thus of overcoming what may be an additional cause of war; withholding of national independence when it is due (a possible cause of revolt and of intervention by foreign powers); combating the Christian religion.

125. Is rearmament justifiable?

Simultaneous and multilateral disarmament is undoubtedly necessary; however, for reasons of just defence it is permissible to rearm to the extent that is absolutely necessary.

[11] The subject and the often heated controversy which it provokes give rise to an attitude on the part of pacifists that is at times quite contentious and intolerant. Frequently they are militant individuals who do not easily admit defeat. This is true also of many Christian and Catholic pacifists, who are not justified in charging their fellow-Christians, who are no less anxiously concerned about

BENEDICT XV (Exhortation to peace, Aug. 1917).

"The very first and most important point must be that the moral force of law will take the place of the material force of arms. Consequently a just agreement of all must be reached on simultaneous and reciprocal disarmament according to agreed rules and guarantees, and allowing for what is necessary and adequate for the maintaining of public order in the individual countries."

PIUS XII (C. B., 1941; C. T. S., p. 2).

"Within the framework of a new order based upon moral principles, there is no room (when the most dangerous breeding-grounds of conflict have once been eliminated) for total warfare or for a reckless race for armaments.... The disproportion between the excessive armament of powerful States and the inadequate armament of weak nations creates a threat to the peace and tranquillity of peoples, and points to the wisdom of reducing the manufacture and storing of offensive weapons to a limit of sufficiency and proportion."

PIUS XII (C. B., 1939; U. A. vol. I, p. 7).

"Conclusions of peace which failed to attribute fundamental importance to disarmament, mutually accepted, organic and progressive both in letter and spirit, and failed to carry out this disarmament loyally, would sooner or later reveal their inconsistency and lack of vitality."

JOHN XXIII (P. i. T. 41–43, 46).

1. SINCE war is no longer a suitable means of politics (Q. 130), everything must be done to prevent it. If the world is to be freed from the scourge of total nuclear war, there must be disarmament, the destruction of existing weapons and no manufacture of new ones are the only solution. The armaments race among the nations

peace, with ignorance or unchristian conduct merely because they consider some other point of view to be right.

means constant danger of war. Only the State that is armed for war will include war as means of politics in its plans, quite apart from the enormous sums put into armaments having to be made to pay dividends. Disarmament can only be successful and effective if it is simultaneous and multilateral, if it is carried out by all States and each contents itself with a limited force for policing purposes. The strength of this force would vary in relation to the size of the State. But no State should thereafter be permitted to have means at its disposal that would place it in a position to start war.

2. To bring about simultaneous and multilateral disarmament we need: i. an international agreement to which all States can subscribe. No State will be prepared to disarm unless others do likewise. ii. we need an international system of control valid for all states and capable of detecting and preventing secret rearmament by anyone. iii. we need an international arbitration court and an international police force. Tension must be resolved in time by an unbiased and binding decision. The armed forces of the community of nations must be strong enough to enforce the execution of any decision, and to prevent any State from preparing for, or starting war. There are also measures of a preventive nature that could act as deterrents: trade restrictions, blockade, sanctions such as the withdrawal of the rights and privileges resulting from membership of the community of nations; military occupation of the State concerned.

PIUS XII (C. B., 1944; N. C. W. C., p. 10).

"The decisions already published by international commissions permit one to conclude that an essential point in any future international arrangement would be the formation of an organ for the maintenance of peace, of an organ invested by common consent with supreme power

to whose office it would also pertain to smother in its germinal state any threat of isolated or collective aggression."

3. So long as any single major power refuses to disarm, the other States are constrained to rearm and to form (defensive) alliances among themselves. Such rearmament may only be defensive and should not therefore exceed what is necessary for this purpose. This will be determined by the fighting strength (number of troops; type, calibre and amount of weapons) of the State that refuses to disarm. No State is obliged to expose itself without protection to the danger of an unjust attack.

Unfortunately the "armed peace" (cf. Pius XII, C. B., I. U. A., p. 122) is a hard and unavoidable necessity, and the saying, "if you want peace, prepare for war", is a sad truth in a world that neither wants nor finds generous and lasting conciliation. Only if peace can be prepared because there is no need to fear war, and if an unarmed peace can guarantee security and prosperity to the nations, will the world have found that "tranquillity of order" which defines the nature of true peace.

126. Is conscription justifiable?

Conscription is justified to the extent to which a State is dependent on it for reasons of self-defence.

CONSCRIPTION means that all men capable of bearing arms are called up for military service and trained for war. In its present form it was first introduced by Napoleon I, and then spread rapidly to other States. Formerly military service was based on voluntary enlistment. The standing army in its present form was unknown.

1. General conscription is certainly a great evil. The Catholic

Church has always urged that general conscription should be abolished as quickly as possible. Cardinal Ottaviani, for example, wrote that by general conscription a great injustice is done to citizens.[12]

General conscription as such is undoubtedly unnecessary; the modern national State with its exaggerated nationalism, national jealousy and rivalry and lust for conquest first brought it into the world. It represents an intolerable interference in the personal liberty of those who for years have to forego training for and the practice of their normal callings; and have to put up with the constraint of barrack life and military drill. The so-called advantages are generally much exaggerated, and could be obtained in other ways. While general conscription is not altogether to blame for war, it is partly to blame for the modern type of warfare, for the extent of the preparations and the conduct of war. Each State tries to outdo the other in military "striking power" in order to be strong enough in the event of war.

2. Nations are entitled to do what the circumstances demand of them. So long as they are able to protect themselves against unjust attacks only on the basis of general conscription, they are not forbidden to introduce it. But the following conditions ought to be observed: i. Numbers, training and armament must serve the purposes of defence, not of attack. Admittedly it is very difficult to fix a limit, since defence and protection of the country can sometimes be achieved only by carrying the war that has been forced on it into the enemy's territory; in such a case defence inevitably changes to attack, but this does not change a defensive war into one of aggression. ii. Greater

[12] Vol. I, p. 151, "*Maxima fit iniuria civibus*".

rights may not be infringed. For example, it is not permissible except in emergencies to take fathers for months and years away from their families. For the family is prior to the State and its rights come before all others. Also the period of service may not be prolonged beyond what is really necessary, since it is man's right to claim that he need not forego his personal liberty for longer than is absolutely necessary. iii. It is the duty of the State to make it possible for servicemen to fulfil their religious obligations, and to see that military service is no danger to morality. God is above the State, and we cannot be dispensed from right and moral conduct on account of military service.

3. Is the individual obliged to join up, or may (must) he refuse to serve?[13] There are Catholic moralists who consider the law of general conscription like an ordinary criminal law (Q. 80, No. 6), and accordingly decide that no one is bound in conscience to military service, but only to serve the sentence that may be imposed on him in case he refuses. Others say – and this is surely the right view – that the law binds in conscience wherever the State is dependent on general conscription. They agree that the State finds itself constrained for the sake of the common good to issue and carry out this law; only in this way can it, in view of modern conditions, take effective measures to prevent an unjust attack, and this it may and must do. Such laws bind the subjects in conscience; because they fulfil all the conditions necessary for a just law (Q. 80). We should add that if greater rights or obligations are infringed or made impossible, the individual must refuse to serve, for example, a father whose family would be destitute without him.

[13] Refusal to do military service is not the same as refusal to serve in time of war, and must not be judged according to the same principles; cf. Q. 136.

127. *What is militarism?*

Militarism is the undue glorification and predominance of the military spirit and ideals, and of readiness for war.

1. MILITARISM overestimates the value of soldierly ability and war. The profession of arms is raised to the highest and leading social rank.

2. The State is not in the habit of maintaining an army as a pastime, but for the defence of the country; according to militarism this means taking the precaution of preparing for war, in planning and preparation to anticipate war as it were. Militarism deliberately fosters the warlike spirit, the readiness for war. Its characteristics are a standing army, universal military service, influence of the generals on the government of the country, infusion of the military point of view in the whole system of education, glorification of war, comprehensive planning of roads and industry for strategic considerations, relatively large items in the budget for military purposes, encouragement of armaments industry, striving after the greatest possible self-sufficiency in the national economy; militarism is not so much preparation for a definite, immediate war of aggression as rather an essential element of what is institutional in society. As we have shown, the institutional is characterized by the tendency towards independence of purpose; in militarism the soldier, readiness for war and upbringing for war, become ends in themselves. This rejection of militarism is, of course, not meant to detract from the value of those virtues which distinguish the upright soldier by a keen sense of duty, or by bravery in the face of extreme danger; patience in inevitable and at times

great privations; love of country; discretion and presence of mind. Cf. the preliminary remarks in the next lesson.

Lesson Three

WAR, MILITARY SERVICE AND CONSCIENTIOUS OBJECTION

1. WAR may be the ultimate means of safeguarding order and law; and because of its devastating effects it must be conducted with all possible restraint, and be ended as soon as possible. Pius XII rightly said that war everywhere presents "the admirable spectacle of indomitable courage in defence of right and fatherland, of sorrow patiently borne, of souls aflame with zeal for the triumph of justice and truth" (C. B. 1941, C. T. S., p. 2). But these values are out of all proportion to the frightful losses and to the demoralization that especially modern war entails (*ibid.*).

2. Quite a number of the questions concerning war have, since the first world war, taken on a completely new aspect. The traditional teaching concerning the "just war" no longer suffices and needs supplementing (Q. 129). Since the Second World War two things stand out: i. War is ideologically conditioned; it is fought with the whole armoury of modern weapons for spiritual values, ideologies and movements. ii. Every war has "worldwide" importance; it threatens to develop into world war.

128. Can war ever be justifiable?

Catholic ethics has always recognized the existence of just and permissible wars.

It cannot be concluded from our reply that any particular war was (or is) just and justifiable, or that a modern war may be just and justifiable (on this point cf. Qs. 130ff).

1. War means that sovereign States fight against one another, the conflict being fought out by major formations with lethal weapons. Thus war essentially includes the distinction between combatants and non-combatants, between military and civil population. It is directed against an external enemy.

2. War may "not be considered a normal means of settling disputes between nations. It should find no place in a perfectly organized international society".[14] Nevertheless war may be lawful: i. States and nations have the right to live in peace and order; so long as they fulfil their obligations towards other States and towards the community of nations, they have a strict claim to inviolability in their rights and liberties (not to be attacked or obstructed; for exceptions cf. Qs. 134/135). If another State should infringe these rights, and the State that suffers the injustice has no other means of redress, it may use force either to defend itself or to compel restoration or restitution. For both on its own and on behalf of its citizens the State is the guardian of law and public order on which depends the common good of the nation. ii. The State may oblige those citizens capable of bearing arms to support a war in a just cause, and to risk their lives. According to Catholic ethics the common good would justify such a risk; death at the hands of the enemy in a just war is genuine evidence of fortitude, service (love of country) and charity.[15]

Though she has warned against war and condemned modern wars of aggression (Q. 132), the Church has never banned war

[14] Malines Code of International Ethics, para. 137.
[15] St. Thomas Aquinas, II–II 123, 5.

as such. Not only the natural reasons already cited, but also the Word of God both in the Old and the New Testament forbid her to do this.

3. According to the Bible: i. War as such is not condemned in the Old Testament; on the contrary, it recognizes both the just, legitimate war of defence or liberation, and the just, legitimate war of aggression and conquest. There are, of course, also unjust, illegitimate wars (Judges 11:27). According to the Old Testament God's will is for peace and not for war; but the just war, including war of aggression, is an instrument in the hand of God, whether for the punishment of the nations, especially of the insubordinate and impenitent people of Israel, or for the implementation of his divine plan of salvation (conquest of the Promised Land). War is expressly attributed to the will of God. In his name, by his command, supported by his aid, the people of Israel (and sometimes also their opponents) fight against his enemies. This reliance on the will of God is sometimes even taken to mean that God has commanded atrocities of war. In these cases the biblical writer failed to distinguish between human and divine elements. The fifth commandment, "Thou shalt not kill" is now regarded as applicable to murder only, and by no means to every killing in the service of the community. ii. Regarding the New Testament views we refer to what has been said in Lesson Six in connection with the right to resist the authority of the State. Concerning war the New Testament must be considered in its entirety. Statements conditioned by the circumstances of the time cannot be regarded as universally valid and binding. Neither Christ nor the apostles condemned war or military service. Christ was sent into the world by the Father in order to establish the messianic kingdom of peace. But men rejected him and his Gospel, and thereby forfeited the

promises that were directly linked with the coming of Christ. Henceforth they had to take up the cross and suffer with Christ all the trouble and hardship of a world that "lies in the power of evil" (1 John 5:19), so that in this way that kingdom of peace may come the bulding of which remained to them as a divinely appointed task. War is one of these great trials and punishments of this life.

To substantiate that the New Testament condemns all wars, the words of Our Lord are cited: "Put thy sword back into its place; all those who take up the sword will perish by the sword" (Matt. 26:52). But we cannot assume that in that hour in the Garden of Olives Christ intended to issue a command to apply to the whole of world history. Our Lord rebuked Peter for his impetuosity and made known once again that he voluntarily surrendered himself to authority. The saying "... all those who take up the sword ...", must be taken in a proverbial sense unless it is to go against experience, for it is a well-known fact that neither all those who instigate war nor all those who take part in war have perished by the sword which they took up. Christ here has recourse to this saying in order to warn his apostle who thoughtlessly and against his will laid about him with his sword. It is noticeable that the account in John 18:11 of this scene in the Garden of Olives agrees with Matthew (Luke and Mark do not report the scene), but the clause which causes the difficulty is missing. St. John has: "Put thy sword back into its sheath", and goes on: "Am I not to drink that cup which my Father himself has appointed for me?" Many commentators, therefore, assume that the clause: "All those who take up the sword ...", is not a saying of Our Lord at all, but rather a reflection of the Evangelist which means to imply that "all those who take up the sword", whether justly or unjustly, risk perishing by the sword.

It is often argued that war is incompatible with the Gospel and the religion of Our Lord, that it is a complete contradiction of the principal command to love God and our neighbour. Our view is that the love which Our Lord preached and exemplified in his life does not abolish but presupposes law and justice (cf. Matt. 7:12, "Do to other men all that you would have them do to you"). It is not right to apply commands of the Gospel which clearly concern the mutual relations of men in the same sense to international relations. The Sermon of the Mount, which is always quoted by the opponents of war, is – at least according to the opinion of leading scripture scholars – to be understood in the sense that Christ there outlines the highest ideal and the highest goal for which his followers should strive; but not in the sense that each of these precepts represents a general norm that is under all circumstances universally binding both for individuals and for mankind in general. After all, it may well be lawful and even necessary to defend our neighbour (relatives, home, country) against attacks and injustice, and this is not always possible without the use of organized armed force.

It lies in the nature of war to bring grave and sometimes frightful suffering upon men. This fact must induce men as far as possible to eliminate or shorten war, and to mitigate its conduct. But its inevitable consequences cannot make war itself either unjust or unlawful, though in judging modern war they must play a decisive part (Q. 130). Nevertheless, Pius XII, who so often expressed his deep anguish at the suffering of humanity, and spoke in no uncertain terms against modern war, said:

PIUS XII (C. B., 1948; U. A. vol. I, pp. 95, 96).

"Resting for support on God and on the order He established, the

Christian will for peace is thus as strong as steel. Its temper is quite different from mere humanitarian sentiment, too often little more than a matter of pure impression, which detests war only because of its horrors and atrocities, its destruction and its aftermath, but not for the added reason of its injustice. . . . This is so true that neither the sole consideration of the sorrows and evils resulting from war, nor the careful weighing of the act against the advantage, avail to determine finally, whether it is morally licit, or even in certain concrete circumstances obligatory (provided always there be solid probability of success) to repel an aggressor by force of arms."

129. *Which war is just?*

Only that war is just which is waged:
1. by a legitimate authority;
2. in a just cause and with a right intention;
3. with the greatest possible restraint and with a prospect of success.

PIUS XII (C. B., 1940; U. A. vol. I, p. 14).

"There is a dismal principle that utility is the foundation and aim of law, and that might can create right. This principle is bound to upset all international relations and is unacceptable to all weaker nations. This conception does not exclude the desire for the honourable improvement of conditions or the right to defend oneself if peaceful life has been attacked, or to repair the damage sustained thereby."

PIUS XII (C. B., 1948; U. A. vol. I, p. 95).

"Every war of aggression against these goods which the divine plan for peace obliges men unconditionally to respect and guarantee and accordingly to protect and defend, is a sin, a crime, an outrage against the majesty of God, the Creator and Ordainer of the world. A people

threatened with an unjust aggression, or already its victim, may not remain passively indifferent, if it would think and act as befits Christians. All the more does the solidarity of the family of nations forbid others to behave as mere spectators, in an attitude of apathetic neutrality."

THIS reply too applies not only to defensive but also to aggressive wars. It refers to general norms concerning war, not to particular wars.

1. Not every authority is entitled to declare and to wage war, but only that which must be considered the highest in temporal affairs and the guardian of order and right. Until we have a genuine authority that is above the states this authority is the State. Naturally the question of what is demanded by right and justice must be most carefully examined. The responsibility for the outbreak of a war is shared by all those whose proper duty it is to work for the maintenance of peace, for example, Parliament, the Cabinet, ambassadors and diplomats, those specially deputed to negotiate etc. A declaration of war is not an absolute part of the nature of just war, and is not required by international law. Yet it ought to be required both on the grounds of humanity and law. Of course, in a war of defence the State attacked has neither the obligation nor often the opportunity of declaring war beforehand, since the unjust attack comes unexpectedly, so that the State suddenly finds itself in a state of war imposed upon it.

2. No war is lawful unless conducted in a just cause and in a right spirit. War must always be conducted in the service of rights that from a moral point of view have been wrongfully denied, infringed or destroyed. In other words, war is always

concerned with injustices that have been committed and proved, or that are actually being committed. Motives such as greed, vindictiveness, territorial aggrandisement, expansionist desires, redressing the balance of power, even "peaceful" domination cannot justify war. Regarding modern war we would add:

i. For modern war to be justifiable, its infinitely greater menace requires an accordingly greater degree of injustice suffered. In this connection the international common good would have a decisive say (Q. 130). ii. A war may well be unjust on both sides, but it can be just only on one side. Justice and injustice must be clearly proven, otherwise the war is not lawful, much less so today and in the future than formerly. To wage war without absolute certainty that its cause is just is to embark upon the gravest crimes against justice and charity.

3. Since war is attended by terrible consequences for both sides the greatest possible restraint ought to be observed in waging it. The safety of the civil population is a first necessity; it must not be subjected to deliberate attacks. If in necessary attacks on important military targets, non-combatants are also killed or wounded, this is a deplorable concomitant which must be kept within bounds. A war is unreasonable and unlawful if there is no prospect of success, and if its final result is a worse fate for the States or of the community of nations concerned. Belligerents ought to be able as far as possible to foresee that they could win and that victory is not achieved at too costly a price of human lives. Of course, no more than conjectures are possible.

130. Which are the marks of modern war?

Modern war
1. is "total" war;
2. causes devastation in no relation to its success;
3. threatens to develop into a world war with unimaginable losses in lives and property.
4. renders impossible any forecast and corresponding preparation.

1. MODERN war is of its nature total, an all-out war.

PIUS XII (C. B., 1941; C. T. S., pp. 2, 11).

"Yet humanity meanwhile is prey to a devastating war. . . . Within the framework of a new order based upon moral principles, there is no room for total warfare or for a reckless race for armaments. Not for the third time must the misfortune of a world war, with its economic and social havoc, its moral turmoil and aberrations, be allowed to afflict humanity."

PIUS XII (C. B., 1944; N. C. W. C., p. 2).

"They are so many silent witnesses to denounce this blot on the story of mankind . . ."

There is no longer any distinction beween combatants and non-combatants. It is true that not everybody can be drawn into the war; for example, children, the sick and the aged are not able to take part; many others may have no direct part in it, by working on the land, nursing the sick, teaching etc. Yet as a general principle war is understood as the conflict of nation against nation; it is a collective entity against which the fighting is directed. Modern war, making full use of the potentials of science, essentially aims at total destruction. The means employed depart more and more from the "weapon", and become positive instruments of destruction (Q. 131); they render it impossible to wage war in a right spirit.

2. Similarly modern war causes material, cultural and moral havoc exceeding all bounds with its mass killing, mass misery, mass devastations. Wars in former times were also often very cruel and terrible in their consequences. But in numbers and gravity there was nothing in former times to compare with the losses caused by modern war. Moreover, the merciless nature of modern war tends to demoralize, indeed brutalize men. Respect for human life, belief in God, trust in the solidarity of men and respect for law disappear; moral principles are undermined (cf. Pius XII, C. B. 1941, C. T. S., pp. 2–3).

PIUS XII (Encyclical of 19 July 1950; on modern weapons C. D. III. p. 23).

"In the progress of time technical science has created and perfected such deadly and inhuman weapons that not only can armies and fleets, towns, country-sides and villages, the irreplaceable treasures of religion, art and culture be destroyed, but also innocent children with their mothers, the sick and the defenceless aged."

PIUS XII (C. B., 1939; U. A. vol. I, p. 6).

"These efforts failed to produce the hoped for effect, chiefly, because of deep and apparently irremovable distrust – distrust which had grown in recent years and which had raised insurmountable spiritual barriers (between peoples)."

PIUS XII (C. B., 1941; C. T. S., p. 5).

"A religious anaemia has spread like a plague and infected many peoples of Europe and the world, creating in souls a moral void which no makeshift for religion, no national or international myth is able to fill."

3. It is very difficult to confine modern war to particular areas; it is always likely to turn into a general conflagration. This is due to the close interdependence of the nations, the division of the world into blocks and to the imperialistic ambitions of some of them. Every modern war constitutes a direct danger to world peace. For this reason modern war ought to be subject to the claims of the common good that is above national interests.

4. There is also the high degree of uncertainty that attaches to modern war. Science can produce new weapons that may determine a completely new turn in the course of the war. The pressure exercised by this or that great power may change considerably the balance of forces.

5. Some important conclusions emerge from these marks of modern war:

i. War has ceased to be, as Clausewitz defined it, "the continuation of politics with other means"; it is unsuitable for settling international disputes.[16] Politics ought therefore to operate with the moral power of law, sanctions, arbitration and threats of retaliation. Cf. C. B. 1944, C. T. S., p. 10.

[16] Materially unsuitable means may, nevertheless, be morally lawful in certain circumstances; cf. Q. 133.

PIUS XII (S. P.; C. T. S., p. 32).

"It is not from outward pressure, it is not from the sword that deliverance comes to nations; the sword cannot breed peace, it can only impose terms of peace."

PIUS XII (C. B., 1944; N. C. W. C., pp. 10–11).

"No one could hail this development with greater joy than he who has long upheld the principle that the idea of war as an apt and proportionate means of solving international conflicts is now out of date. No one could wish success to this common effort, to be undertaken with a seriousness of purpose never before known, with greater enthusiasm, than he who has conscientiously striven to make the Christian and religious mentality reject modern war with its monstrous means of conducting hostilities."

PIUS XII (C. B., 1946; N. C. W. C., p. 6).

"The utter depth of misery into which the horrible war has thrown humanity calls for help and imperiously demands to be healed by means of a peace that is morally noble and irreproachable; such a peace that may teach future generations to outlaw every trace of brutal force and to restore to the idea of right the priority of place from which it was wickedly dislodged."

ii. Decisions over war and peace can no longer be left to individual States, hence once again the demand for an effective international authority strong enough and authorized to prevent wars (Q. 113).

iii. The only possible "humanization" of war today is to abolish it. Modern international agreements of the nineteenth and twentieth centuries have created legal norms and usages that have humanized war in many respects. But the latest developments of science and those yet to come lead to the conclusion that modern war cannot be humanized.

131. *Is the use of modern weapons morally permissible?*

There is at most only one ground for using modern weapons, in cases of ultimate self-defence in a just war of defence.

JOHN XXIII (P. i. T. 46).

PIUS XII (Address of 19 July 1950; text quoted in Q. 130, No. 2).

i. We are concerned here with the fundamental question whether it is bad in itself for modern weapons to be used. If this is so, then these weapons may not, and may never be used on any account not even in defence against an attack however unjust and overwhelming it may be.

ii. We refer to those weapons which of their nature are likely to cause injury to defenceless persons, or to harm the belligerents unnecessarily; thus all ABC weapons, nuclear bombs and missiles, bacteriological and chemical warfare.

1. Modern weapons differ from all others not only in degree but essentially. They are explicitly means of indiscriminate destruction. They cause damage far beyond any necessary scale. Nuclear weapons cause total destruction of cities and regions. They are more or less beyond human control as regards target, effects and after-effects. An area is hit or infected in which the target lies or is presumed to lie; there is no knowing the havoc caused, nor can the effects be prevented: radiation and its possible genetic effects, the spreading of infectious diseases etc. There is a great temptation to use these weapons unconditionally. Especially if both sides are in possession of these weapons there

is the risk of their being driven to use them unscrupulously. The indiscriminate use of modern weapons of destruction must lead to the brutal extermination of mankind.

2. Does this mean that it is never lawful to use modern weapons of destruction, nuclear weapons above all? Catholic moral theologians who have so far considered this question are not unanimous in their opinion:

i. Some state very definitely that modern weapons of destruction are in themselves immoral means of waging war and consequently are never lawful, either in aggressive or defensive war, either as a means of shortening and mitigating war, or as a last resort in order to escape certain and terrible defeat. They argue that man has no right to employ means which of themselves cause total destruction, abolish all distinction between combatants and non-combatants, are beyond all effective control. There are limits beyond which man may not go.

ii. Others point out that by means of these weapons war is ended much more quickly, and consequently far greater losses can be prevented. And there is also the possibility of hitting important military targets without harming the civilian population, for example, in a naval attack, in raids on the armaments industry situated away from inhabited districts. It is stressed that these weapons are not by their nature intended for the killing of innocent people. The death of thousands of innocent people, which may result from the use of these weapons, is not willed in itself but only tolerated as a concomitant effect unavoidably linked with the military objective.

3. Which opinion is right? Surely there is only one single reason which can justify using these methods of war, and that is if an

aggressor uses them first and if it is certain that there are no other means of saving the State thus threatened. In other words, ABC weapons may only be used in a just war of defence, and then only as the last means of self-defence to escape total extermination. All other reasons are thus eliminated as insufficient. These weapons may never be used against a population that can only indirectly participate in the war, nor in the hope of breaking the opponent's morale by the horror of mass victimization through nuclear bombs.

132. *Is war of aggression lawful?*

War of aggression, no matter on what grounds it is waged, today must be considered immoral and be rejected.

PIUS XII (C. B., 1944; N. C. W. C., pp. 10, 11).

"There is a duty, besides, imposed on all, a duty which brooks no delay, no procrastination, no hesitation, no subterfuge. It is a duty to do everything to ban once and for all wars of aggression as legitimate solution of international disputes and as a means towards realizing national aspirations. Many attempts in this direction have been seen in the past. They have all failed. And they will all fail always, until the saner section of mankind has the firm determination, the holy obstinancy, like an obligation in conscience, to fulfill the mission which past ages have not undertaken with sufficient gravity and resolution.

If ever a generation has had to appreciate in the depths of its conscience the call: 'war on war', it is certainly the present generation. . . .

Unquestionably the progress of man's inventions, which should have heralded the realization of greater well-being for all mankind, has instead been employed to destroy all that had been built up through the ages.

But by that very fact the immorality of the war of aggression has been made ever more evident."

1. IT IS difficult to state exactly which wars should be considered wars of aggression. Wars of aggression are not confined to unjust, wilful attacks, for they may have just causes, such as the infringement or the denial of essential rights (cf. No. 2 below). Those who open hostilities cannot in every case be described as the aggressors, for a State or a group of States may be forced into a situation when it has to anticipate the attack of the opponent (cf. Q. 133, No. 4 on the "cold war"). It is simplest to consider as a war of aggression one that is declared to be such by an international tribunal. But this definition is strictly speaking of a merely formal nature; it states nothing concerning the true nature of war of aggression. Nevertheless, if the tribunal fulfils all the conditions for a really unbiased and objective judgment, then its decisions must be recognized as valid and be obeyed by all States and by the community of nations. This seems the only practical solution. In view of the new situation today there would seem to be only one way of defining war of aggression; we must proceed from its opposite and say that today every war that is not forced on States or on the community of nations in order to protect themselves and their most sacred rights must be considered one of aggression. Thus we distinguish between the lawful, that is, the just war of defence (Q. 132f.), and the unlawful war of aggression (no matter on what grounds it is fought).[17]

[17] According to this definition war of aggression also includes the unlawful war of defence; because a war of defence for which the States or groups of States waging it have no valid justification, has in fact, if not according to its form, the character of a war of aggression. The manner here chosen of determining the limits of war of aggression is undoubtedly unusual; but I see no other way of avoiding misunderstanding.

Most Catholic moralists who have expressed an opinion on the matter agree in unreservedly condemning every modern war of aggression; they hold that the circumstances on which this judgment is based (No. 2) are today present in every case. The greatest difficulty lies in the question whether the so-called "war of liberation" is to be considered a war of aggression or of defence; on this point cf. Q. 133.

2. The reasons for the immorality of a war of aggression lie in the essential nature of modern warfare. The convulsions, losses and dangers are out of all proportion to the gain which a war of aggression may achieve. Of special consequence (Q. 130) are:

i. the terrible sacrifice and destruction on every side caused by weapons of destruction in a modern war; losses among the civilian population, as witness Hiroshima, Dresden, and Korea; the decay of morality; ii. the menace to world peace; every region today even in the most remote corner of the earth lies within the sphere of interest of the few big powers; the most senseless local conflict can easily develop into a world war. Even before an organized community of nations has been formed, the States are obliged in justice and charity to preserve the common good of mankind from being gravely endangered.

3. With the banning of wars of aggression States and nations are called on not only to refrain from all war of conquest, but even patiently to endure injustice rather than to seek redress by force. For it cannot be maintained that the customary international provocations constitute an extreme case of self-defence which alone may still justify war (Qs. 133/134).

4. The question whether, and to what extent, modern weapons are controllable or uncontrollable is one of fact that can be an-

swered only by the experts. Scientists are working with success on the production of "clean" bombs, the effects and after-effects of which could be controlled.

It is irresponsible and morally wrong to neglect the production of conventional weapons and to restrict rearmament to nuclear weapons "as a deterrent"; for the risk is that, when nuclear weapons are the only means of defence, States will be compelled to use them in order to repel an attack even by conventional weapons.

The decisive factor is not the scientific and technical but the "moral" control. What is to be defended must stand in some relation to the inevitable evil and losses. If the other conditions for waging just war (Q. 128) are fulfilled, even unusually great damage can be justified.

We must distinguish between the moral justification of nuclear war and that of nuclear weapons. It is quite possible that certain types of nuclear weapons may be controllable and hence their employment justified for reasons of defence and on the conditions already mentioned. But a nuclear war cannot be justified if, and because, it is not restricted to these weapons, but includes the use of all, even uncontrollable, nuclear weapons.

States are strictly obliged, i. to agree to effective measures of control, that is to allow independent inspection of their own territory for this purpose; ii. to make timely provision for extensive measures of air-raid protection, so that as far as possible the danger to the population may be reduced; according to the latest scientific investigations a very considerable reduction of this danger is possible, though at great financial cost.

133. Is defensive war lawful?

A purely defensive war is lawful even today under the following conditions:

1. There must be an unjust, actual attack that cannot otherwise be met.

2. The aggressor must not be harmed more than is necessary.

3. The defence must have a prospect of success, and no higher goods must be jeopardized than those which have to be defended.

CATHOLIC moralists are practically unanimous on this issue.

PIUS XII declared (C. B. 1949, I. U. A., pp. 95/96).

"A people threatened with an unjust aggression, or already its victim, may not remain passively indifferent, if it would think and act as befits Christians. All the more does the solidarity of the family of nations forbid others to behave as mere spectators, in an attitude of apathetic neutrality. . . . This is so true that neither the sole consideration of the sorrows and evils resulting from war, nor the careful weighing of the act against the advantage, avail to determine finally, whether it is morally licit, or even in certain concrete circumstances obligatory (provided always there be solid probability of success) to repel an aggressor by force of arms. One thing, however, is certain: the commandment of peace is a matter of Divine law. Its purpose is the protection of the goods of humanity, inasmuch as they are gifts of the Creator. Among these goods some are of such importance for society, that it is perfectly lawful to defend them against unjust aggression. Their defence is even an obligation for the nations as a whole who have a duty not to abandon a nation that is attacked. The certainty that this duty will not go unfulfilled will serve to discourage

the aggressor and thus war will be avoided or, if the worst should come, its sufferings will at least be lessened."

The right of self-defence exists not only for the individual, but also for nations and States. For brute force would otherwise be placed above right, and predatory war and armed aggression would have to be regarded as "just". In certain circumstances the State is even more obliged to resist than the individual who may be responsible only for his own life and conduct, whereas the State is entrusted with the protection of many individuals and groups, especially families, of goods and values such as justice, tradition, civilization. Moreover, it ought in the name of God to protect the sanctity of the moral order in the world against injustice and harm (cf. Rom. 13:4).

The conditions that apply to any just self-defence (Q. 41) must be applied correspondingly to defensive war:

1. Defence in the form of armed resistance, which may involve heavy sacrifices in lives and property, is only permissible if an unjust attack is threatening or already in progress, and if all other means have been tried; in short, it must be a case of the ultimate resort.

What is essential is that the aggressor must be in the wrong, the defender in the right. A State that is attacked because of an injustice which it has itself committed and has not made good, must bow to the justice that is meted out to it. Pius XII expressly stated that there are some human values which would justify a defensive war even today. Such human values are the existence of an ordered political community and man's fundamental rights and liberties (I, Qs. 84 and 87), and especially Christian faith and morality. Before arms are taken up all other solutions must have been tried. Defensive war is only an *ultima ratio,* a last resort, if neither negotiations nor threats nor the intervention of other powers or of the community of nations are successful. Aggression must be actual; the State must be "threatened with an unjust aggression, or already its victim" (Pius XII). Like an individual, the State need not wait until it is too late; "actuality" exists when it is morally certain that the aggressor is making final preparations for an attack and does not desist in spite of sufficient warning; usual indications are troop concentrations; suddenly increased press campaigns which suggests that a fitting cause for war is being invented etc.[18]

It follows from what has been said that so-called preventive war is not permissible. A preventive war is waged in order to ward off a later, possible, perhaps probable attack. There is reason, or so it is thought, to fear that a State is preparing for war and will in the near future begin the war as soon as a favourable opportunity presents itself.

2. To defend, to repel, ought not to imply ruthless destruction. Self-defence does not entitle one to ruthless severity. Modern war in itself is hard and cruel enough. The one who has been unjustly attacked must do what he can to end the conflict as quickly as possible and not to inflict more wounds on the opponent than is necessary.

[18] Moral certainty has been attained when a person by making conscientious use of all sources of information has sufficiently informed himself in relation to the seriousness of the matter. No person in such situations can foresee the future with infallible certainty. The situation may change at the last minute through the sudden death of a dictator, rebellion and disunity among the enemy, the completely unexpected postponement of a campaign which had seemed to be determined. But men are able to act only in accordance with their own possibilities; they may (and must) accept the risk of anticipating the attack if everything points in that direction; we then have a genuine defensive war.

3. The third condition is that there must be a prospect of success, a solid probability (Pius XII, C. B. 1948, I. U. A., p. 96) that the defence will succeed in repelling the aggressor. The defenders may not jeopardize higher values in order to save lesser ones. Precisely in the case of a war of defence it is often difficult to foresee success, since the State attacked must often act with the utmost speed.

4. In the "cold war" as it exists since 1945, there is no conflict of arms. Yet the cold war so resembles the hot, that it has been called the "continuation of war by other means". It is not a case of two opponents fighting each other, but of one nation forcibly suppressing another or several others. The cold war operates chiefly by ideological subversion ("peaceful penetration") combined with systematic popular agitation, and by occasional acts of violence.

PIUS XII (Address of 13 September 1952).

"The attack in the form of the 'cold war' must be unconditionally condemned morally. But should it be made, the peaceful nation or nations attacked have not only the right, but also the duty to defend themselves. No State or group of States can peacefully accept political servitude and economic ruin. They owe it to the common good of their peoples to assure its defence. This tends to stem the attack and to ensure that political and economic measures will be fairly and completely adapted to the state of peace that obtains in a purely juridical sense between attacker and attacked."

Pius XII here stated the following:

1. The victim of an attack in the form of a cold war may and must resist; he is acting in just self-defence.

2. This right belongs both to individual States and to groups of States; it is based on the common good, that is, on the obligation of the nations towards their common good; it exists regardless of whether the cold war is causing, or threatening to cause, political or economic collapse.

3. The defence must aim at stopping the attack and restoring law and order to such an extent that politics and economic life can develop properly.

Did Pius XII also answer the question whether armed resistance is lawful? Are we entitled to interpret his words as sanctioning wars of liberation? Or did he merely envisage a defence with moral and spiritual weapons? He did not express an opinion, and we know of his warning against "hot war" which today may very easily develop into a world war even when it does not begin as such. But the words which the Pope used show that he was thinking of an effective resistance, that is, one likely and strong enough to halt the cold war attack and to restore law and order to the unjustly attacked nation. Now it may well be that this goal can be achieved only by a war of liberation waged by the people or by several nations, that is, when all other possibilities are either impracticable or have been tried, and when in spite of all warnings and threats there is no end of the cold war in sight.[19]

[19] I wish to emphasize that in my personal opinion the words of the Holy Father bear this interpretation. Pius XII spoke of the unjust attack and of the right and the duty of defence which in this case is clearly just self-defence. The nations oppressed in a cold war may not tolerate such a situation so far as they are at all able either by themselves or with the help of other nations to free themselves; if they resort to force because every other way is barred, then they are not waging a war of aggression, but one of genuine defence. I do not maintain that the Holy Father himself wished to draw this conclusion and approve of it.

134. *Can a war of liberation be permissible?*

If it is of defensive, not of aggressive character, a war of liberation is permissible and perhaps even a duty.

THIS is one of the most delicate questions in the whole ethics of war. By war of liberation, including what is called war of invasion, is meant one that is undertaken in order to liberate countries from unjust foreign rule or occupation, or from an extremely grave menace. In some cases it may resemble a war of aggression or a preventive war, since it is begun in order to drive out a foreign power, or to prevent it from continuing the menace. Is such a war of liberation to be considered a war of aggression or a preventive war? The question has to be answered; for the totalitarian powers are not only causing widespread confusion by their completely unjust claims and methods, but also material and even worse intellectual and moral misery. May the free world turn the cold into a hot war if there is no other way out than slavery? Two possibilities will be dealt with here:

THE LIBERATION OF INDIVIDUAL NATIONS

1. Let us suppose that a country is unjustly occupied and ruled by another. The occupation may take place in the course of an unjust war or for preventive reasons (for the "protection of neutrality"); authority is exercised without any consideration for right and justice: terror, suppression of the nation's individuality and self-government, political parties that are subservient to foreign dictators and parties, denial of human rights, suppression of liberty, etc.

2. Such a situation is clearly unjust; it is a continuous aggres-

sion against the nation, its existence, honour and most sacred rights. The methods of such a "system" or occupation are in fact not different from unjust military attacks. Certainly the principles governing just resistance to the State (cf. Qs. 106ff.) apply; for this is a matter of foreign interference, of usurpers invading foreign territory and coercing a foreign nation. Therefore it is clearly a case of self-defence against actual, unjust aggression.

The sense of mutual dependence among the nations ought to support the struggle for liberation of a people subjugated in this manner. The common good of the whole world may be involved; and apart from this there exists an obligation of the nations and States to help (cf. Q. 135).

The War of Liberation for Peace and Freedom in the World

1. Let us suppose that a totalitarian power, completely materialist in outlook and consciously atheistic, in theory and practice professes world imperialism. This great power has such enormous resources in power and so many powerful supporters in satellite States and among its allies and followers in other countries that it constitutes *the* world danger. Its ideological basis is a ruthless collectivism recognizing no human dignity and rights. We are aware that this great power disturbs world peace wherever and whenever it can, and with all its strength is preparing an armed struggle for world domination; that wherever it has established its rule, the people are forcibly robbed of their most sacred rights by oppression and terror; education of youth to atheism; fight against God, Christ and the Church; uniformity of thinking, absence of any legal order and security.

This great power is at work enslaving other nations (adjoining territories and satellites) or undermining them, for example, by means of fifth columns, political parties influenced and commanded by the financial, intellectual support of the major power in question etc. There are occasional strikes, acts of sabotage, including political murder, and, above all, local wars are unleashed. These wars, as the major power openly admits or by its actions clearly shows, are in reality waged against the community of nations and against the free world; consequently they have the character of acts of aggression against world peace.

The question now is this: Under these circumstances has the world the right to armed self-defence, to a war of liberation? Or must humanity, that is, all the other nations as a whole, wait until the great power has struck? And if the nations foresee with certainty that due to the inequality of forces they might soon no longer be in a position to defend themselves, ought they to resign themselves to the inevitable fate of defeat later on and the enslavement to follow?

2. Some consider a war of liberation in these circumstances a defensive war imposed upon the free world and therefore lawful. They argue that since mankind has a natural, God-given right to its existence, fundamental freedoms, to peace and order, it has a right also to protect itself and its most sacred rights in good time against unjust attacks. It may not allow these rights to be flagrantly wrested from it. Unjust aggression by the other side against world peace and the most sacred right of mankind is already taking place with weapons not only of the cold, but also of the hot war; nations are held in subjugation, there is subversion, there are local wars etc.

This state of affairs has no precedent. The very existence not only of an individual nation but of mankind as a whole is at stake, and the case of self-defence in extreme necessity exists not only when the major armed offensive is already in progress, but already when this major offensive is inevitably approaching and through individual acts has already begun. Failure to act must not be allowed to lead to the loss of all rights. Responsibility for the resulting world war and its victims clearly lies with that great power which systematically aims at the enslavement of the world. In order that this great power should realize its responsibility, and at the same time in order that everything possible may be done to avoid war, we demand that it should first be called upon to desist from its unlawful activities; otherwise the nations as a whole would consider themselves forced to take action. When the official organ of the community of nations has expressed this warning and has forbidden further preparations for war, the great power concerned may, and unless it submits, must be considered and treated as an unjust aggressor. When and where pressure can be exerted and is likely to be successful, it must be used, for example by breaking off diplomatic relations, imposing economic sanctions etc.

To be permitted such war of liberation too must have prospects of success. Since the good and ill of all humanity is at stake, all States and groups of States are obliged to participate if necessary, and the organized community of nations has undoubtedly the right to impose this obligation. Real interdependence among the nations should form the most effective defence and be most likely to avert such a war of liberation. Power that tends to disrupt can only be kept in check by the threat and the readiness for defence of a bigger power.

3. Others, in direct opposition to the first opinion, quite definitely deny that a war of liberation of the kind mentioned could be legitimate; they consider it an unlawful war of aggression or a preventive war. They would argue that a war of this kind, an unjust aggression involves the deliberate murder of

innumerable innocent persons on both sides. We may never kill or harm for preventive reasons, not even when we fear that we might be attacked at some later time and would not then be strong enough to withstand it. In such a case, there is only one way out, which is to be cautious and to invoke the protection of a higher authority.

Such a war of liberation cannot compensate for the frightful sacrifices which it entails, and its prospects of success are too slight. In other words, we do not know if the conflict will be brought to a victorious conclusion, and even if it is, then it would be only at the price of proportionately great losses; and finally, what goods and institutions worth defending will the equally dechristianized and materialistic "liberators" bring in their train?

The fate of mankind must be entrusted to God in an heroic attitude of endurance and hope. God can so arrange things that the totalitarian power will listen to reason and abandon its aggressive plans, that the situation will in one form or another radically change, that new weapons will be invented which will deter the aggressor from his purpose. In short, it is possible, but not inevitable that the aggression will take place.[20]

135. Is neutrality justifiable?

If a State has no obligation to repel, or help to repel, an unjust aggression, it undoubtedly has the right to remain neutral.

[20] I have purposely placed both opinions with their arguments and counter arguments side by side. I personally favour the first opinion. It does not seem to me to be right, either from a natural or Christian point of view, that mankind may not effectively and in time protect its most sacred rights from being destroyed. Naturally, as we emphasized, other possibilities must be tried first.

PIUS XII (C. B., 1941; C. T. S., pp. 9–10).

"If it is inevitable that the great States should, by reason of their greater resources and their power, lead the way in forming economic groups between themselves and the smaller and weaker nations, nevertheless what holds for all in the sphere of the common interest holds also for these smaller nations: that they possess an unquestionable right to have their political freedom respected; a right to the effectual safeguarding of that neutrality in conflicts between other States which belongs to them in virtue of the natural law and the law of nations; and a right to the protection of their economic development. Only in such circumstances can they adequately secure the material and spiritual well-being of their respective peoples."

1. Neutrality means keeping out of a quarrel, supporting neither one side nor the other in a war:

i. Permanent neutrality implies that a State is once and for all determined not to wage war, and not to assist any other State to wage war. It will have to renounce all alliances and guarantees, but it may defend itself if unjustly attacked. There are also cases of temporary neutrality.

ii. Armed neutrality exists when a State makes all provision for military preparation against attacks and infringements of its rights (Switzerland).

iii. Neutralization means imposed neutrality. A territory is ordered to remain neutral; for this it receives under treaty the assurance that it will be defended against enemy attacks.

iv. There is a distinction between neutral States and those which, while they do not declare war or directly participate in the fighting, morally and economically support one side in the war.

2. States, whether big or small, have a natural right to remain neutral in the military conflicts of other States. Because their first obligation is to their own common good and to their own people. It is their duty to do that which will guarantee order and prosperity to themselves. But they must really pursue a policy of non-intervention. Pius XII argued from the "solidarity of the nations" that, when a nation or group of nations is not of itself able to repel an unjust attack, the other nations are in duty bound to render it assistance (C. B. 1948, I. A. U., p. 95; for the text cf. Q. 134). This obligation may in certain circumstances involve armed intervention which is only possible by the abandonment of neutrality. But no State is bound to come to the assistance of another, if by doing so it may itself perish or have to make unduly great sacrifices. Neutrality is of the greatest importance for the common good of the nations. A neutral State can act as intermediary in peace negotiations; it can look after the interests of the wounded and of prisoners. The good work of the Red Cross organization is an example. It can help the establishment of neutral courts. The trial of war criminals ought to be transferred to such neutral courts. By remaining neutral, a State can sometimes do more for a nation unjustly attacked than by taking part in the fighting.

It is a very difficult question whether, and when, an infringement of neutrality is justifiable. May a State that cannot otherwise successfully defend itself against an unjust aggressor demand passage through neutral territory, or in case of refusal, enforce it? It seems necessary nowadays to make the following distinction: Armed forces of the organized community of nations must undoubtedly have the right of passage anywhere; this also includes full freedom of movement for air and naval forces. The neutral State that in a modern war of State against State would permit a march through, would, in view of the destrucive power of modern weapons, expose its territory and peoples to possible extermination or to frightful devastation and sacrifices. The enemy State would perhaps retaliate with mass air attacks or with atomic bombs. It is impossible to expect any State to suffer such a fate for the benefit of another.

3. The political neutrality of the Catholic Church has a special character of its own of which Pius XII spoke in his Christmas broadcast of 1951 (I. U. A., pp. 118ff.). The Pope stressed that the Church is a supra-natural society with supra-natural aims and functions. Hence she thinks, evaluates and decides not according to secular, political standards, but rather according to supernatural, eternal norms and points of view. She cannot be politically neutral for the reason that she is not a political instrument. In accordance with her mission, outlook and responsibility she can never be neutral. For the Church it is always a question of what is in accordance with the will of God; always and everywhere she must defend good against evil; and exhort men to build a Christian world order which is essentially peaceful.

136. Is it an obligation to serve in wartime?

Depending on the circumstances, the citizens of a State may be obliged or at least entitled, to serve or refuse to serve in wartime.

THE question of refusing active service has many aspects and is very complex. In Catholic ethics also there are differences of opinion, although agreement in essential points seems to be growing.[21] The whole question ought to be considered from

[21] Complete rejection of active service is rare among Catholic moralists. Those who regard all wars as wrong must logically declare the refusal of active

the following basic premises; i. Political authorities that impose an obligation to active service are not entitled to send troops into action that are insufficiently armed and trained. This would be contrary to all sound reason. ii. The necessities of the national or international common good may demand very heavy sacrifices. But they do not justify ignoring superior natural or supra-natural rights, and sacrifices that can be avoided. Consideration is due to the family, to religious and moral obligations, the claims of the Church (exemption of clerical students and priests from military service). iii. The political authority declares and wages war, but each individual must take personal responsibility for his part in it as for everything he does; hence he must form his own judgment on whether the war is lawful or not. This judgment often is admittedly very difficult, if not impossible, for the individual. But circumstances today make it easier compared with former times. World-wide communications can speedily provide information, and the unjust aims of certain regimes can be recognized by every fair-minded person. Wars of aggression have been outlawed both by international law (the world conscience) and by unequivocal statements of the highest authority in the Church. Nevertheless, in individual cases it may often be difficult to have a clear grasp of the true situation.

There are various categories of objectors to war service: i. There are those who consider no war to be justifiable and reject any kind of military service as immoral. Objectively speaking these people are mistaken (Q. 128); on the other hand their motives, their courage and self-sacrifice deserve all respect

service to be an universal obligation that is absolutely binding. There have been, and are, moralists who consider the law concerning military service to be an expedient, that it does not bind in conscience, but merely obliges the individual to suffer the sentence imposed on him for contravening the law (Q. 80).

and consideration. (ii) There are those who are convinced that a righteous war is possible, that there have been righteous wars in the past, but that today and in future war can no longer be just and righteous because of modern weapons and the losses which they cause. Hence they would refuse to do active service even when the country for which they should fight is in the right. iii. The third category consists not so much of conscientious objectors as of those who adopt a course of civic disobedience. They would distinguish between lawful and unlawful military actions; and reject the latter no matter against whom, or on what grounds the war is being fought.

1. In war no one may do what is bad in itself and(or) is judged by him clearly to be such.

EXAMPLES. Direct killing of hostages and prisoners; mass air attacks on open cities; suicidal actions; mercy-killing of wounded comrades; torture and brain-washing; mass murder, a policy of extermination on racial or religious grounds. Naturally it is not lawful for military commanders to order what is bad in itself, either explicitly or tacitly. Phrases like "orders must be obeyed regardless" make a mockery of law and morality.

2. The political community ought not to force those who can show serious grounds of conscience for refusing active service to serve with the fighting troops. Not any and every defence and assertion that is made on grounds of conscience can be considered as valid; a true and deep religious conviction is likely to be such. Sometimes it is very difficult to distinguish between genuine conscientious objection and objection on grounds of cowardice or selfishness. The conscientious objector ought to be aware that the burden which he rejects will fall on others. In the case of a lawful war the authorities are entitled

properly to examine whether conscientious objection is actually due to reasons of conscience, and to find other duties for such persons, for example, as nurses, air-raid wardens, farm workers, etc.

Here we ought to recall the Catholic teaching on the binding force of an erroneous conscience. The individual must earnestly strive to have a right conscience. But whoever is in error through no fault of his own, and is unable in spite of sufficient effort to overcome this error, may, and must act in accordance with his conscience. It is true that his actions may be objectively wrong; but since he personally believes he is doing right, and does not act unscrupulously but conscientiously, he may (and must) follow his conscience (cf. I, Qs. 17, 42, 77).

3. Everyone must refuse active service when the war is unlawful, or when he cannot be convinced that it is not unlawful. The argument is simple and clear: Whoever fights in an unlawful war, formally and directly takes part in the injustice that is done. The principle must be extended to cover the case where it has obviously become senseless to continue the war, thus where the military situation shows to every fair-minded person that further sacrifices are futile.

Care of the wounded, making provision for food supplies and protecting the civilian population would not formally and directly serve the war effort. It would benefit the people who are (unfortunately) involved in the war or threatened or injured by it. It is true that they indirectly influence the course of the war, but this is not their proper and primary purpose. Manufacture of armaments, troop training, securing rear lines of communication (guarding bridges and railways), provisioning the troops with ammunition and stores and similar tasks, however, are quite a different matter.

4. In a righteous war no one may refuse the active service to which he is obliged by lawful authority. In other words, active service in a righteous war is an obligation in conscience. Our view is based on the one hand on the obligation which every member of the all-inclusive community has towards the common good, and, on the other hand, on the right of the State authority (or super-State authority) to protect the common good and to demand corresponding sacrifices. The servants of the Church are chosen, consecrated and commissioned by God himself to preach and to spread his Gospel and kingdom of peace. Hence the Church is quite within her rights in demanding that her priests should not be called up to serve as combatants. Particularly in modern warfare they have sufficient opportunity of showing bravery and a spirit of sacrifice as chaplains or in other non-combatant functions.

A lawful war becomes unlawful when men are unnecessarily sacrificed. No State is entitled to expose its citizens to mortal danger without necessity. If it obviously does this, no one is obliged to obey.

5. Those who are merely in serious doubt about the lawfulness of a war are not excused from active service. One who is in doubt has not (yet) attained certainty, his judgment remains suspended. In the case of war this may be due to the fact that he is unable to decide whether it is a war of aggression or a defensive war, whether a just cause is really being defended, or whether the war is being fought with unlawful means and with unnecessary severity.

In such an important matter the individual must seek, by all the means at his disposal, to resolve the doubt, for instance, by prayer, by the advice and example of well-informed men, by thoroughly informing himself through press and radio. If he does not succeed, he is obliged to active service. For it is for lawful authority in the first place, as carrying the chief responsibility, to judge the necessity and lawfulness of a war; this judgment binds the subjects as long as they do not find after unbiased and careful examination that they cannot agree with it.

Pius XII expressly stated in his Christmas broadcast of 1956 that a Parliament or a freely elected Government does not act immorally when in a case of extreme necessity it decides on defence measures using the legitimate means of foreign and home policy, and makes the preparations it considers necessary; in such cases a Catholic citizen cannot appeal to his conscience in order to refuse to do active service and to fulfil the obligations laid down by law.

137. What is true peace?

Only a peace that is concluded in justice and wise moderation can be true and lasting.

PIUS XII (C. B., 1941; C. T. S., p. 8).

"The lesson of history is that peace treaties concluded in a spirit and with conditions contrary to the moral law and true political wisdom have had a short and precarious life; thus giving evidence of a miscalculation which, though human, has been none the less disastrous in its results."

1. MUCH would be gained if men could agree on the following points:

i. War, peace negotiations and peace terms are only means; their goal is "a peace that is morally noble and irreproachable" (Pius XII, C. B., 1946; I. U. A., p. 77). Peace, whether it is imposed or agreed upon, is not an act of revenge, but one of social and penal justice. It may be severe, but it must never be unjust.

PIUS XII (C. B., 1946; U. A. vol. I, p. 77).

"Nevertheless, all the measures of repression and prevention should keep their character of means and hence remain subordinate to the lofty and ultimate purposes of a true peace which, while providing the necessary guarantees, contemplates the gradual co-operation of conquerors and conquered in the work of reconstruction to the advantage of the entire family of nations as well as of each of its members."

ii. A peace treaty that must inevitably work out unfavourably for the good of mankind stands self-condemned.

iii. It is as short-sighted as it is unjust to force nations, including the defeated, to acknowledge untrue and for themselves degrading declarations (War guilt).

iv. The defeated nation is not without rights (Pius XII, C. B., 1944; I. U. A., p. 61). Entry into the community of nations and States ought not to be barred to it by the victors. Unconditional surrender is clearly an unjust demand.

2. The side which has conducted an unjust war must be responsible for all the damage and costs that are incurred by his opponent. It is bound to make reparation and restitution, and in addition it is liable to a just punishment, because it has in a culpable manner violated the order of justice. The amount of reparation must be determined by the extent of the guilt and – a matter that is usually overlooked – by the amount of damage unjustly caused by the other side. Even the side that is in the right has no licence to commit injustice such as the systematic destruction of open towns. Reparations to the full equivalent value are

usually quite impossible in view of the destruction caused by modern warfare, and they could not be borne by the international economic structure.

PIUS XII (Address of 1 June, 1946).

"We know, of course, that the strict letter of international law only obliges the victor to release the prisoners after the conclusion of peace. But the spiritual and moral distress of the prisoners and their families increases from day to day. The sacred rights of marriage and the family cry louder to heaven than all legal documents. They demand that an end should be made of the system of prisons and concentration camps. If a victorious State believes it cannot, for economic reasons, do without the labour of its prisoners, the question should, nevertheless, be examined whether they could not with as much or even greater advantage be replaced by voluntary workers from the home countries to whom just and human living and working conditions are granted."

3. War does not justify the expulsion of innocent people from their homes. If resettlements are necessary, they ought to be carried out with the proviso: i. that they are preceded by positive agreements with countries where those forced to resettle will be able to find a living; ii. that those being resettled are allowed to take their lawfully gained property with them or are compensated for it; iii. that the resettlement is carried out in a reasonable manner.

PIUS XII (Letter to German Bishops, 1 March 1948).

"But was it right as a counter measure to expel 12 million people from their homes and to sacrifice them to certain death? Are not the victims of that counter measure in the overwhelming majority men and women

who had no part in the events and crimes of which we spoke and had no influence upon them? And was that measure politically right and economically responsible when we think of the necessities of life of the German people as much as the welfare of the rest of Europe. Is it unrealistic when we desire and hope that all concerned may, on calm reflection, try to undo what has been done in so far as that is still possible?"

138. Who should be punished for war crimes?

Only those convicted of personal guilt for crimes ought to be punished as war criminals.

1. THE courts can only deal with offences which a man has certainly committed and by his own free will, or which he did not prevent although he could and should have done so. But it must be clearly proved both that he committed the crime and that he was fully responsible for it.

2. Only individual persons, and not collective entities may be tried and condemned. Human courts may only pass sentence on several or a large number of persons if each one of them can be proved personally to be partly or wholly responsible for the crime.

PIUS XII (C. B., 1944; N. C. W. C., pp. 12–13).

"No one certainly thinks of disarming justice in its relations to those who have exploited the war situation in order to commit real and proven crimes against the common law, and for whom supposed military necessity could at most have offered a pretext, but never a justification. But if justice presumed to judge and punish not merely individuals but even whole communities together, who could not but see in such a procedure a violation of the norms which guide every human trial?"

3. A judgment to be valid must be passed by a competent court according to proper procedure. According to the principle that no one ought to be judge in his own cause, members of a court of justice that has to deal with such delicate questions should be taken from strictly neutral States. The community of nations ought to have its own criminal court which would be competent to deal with these matters.

It is part of a proper procedure that confessions may not be extorted by violence, that the defence should be given timely and adequate access to all the files of the case; that all witnesses for the defence should be heard and their evidence be taken into account; that no positive penal laws should be issued with retroactive force.

Justice demands that all war criminals should be tried and punished according to the same standards, whether they belong to the victor or to the defeated nations.

4. A crime against peace means unleashing and continuing an unjust war of aggression. The prosecution brings those to trial who are directly responsible for the war and consequently for the horror and misery caused by it. The position in positive law has not yet been clarified, but the moral conscience of humanity must today be considered perfectly clear in regard to the principles that condemn war of aggression as a political means.

5. Crimes against humanity are grave misdeeds that conflict with the most important fundamental rights of man, for example, the murder of innocent people; confiscation and destruction of property; looting in occupied territories; keeping people in inhuman conditions (concentration camps); betrayal to the political secret police and the like. When such crimes are intentionally committed they must undoubtedly be punished with corresponding severity.

There are instances from the last World War where military commanders of irreproachable personal character found themselves in the difficult position of having to pass on, or to carry out, higher orders which they themselves condemned. They could have resigned; and in this way they would have avoided a grave conflict of conscience, but at the same time they would have sacrificed those in their charge to greater violence. In order to spare the occupied territory from this fate they chose the lesser evil. Circumstances such as these ought to be taken into account by war crimes' tribunals as by any ordinary court of law.

BIBLIOGRAPHY

General Works

Casserley, J. V. L., *The Bent World* (Oxford University Press, London and New York, 1955).

ALTHOUGH the main preoccupation of this work (by the Professor of Dogmatic Theology at the General Theological Seminary, New York) is the conflict between Russian Marxism and Western civilization, it contains some penetrating chapters on the West in theory and practice. Of special value are the chapters on democracy, secularism and the family.

Cronin, John F., *Social Principles and Economic Life* (Bruce, Milwaukee, 1959).

THIS work replaces Father Cronin's highly praised *Catholic Social Principles,* which has been entirely rewritten and three further chapters added. These deal with the economic problems of the family, international political and economic life, racial discrimination and racial justice. It is a major contribution to the application of papal principles to social and economic problems. Not the least of its features are the lavish quotations from papal documents.

Guerry, Archbishop Emile, *The Social Doctrine of the Catholic Church* (St. Paul Publications, New York, 1962).

THIS survey of papal teaching from Leo XIII to John XXIII is influenced by the fact that the Archbishop of Cambrai has for some years exercized episcopal responsibility for the Catholic worker movements in France. Scholarly though his approach is, his conclusions are severely practical through his association with *la mission ouvrière.*

Leclercq, Jacques, *Leçons de droit naturel* (2nd edition, Louvain-Namur, 1946–50).

THIS comprehensive work is in four volumes which deal respectively with the Basis of Law and Society, State and Politics, the Family, Individual Rights. The author manages to combine traditional Catholic teaching on the Natural Law with a modern approach and present-day examples. A valuable contribution to the study of Christian social ethics.

Maritain, J., *The Rights of Man and the Natural Law* (Scribner, New York, 1943; Bles, London, 1943).

BEGINNING with the vocation of the person, a spiritual and free agent, to an order of absolute values and to a destiny superior to time, J. Maritain deduces the various rights, personal, civic and social, which are significant (perhaps because they are attacked more often than they are upheld) in the world of today.

Messner, J., *Social Ethics* (Herder, Saint Louis, 1949).

THIS is an essential work of reference, one of the most profound studies in social philosophy in the English language. The social principles which are elaborately established are applied in detail to economic and political relations, with particular reference to current problems. In general the author inclines to a conservative standpoint while remaining within the broad stream of Catholic social thought.

Ottaviani, Alaphridus Cardinal, *Institutiones juris publici Ecclesiastici* (Roma, 1947–48).

THIS work deals with most of the questions that arise through man's life in society. Cardinal Ottaviani writes with rare expertness, clarity and judgment on the difficult questions of our time, *e.g.*, Aggression, War and Peace, Education.

Part One

Marriage and the Family

Burke, Louis H., *With This Ring* (McGraw-Hill, New York, 1958).

The author is presiding judge of the Los Angeles Supreme Court. He analyzes a number of case histories of marriages which were breaking up, and shows how his well-known Reconciliation Agreements have gone a long way to cement these marriages.

Cervantes, Lucius and Zimmerman, Carle C., *Marriage and the Family – A Text for Moderns* (Regnery, Chigago, 1956).

Acclaimed on all sides when it first appeared, and still after a number of years one of the best works on the subject published in the United States. Its special contribution is the development of the idea of complementarity at all levels in married life as an antidote to tensions.

Fitzsimons, John, *Woman Today* (Sheed & Ward, London and New York, 1952).

A further development of the theme of complementarity, bringing in the idea of active submission, at the same time showing that woman's place in modern society is not meant to be confined to Church, children and cooking.

Gallagher, Donald and Idella (Ed.), *The Education of Man* (Doubleday, New York, 1962).

A lively presentation of the educational philosophy of Jacques Maritain. An exposition of the best in the neo-Thomist attitude to the educational theories of today and yesterday. An indispensable companion to M. Maritain's political thought.

Keenan, Alan, O. F. M. and Ryan, John, *Marriage: A Medical and Sacramental Study* (Sheed and Ward, London and New York, 1955).

THIS work is the fruit of collaboration between a priest and a physician. Their basic thesis is that in marriage, as elsewhere in creation, good morals is good medicine and good medicine is good morals. Its major contribution is its positive attitude, full of hope and of humanity.

Leclercq, Jacques, *Marriage and the Family*. Translated by T. A. Hanley, O. S. B. (Pustet, New York, 1945).

THE author in his introduction says: "nothing is more repetitious than the literature on the family. It is enough to select a few representative authors to have the whole doctrine." This book certainly earns its place in such a select group, if only for the comprehensive view of the whole picture which it presents. The statistics are now out of date but the solid doctrine is perennial.

Lestapis, Stanislas de, S. J., *Family Planning and Modern Problems: A Catholic Analysis*. Translated from the French by Reginald F. Trevett (Burns Oates, London, 1960; Herder & Herder, New York, 1960).

A SCHOLARLY book, packed with facts and figures. The author discusses one of the most acute questions of our time against the background of the Catholic faith. Already a classic. The author has been for some years Professor of Family Sociology at the *Institut Catholique* of Paris.

Suenens, Leo Joseph Cardinal, *Love and Control* (Burns Oates, London, 1961).

THE pastoral approach to problems of marriage and the family as seen by a warm-hearted but clear-thinking shepherd of souls. The fundamental solution which Cardinal Suenens proposes is a return to the true meaning of love. His detailed analysis shows courage, originality and progressive views.

Thomas, John L., *The American Catholic Family* (Prentice-Hall, New York, 1956).

THIS is the best and most documented work on the subject published so far. It will appeal to the professional sociologist, as the approach is thoroughly scientific, with a great deal of originality in the interpretation of the facts.

—., *Education* (St. Paul Publications, London and New York, 1961)

—., *Woman in the Modern World* (St. Paul Publications, London and New York, 1962).

Compilations of papal pronouncements by the monks of the Abbey of Solesmes and translated by the Daughters of St. Paul.

Part Two

Vocational Order

Barker, Ernest, *Principles of Social and Political Theory* (Oxford University Press, Oxford, 1951).

In the course of his discussion of Society and the State, Sir Ernest Barker devotes a section (pp. 77–88) to "The Idea of a Social Parliament". He deals with it in theory, and then quotes various authorities who have advocated such a "Third House". They include such different personalities as the Webbs and Sir Winston Churchill.

Calvez, Jean-Yves, S. J. and Perrin, Jacques, S. J., *The Church and Social Justice*. Translated by J. R. Kirwan (Burns Oates, London, 1961).

This major commentary on papal social teaching from Leo XIII through Pius XII confines itself to the economic order and is a systematic analysis of economic society in the light of Christian teaching. The final chapter is a magnificent exposition of the growth of the Industry Council Plan in papal teaching over the past seventy years.

Dion, Gerard, *The Industry Council Plan* (Social Justice Review, St. Louis, 1962).

THIS reprint of an article (which first appeared in the Review in January, 1962) deals with the state of the economy and the advisability of introducing the Industry Council Plan. Its value is enhanced as it comes from an "outsider", the author being head of the Department of Industrial Relations at Laval University, Quebec.

Eberdt, M. L. and Schnepp, G. J., *Industrialism and the Popes* (Kennedy, New York, 1953).

AN EXPOSITION of social principles, drawn from papal documents, related to the fundamental idea of subsidiary function with special reference to the Industry Council Plan. It is a little too cut-and-dried in dealing with Councils which can only come about through organic growth, but it has an excellent bibliography and reading lists.

Gearty, Patrick W., *The Economic Thought of Monsignor John A. Ryan* (Catholic University of America Press, Washington, 1953).

IT WAS Ryan's conviction that the Industry Council Plan provides the most effective means for safeguarding freedom and human dignity in the context of economic justice. This doctoral thesis, fascinating in its detail and profound in its grasp of economic fact, explains how he arrived at this conclusion in the twenty years before the publication of the encyclical *Quadragesimo anno*.

Munier, Joseph, *Some American Approximations to Pius XI's 'Industries and Professions'* (Catholic University of America Press, Washington, 1943).

THERE are many elements in the American scene which would facilitate the emergence of the papal Industry Council Plan, and there has been legislation (*e.g.*, the ill-fated National Industrial Recovery Act, passed in 1933 and declared unconstitutional in 1935) which also has favoured such developments. Fr. Munier assembled this material for a doctoral dissertation twenty years ago, but it is still useful to the student.

Newman, Jeremiah, *Co-responsibility in Industry* (Gill, Dublin, 1955).

THIS book discusses in detail the development of industrial relations in

Belgium, Germany and Great Britain, but its chief relevance here is a chapter (pp. 95–110) on the movement for Industry Councils in the U. S. A.

Part Three

Political Order

Cranny, Titus, S. A., *The Moral Obligation of Voting* (Catholic University of America Press, Washington, 1952).

This obligation is one that derives from natural morality, and it is in dealing with this that Fr. Cranny is at his best. Wherever there is universal suffrage, what he has to say needs careful attention.

D'Antonio, William F. and Ehrlick, Howard J. (Ed.), *Power and Democracy in America* (University of Notre Dame Press, Notre Dame, 1960).

A symposium in the course of which Professors Peter F. Drucker of New York, Delbert C. Miller of Indiana and Robert A. Dahl of Yale discuss the possibilities of achieving that delicate balance between power and democracy which is called for in a society jealous of its freedom.

Fogarty, Michael P., *Under-governed and Over-governed* (Geoffrey Chapman, London, 1962).

This is an application of the principle of subsidiarity to the British scene. Professor Fogarty desribes the present situation as being the Executive State, *i. e.,* where the State over-governs in matters of detail. He points the way towards the Educational State, where government will turn its attention to the larger issues where at present there is under-government.

Kerwin, Jerome G., *Catholic Viewpoint on Church and State* (Hanover House, New York, 1960).

The main part of this work is devoted to the more specialized subject of Church-State relationships, but all along the line Professor Kerwin, drawing on a lifetime's meditation on political theory provides some very sound ideas on political authority and the State.

Lachance, Louis, O. P., *L'humanisme politique de S. Thomas* (Recueil Sirey, Paris, 1939).

THIS work deals with the relationship between the individual and the State, with a wealth of references which cannot be found elsewhere.

Maritain, Jacques, *Christianity and Democracy* (Bles, London, 1945).

THE object of this little work is to show how peace can come through the reconciliation of the democratic and Christian idea. Only in this way can man be rescued from the grip of the omnipotent State.

Maritain, Jacques, *Man and the State* (University of Chicago Press, Chicago, 1951; Hollis and Carter, London, 1955).

THE most comprehensive statement by Maritain of his political philosophy, linking the rationality and freedom of the human person with the spiritual meaning and purpose of the organized political community, and at the same time establishing the principles and aims of Christian democracy.

Rommen, Heinrich A., *The State in Catholic Thought* (Herder, St.Louis, 1945).

A STANDARD work, due to its comprehensive treatment of social ethics as applied to man and the State.

PART FOUR

International Order

Code of International Ethics (Newman Press, Westminster, 1953).

THE International Union of Social Studies, meeting at Malines, first drew up this Code in 1937. It was subsequently revised at meetings in

1947 and 1948, and was approved in 1949. This present edition is a translation made by John Eppstein who has added a valuable commentary. In the appendix may be found the Charter of the United Nations and the Declaration of Rights drawn up by a committee appointed by the National Catholic Welfare Conference in 1947.

Drogat, Noel, S. J., *The Challenge of Hunger* (Burns Oates, London, 1962).

This work examines the paradox of the West's growing technological mastery and the rising malnutrition rates in Asia and South America. It deals with social and economic remedies through science and education, and pays special attention to the work being done by the UN's Food and Agriculture Organization. The book is introduced by the Assistant Director-General of the FAO.

Flannery, Harry W. (Ed.), *Pattern for Peace: Statements on International Order* (N. C. W. C., Washington, 1962).

A completely indexed book of statements on peace and international life from Leo XIII to John XXIII. This is the most comprehensive collection of documents, commentaries and speeches that has so far been published in English. It is indispensable both for a study of the principles of papal thought on order in international affairs, and for the specific recommendations and suggestions made by the Holy See.

McCormack, Arthur, *People, Space, Food* (Sheed & Ward, London, 1960).

The author faces the problems raised by the population explosion and takes an optimistic attitude, taking into account population trends, food supplies, underdeveloped areas, technology, birth control etc. The study is well documented, especially from statistics and surveys provided by the United Nations.

Nagle, William J. (Ed.), *Morality and Modern Warfare* (Helicon Press, Baltimore, 1961).

A symposium of nine essays on the various aspects of traditional morality as applied to war and peace in the nuclear age. It includes a valuable bibliography entitled "The Moral Problem of Modern Warfare".

Stein, Walter (Ed.), *Nuclear Weapons and Christian Conscience* (Merlin Press, London, 1961; Sheed & Ward, New York, 1962).

THIS is a collection of essays, the work of five Catholics, philosophers and historians from various English universities, and is a systematic examination of the moral questions raised by nuclear weapons in the light of traditional Christian teaching. The findings of the authors is that a Christian should be committed to unilateral nuclear disarmament.

Thompson, Charles S. (Ed.), *Morals and Missiles* (Clarke, London, 1959).

A COLLECTION of essays by Catholics on the problem of war today. The authors include Fr. Stratmann, O. P., Archbishop Roberts and Dom Bede Griffiths, O. S. B. While these are expressions of personal attitudes and are in no way authoritative, they are useful in giving a many-sided approach to the problem.

Zimmerman, Anthony F. *Overpopulation* (Catholic University of America Press, Washington, 1957).

A DOCTORAL dissertation which carries the subtitle "a study of papal teachings on the problem, with special reference to Japan". The positive doctrinal sections of this work are thorough and competent and give an exhaustive survey of the pronouncements of the Holy See on the subject.

World Justice

THIS is a quarterly review published from the Research Centre for International Social Justice at the University of Louvain. It is indispensable for the student who wishes to keep abreast of Catholic ideas and Catholic initiatives in the international sphere.

Index